THE LEGENDS OF
ASTON VILLA

THE LEGENDS OF
ASTON VILLA

by Tony Matthews

First published in Great Britain in 2007 by
The Breedon Books Publishing Company Limited
Breedon House, 3 The Parker Centre,
Derby, DE21 4SZ.

© TONY MATTHEWS, 2007

All Rights Reserved. No part of this publication may be reproduced, stored in a retrieval system, or transmitted in any form, or by any means, electronic, mechanical, photocopying, recording or otherwise without the prior permission in writing of the copyright holders, nor be otherwise circulated in any form or binding or cover other than in which it is published and without a similar condition being imposed on the subsequent publisher.

ISBN 978-1-85983-580-7

Printed and bound by MPG Books, Bodmin, Cornwall.

Contents

Introduction and Acknowledgements	7
Charlie Aitken	8
Peter Aldis	10
Jimmy Allen	12
Willie Anderson	14
Charlie Athersmith	16
Joe Bache	18
Gareth Barry	20
Frank Barson	22
Joe Beresford	24
Danny Blanchflower	26
Des Bremner	28
Frank Broome	30
Ernie Callaghan, BEM	32
Len Capewell	34
James Cowan	36
Gordon Cowans	38
Jimmy Crabtree	40
Vic Crowe	42
George Cummings	44
Tony Daley	46
Alan Deakin	48
Jack Devey	50
Johnny Dixon	52
Arthur Dorrell	54
Dion Dublin	56
Andy Ducat	58
Jimmy Dugdale	60
George Edwards	62
Ugo Ehiogu	64
Albert Evans	66
Allan Evans	68
Trevor Ford	70
Billy Garraty	72
Billy George	74
Colin Gibson	76
Jimmy Gibson	78
Andy Gray	80
Ray Graydon	82
Albert Hall	84
Harry Hampton	86
Sam Hardy	88
Jimmy Harrop	90
Tony Hateley	92
Gerry Hitchens	94
Dennis Hodgetts	96
Eric Houghton	98
Archie Hunter	100
Billy Kirton	102
Alex Leake	104
Brian Little	106
Andy Lochhead	108
Stan Lynn	110
Tommy Lyons	112
Paul McGrath	114
William McGregor	116
Ken McNaught	118
Peter McParland, MBE	120
Con Martin	122
Alex Massie	124
Freddie Miles	126
Dr Vic Milne	128
Tony Morley	130
Tommy Mort	132
Dennis Mortimer	134
Harry Morton	136
Frank Moss, senior	138
Frank Moss, junior	140
Chris Nicholl	142
Harry Parkes	144
David Platt	146
George Ramsay	148
Jimmy Rimmer	150
Bruce Rioch	152
Ian Ross	154
Dean Saunders	156
Ron Saunders	158
Jackie Sewell	160
Gary Shaw	162
Nigel Sims	164
Tommy Smart	166
Leslie Smith	168
Gareth Southgate	170
Howard Spencer	172
Nigel Spink	174
Ronnie Starling	176
Steve Staunton	178
Clem Stephenson	180
Alec Talbot	182
Joe Tate	184
Ian Taylor	186
Andy Townsend	188
Billy Walker	190
Charlie Wallace	192
Mark Walters	194
Tom 'Pongo' Waring	196
Fred Wheldon	198
Gary Williams	200
Peter Withe	202
Dicky York	204
Dwight Yorke	206

Introduction and Acknowledgements

To choose 100 legends from any one club that has been in existence for more than 130 years is no easy task. Therefore, I am expecting a few supporters to ask the question, why wasn't his or her favourite player included?

If I had been allowed to feature 200 legends, I don't think there would be any problems, no queries as to who should and shouldn't be included, but I went for men who I believe gave Aston Villa football club excellent service over a number of years.

John Farrelly, an ardent Villa supporter and collector of club memorabilia, and now a good friend of mine, asked me to include certain players who he believed warranted an entry, having worn the claret-and-blue strip with pride and commitment. I had no objection at all, especially when he mentioned the likes of Willie Anderson, Andy Ducat, Andy Lochhead and Dwight Yorke.

I would like to thank John for supplying most of the photographs used in this book; also, thank you to Charlie Pountney, a collector of old football photographs who has loaned quite a few, Steve Caron and Michelle Grainger at Breedon Books and also love and thanks to my darling wife Margaret, for her terrific support and, indeed, patience!

And last but my no means last, I say thank you to the 100 legends themselves...if it hadn't been for them, this book would have been rather nondescript!

Read and enjoy.

Tony Matthews, 2007

Charlie Aitken

Date of birth: 1 May 1942, Edinburgh

Aston Villa record:

Appearances: League 559+2, FA Cup 34+1, League Cup 61, Europe 2, Charity Shield 1

Goals: League 14, FA Cup 1, League Cup 1

Debut: League, 29 April 1961 v Sheffield Wednesday (h) won 4–1

Also played for: Gorsebridge Juniors, Edinburgh Thistle, New York Cosmos, Worcester City, Talbots Tankards FC, Aston Villa Old Stars, Scotland (3 Under-23 caps)

On the final day of the 1960–61 season, Johnny Dixon made his last senior appearance for the club in a 4–1 home win over Sheffield Wednesday. As one great servant bowed out, so another – full-back Charlie Aitken – stepped forward to make his Football League debut in the same game.

Charlie, when a pupil at George Watson's school in Edinburgh, played rugby on a Saturday morning and football in the afternoon, and occasionally on a Sunday.

As time progressed he decided against the oval ball game and signed up to play for the local intermediate soccer club, Gorsebridge Juniors. Soon afterwards he registered with Edinburgh Thistle, one of Hibernian's junior teams, and was asked to train at the Easter Road ground twice a week.

Charlie recalled 'I certainly enjoyed my time with Hibs, brushing shoulders with several Scottish internationals as well as being looked after very well indeed. When I was 16, I was asked if I would like to travel down to Birmingham and have a trial with Aston Villa.

'I jumped at the chance and did pretty well, but at that time I wasn't really bothered about joining an English club, certainly not one based 300 miles away from home, as I wanted to try and pass my exams and go to university. However, I chatted with my parents and decided to give it a go for a year, signing as an amateur at Villa Park.

'There were around 50 professionals at Villa Park when I arrived there, and believe me some of them didn't look at all that fit. I will admit that I was certainly fitter and quicker than most of them, and I played for the third team initially, earning £8 14s [£8.70] a week at that time – half of what I had been picking up grouse-beating in the Scottish Highlands in the summer months. And £4 went on board and lodgings.

'I learned a lot from the Villa manager and former England international Joe Mercer, and after my first year I knew I had made progress and decided to stay on for another 12 months, signing as a full-time professional at the age of 17, along with my friend from Edinburgh Wilson Briggs. I never looked back after that.'

Indeed he didn't. Charlie became one of the finest full-backs ever to wear the famous claret-and-blue strip. Over a period of 17 years he appeared in a club-record 660 first-class matches (561 in the Football League), gained a League Cup-winners' tankard in 1975 and two runners'-up prizes in the same competition in 1963 and 1971. He was also a key member of Villa's Third Division Championship-winning side in 1972 and helped the club back into the First Division in 1975, the same year he was voted Midlands Footballer of the Year.

Charlie represented Scotland in three Under-23 internationals, gaining his first cap against England in 1961, with the other two both coming against Wales soon afterwards, and he also played for a Scottish XI in 1962.

A clean kicker of the ball, he had great mobility, was an excellent positional player and very rarely, if ever, put in a reckless challenge.

A colleague of his, former centre-half Dick Edwards, said in 1968 'Charlie was a master in his position. Able to contain the most formidable opponent, he was scarcely given the runaround by a winger and always found time to assist his forwards. His timely interventions were of the highest quality. A tremendous left-back – one of the best I have ever played with.'

Five times an ever present (1962–63, 1964–65, 1965–66, 1968–69 and 1974–75), Charlie in fact missed only 18 out of a possible 252 First Division matches between his debut in April 1961 and May 1967. Captaining the side several times, he was both enthusiastic and totally committed, and in 1970, with less than 400 appearances under his belt, he was rewarded with a testimonial match at Villa Park versus Coventry City.

After helping Villa re-establish themselves back in the First Division, and ironically playing his last game for the club against his debut opponents Sheffield Wednesday, Charlie bid farewell to England for a while and signed a short-term contract with New York Cosmos in May 1976.

He returned from the States in 1977 to assist non-League side Worcester City and thereafter played in several charity matches for the Aston Villa Old Stars XI, also turning out for Talbot Tankards, before officially hanging up his boots in 1986 to concentrate on his antiques business, initially based in Acocks Green, Birmingham.

Peter Aldis

Date of birth: 11 April 1927, Kings Heath, Birmingham

Aston Villa record:
Appearances: League 262, FA Cup 32, Charity Shield 1
Goals: League 1
Debut: League, 29 March 1951 v Arsenal (a) won 3-1

Also played for: Hay Green, Hinckley Athletic, Slavia FC (Australia) player-coach, Wilhelmina (Australia) player-coach, Alvechurch player-manager, Mitchell's & Butler's FC
Managed: Melbourne Lions (Australia) coach-manager

Full-back Peter Aldis, like his 1950s teammate Danny Blanchflower, had a sunshine smile and he was also a very useful footballer, who made almost 300 senior appearances for Aston Villa during his 12 years with the club. His only goal was a fluke – a 35-yard header planted into the Sunderland net during a League game at Villa Park in September 1952, which helped set up a 3-0 win.

Peter started playing football with the Pineapple School team in Kings Heath. During the latter stages of the war, he worked at Cadbury's chocolate factory before joining Villa as an amateur centre-half from the local junior side Hay Green in November 1948, turning professional in January 1949 after half a dozen impressive displays in the intermediate and reserve teams.

Developing his game in the Central League, Peter finally made his League debut at the age of 24 against the reigning FA Cup holders Arsenal in front of almost 44,000 fans at Highbury in March 1951, when he lined up at left-back as partner to Stan Lynn.

His second outing a week later at home to Burnley was as a centre-half, but after that – injuries apart, including a cartilage operation in December 1951 – he always lined up wearing the number-three shirt, partnering Harry Parkes on a regular basis up to 1954–55 when the aforementioned Lynn took over on the right flank.

Peter and Stan played superbly well together until 1959. They actually lined up as full-back partners more than 160 times and were both superb when helping Villa win the FA Cup in 1957. They beat the League champions Manchester United 2-1 in the Final, Peter dealing with the threat from Johnny Berry down the right, while Stan kept David Pegg at bay on the left.

Sure-footed, with good balance and technique, Peter eventually lost his place in the Villa line up to new signing John Neal at the start of the 1959-60 season. He remained with the club for a further 12 months before moving into non-League football with Hinckley Athletic, linking up with another former Villa player, Eddie Follan (July 1960).

During his time with Alvechurch, Peter equalled the FA Cup record for appearing in 13 different rounds of the competition by playing through all the qualifying stages and competing in rounds one and two, having previously starred in rounds four, five and six, plus the semi-final and Final with Aston Villa.

In February 1964, intrigued by what he had heard from several former Football League players (and coaches), Peter chose to change his lifestyle and signed up as player-coach of Australia's Victoria State League side, Slavia based in Melbourne.

For season 1965-66, remaining in Melbourne, he served as player-coach with the strong Wilhelmina club, being awarded with the Australian Footballer of the Year trophy for his performances on the field and behind the scenes, even though he was 39 years of age.

After his exploits there, Peter spent three years as coach of Melbourne Lions, returning to England to take over as a part-time player and coach of Alvechurch, where he linked up with one of the Midlands' great personalities from non-League football, Graham Allner. He remained with the 'Church until the summer of 1970 when he switched his allegiance to Mitchell's & Butler's, for whom he played occasionally when in his 40s, finally taking off his boots in 1972.

After his football days were over, Peter, who still kept in touch with Villa but chose to watch matches from the comfort of his armchair, worked for a firm in Earlswood, was employed as an education and welfare officer in Redditch and also assisted as groundsman at a Solihull school.

The former editor of the *Sports Argus*, Dick Haynes, once referred to Peter as being '...eminently consistent, clever and stylish, cool and unruffled who loved to engage in an occasional upfield attacking foray. He also had an artistic streak to go with his consistency.'

Jimmy Allen

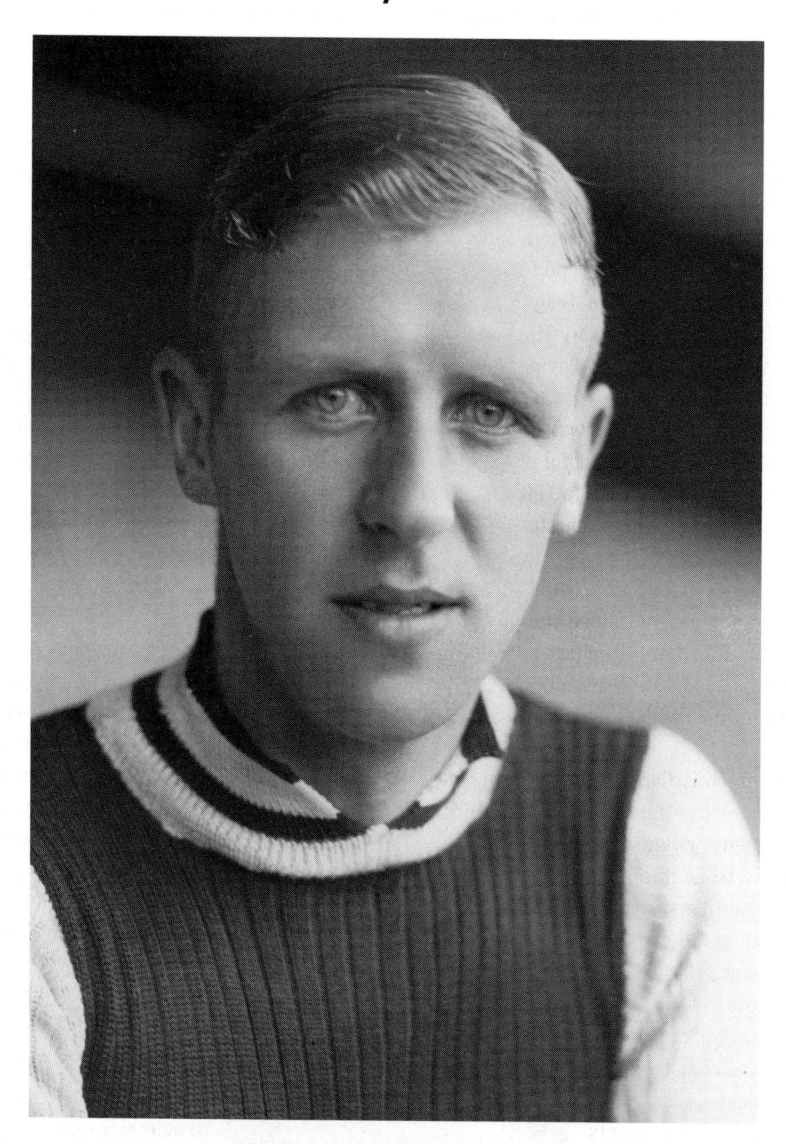

Date of birth: 16 October 1909, Poole, Dorset
Died: 1 February 1995, Southsea

Aston Villa record:
Appearances: League 147, FA Cup 13, Wartime 3
Goals: League 2, FA Cup 1
Debut: League, 25 August 1934 v Birmingham (a) lost 2-1

Also played for: Poole Central, Poole Town, Portsmouth, England (2 full caps)
Managed: Colchester United

In their book *A Century of English International Football: 1872-1972*, authors Morley Farror and Doug Lamming described Jimmy Allen as being 'A thoroughly sporting player and a centre-half of largely defensive bent. He was a big, tall man, ideally built for the "stopper" duties dictated by the tactics of his time.'

After attending Longfleet St Mary's School, Jimmy played for two local clubs as a teenager and once scored a goal from fully 60 yards for Poole Town. He joined Portsmouth as a 20-year-old professional in February 1930 and made his Football League debut in a 2-1 defeat at Birmingham in January 1931, netting his only goal in 145 outings for Pompey against Wolves in September 1932.

An ever present that season, he was in fine form again in 1933-34, missed only a handful of matches, and helped Pompey reach the FA Cup Final, only to collect a runners'-up medal as Manchester City won the Wembley showdown 2-1.

While with Pompey, Jimmy won two full international caps for England, lining up at centre-half against Northern Ireland in Belfast and against Wales at Newcastle in October/November 1933. He also played twice for the Football League in that same season.

Seven weeks after his Cup Final disappointment, Jimmy was transferred to Aston Villa for a then British record fee for a non-forward of £10,775. With the money received, Portsmouth built a new stand at Fratton Park and, to this day, some of the older supporters still refer to it as the 'Jimmy Allen Stand'.

As he had done with Portsmouth, Jimmy, who replaced Alex Talbot at the heart of the defence, made his debut for Villa against rivals Birmingham in front of 54,000 fans at St Andrew's at the beginning of the 1934-35 season. Despite Blues winning 2-1, he made a solid start, although, in truth, he took quite some time to settle into his new surroundings.

Nevertheless, overall he had a decent first season with Villa, making 34 appearances. He added 23 more to his tally in 1935-36 when both he and the rest of the team struggled as Villa suffered relegation to the Second Division for the first time in the club's history.

The outfield defence, which at various times featured George Beeson, Tom Griffiths, Danny Blair, Jimmy Gibson, Alex McLuckie, Ernie Callaghan, George Cummings, Tom Wood and, of course, Jimmy himself, conceded 110 goals, 56 at home, including two sevens and a six.

In an interview shortly after demotion, Jimmy said simply 'We were awful on occasions and played throughout most games as though we were all strangers to each other. Let's hope we can improve next season.'

Unfortunately, Villa didn't really perform at all well in 1936-37, but with Jimmy as captain they came good again in 1937-38 and clinched the Second Division Championship, finishing four points clear of Manchester United, with Jimmy missing only two games while also helping the team reach the semi-final of the FA Cup (beaten by Preston).

With the war clouds building over Europe, Jimmy played in 44 competitive games in 1938-39 and the first three League fixtures the following season before the fighting began. Although he remained a registered player with Villa throughout the hostilities, Jimmy played all his football elsewhere, having outings with Birmingham, Chelsea and Southampton.

He retired through injury in May 1944 and after the hostilities took employment as a sports and welfare officer with Gaskell & Chambers. He then took a coaching position with Villa, looking after the colts team before being lured back into senior football as manager of Southern League side Colchester United in July 1948. Despite operating under strict financial constraints, he was still able to guide the Layer Road club into the Football League in 1950.

However, when he was pressed by the club's directors to utilise more part-timers and blood some youngsters, he quit and moved nearer to home, taking over the Festing Arms pub in Southsea.

Willie Anderson

Date of birth: 24 January 1947, Liverpool

Aston Villa record:
Appearances: League 229+2, FA Cup 11+1, League Cup 23, Charity Shield 1
Goals: League 36, FA Cup 1, League Cup 8
Debut: League, 21 January 1967 v Chelsea (a) lost 3-1

Also played for: Manchester United, Cardiff City, Portland Timbers (NASL)

A throwback to the old-fashioned winger, the fast-raiding Willie Anderson could unhinge defences with a combination of delicate footwork and teasing crosses.

He was certainly quick over the ground and very direct in his approach and was also blessed with film-star looks and a massive female following.

He joined Manchester United as a 15-year-old soon after representing both Liverpool and Lancashire Schoolboys. He signed professional forms in February 1964 and two months later gained an FA Youth Cup-winners' medal. His wing partner at the time was George Best and in goal was future Villa star Jimmy Rimmer. Also in the Reds team were John Fitzpatrick, David Sadler and Johnny Aston, all of whom went on to give United excellent service.

Willie, who quickly won an England Youth cap, had been handed his League debut by Matt Busby in December 1963 (v. Burnley), but he faced some stiff competition at Old Trafford with the likes of Best and Aston, John Connolly, Ian Moir and even Bobby Charlton, all of whom enjoyed playing on the wing – with some of them able to occupy both flanks.

Willie stuck in there though, hoping to make a name for himself, but after just 12 first-class appearances, including outings in the semi-final of the 1966 FA Cup against Everton and the European Cup versus FK Partizan Belgrade, he was transferred to Aston Villa for what was to prove a bargain fee of £20,000 in January 1967.

Villa were struggling desperately at the time, having just been demoted to the Second Division for only the third time in the club's history, and as manager Tommy Cummings set about revamping his squad he placed Willie straight into the team on the left wing (as partner to former England international Peter Broadbent) with ex-Arsenal man Johnny MacLeod on the right.

Unfortunately, although he was an ever present, Willie's first season was not a good one, with Villa finishing a poor 16th in the table, and it was to get worse. After a double change of manager, which saw Tommy Docherty move into the hot seat to soon be replaced by Vic Crowe, at the end of the 1969-70 campaign the club were relegated to the Third Division, and for Willie it seemed as if the world of football had collapsed around him. Four years earlier, he had played in front of 62,500 fans at Old Trafford, but in March 1970 fewer than 9,000 hardy supporters attended a mid-week League game at Boothferry Park, Hull.

Willie, nevertheless, still produced some wizardry on the left wing and once again played in every game of the 1970-71 season, with his brilliant performances helping Villa reach the League Cup Final, which they lost 2-0 to Tottenham Hotspur.

The following season was his best for the club in terms of goals scored – his tally of 10 in 40 League matches helped Villa to win the Third Division Championship.

Twelve months later, having taken his overall total of senior appearances for Villa past the 260 mark (45 goals scored), he was sold to Cardiff City for £60,000.

He continued to do the business with the Bluebirds, tantalising defenders on both sides of the field and laying on chances galore for his teammates as the Welsh club gained promotion to the Second Division in 1976.

The following season, with America beckoning ball-playing forwards, Willie opted to sign permanently for Portland Timbers for £22,000, having been on loan with the same club between May and August 1975. He teamed up with his former playing colleague at Villa Park Brian Tiler at the Oregon-based club.

Retiring in May 1979, Willie and his family chose to remain in the US, where he became an executive with a commercial radio station in Oregon. He very rarely ventures abroad these days, but still maintains a huge interest in Aston Villa football club.

Charlie Athersmith

Date of birth: 10 May 1872, Bloxwich, Staffordshire
Died: 18 September 1910, Shifnal, Shropshire

Aston Villa record:
Appearances: League 270, FA Cup 38, Charity Shield 3
Goals: League 75, FA Cup 10, Charity Shield 1
Debut: League, 9 March 1891 v Preston North End (h) lost 1-0

Also played for: Bloxwich Wanderers, Bloxwich Strollers (2 spells), Unity Gas FC, Birmingham, Grimsby Town (registered player for one season, then trainer), England (12 full caps)

One of the most famous names in football during the latter part of the 19th century, Charlie Athersmith was highly regarded among the quickest wingers in Britain, prompting columnist Simon Tappertit of *The Grasshopper* to write 'He is one of those performers who can play equally well at home or abroad, and, once on the run, he fears no foe; and he is remarkably skilful and well trained, it is seldom that a match passes without him doing some memorable things in it.'

Yes, indeed, Charlie was a supreme footballer. Wonderfully consistent, he regularly charged 50 yards down the wing without anyone getting near him, always rising to the big occasion. He contributed considerably on the goals front, reaching double figures in five seasons for Villa, his best haul being 12 in 1896-97.

Contemporary newspaper reports reveal that if it hadn't been for the likes of West Bromwich Albion's flying winger Billy Bassett and Sheffield Wednesday's flank man Fred Spiksley, then Charlie would certainly have gained many more senior caps for England than he did.

Football mad at Walsall Road Council School, Bloxwich, he joined Aston Villa as a full-time professional in February 1891 following a decent spell with the Unity Gas team, for whom he scored over 40 goals, including 20 in one season.

He went on to serve Villa splendidly for 10 years, notching up 86 goals in 311 appearances, gaining five League Championship-winning medals (1894, 1895, 1897, 1899 and 1900) and two FA Cup-winners' prizes (1895 and 1897), and he was instrumental when the League and Cup double was achieved in 1897. As an ever present that season he was brilliant. He had a hand in every goal when Blackburn Rovers were defeated 5-1 at Ewood Park, scored one and set up four more when Bolton were crushed 6-2, and he laid on three (two for Bobby Campbell) in a 5-0 drubbing of Wolves.

Charlie was on the losing side only twice in 12 international appearances for England between March 1892 and April 1900. He scored three goals, including one in the record 13-2 victory over Ireland in February 1899. His England debut was on the right wing against the Irish in Belfast when he lined up alongside two of his Villa colleagues, Dennis Hodgetts on the left flank and Jack Devey at centre-forward, in a 2-0 win, Charlie having a hand in one of Harry Daft's two goals. He also appeared in two England international trials (1899 and 1900), played twice for an England XI and represented the Football League nine times, eight against the Scottish League, between 1894 and 1901.

In a memorable a League game against Sheffield United in October 1894, Charlie and the Villa goalkeeper Tom Wilkes both borrowed umbrellas from supporters in the crowd to protect themselves from the torrential rain but unfortunately Villa lost 2-1.

In June 1901 Charlie moved across the city to join arch-rivals Birmingham, who wanted him to replace the injury-prone Billy Bennett at outside-right.

He continued to deliver the goods, having an excellent first season when he appeared in 33 senior games and scored four goals, the first two coming in a convincing 5-1 home League win over Sheffield United in mid-October. His other three strikes all earned points from 1-1 draws against Stoke, Sunderland and Nottingham Forest.

A further six goals were scored the following season (in 31 starts), helping Blues finish runners-up behind Manchester City in the Second Division.

Not getting any younger – he was now well into his 30s and losing some of his pace – Charlie still managed to perform pretty well at the highest level, missing only one League game (away to Notts County on Boxing Day) as Blues established themselves in the top flight.

Charlie remained at the club for one more season (1904–05), which saw him make his 100th and final League appearance for Blues.

Unwilling to retire, he was selected for the unsanctioned Tagg and Campbell FA tour to Germany in the summer of 1905. He regretted going in the end because he and several other players, many of them internationals, were subsequently suspended and, in effect, Charlie's career at the top level ended there and then.

He later played briefly for one of his former clubs, Bloxwich Strollers, during the 1906–07 season while still serving out his ban, and when that was lifted he became senior trainer at Grimsby Town, offering to play if required, but he never made the Mariners first team.

He remained as head trainer at Blundell Park until May 1909 when he became ill and moved to Shifnal. Charlie was only 38 when he died.

THE LEGENDS OF ASTON VILLA

Joe Bache

Date of birth: 8 February 1880, Stourbridge
Died: 10 November 1960, Birmingham

Aston Villa record:
Appearances: League 431, FA Cup 42, Charity Shield 1, Wartime 2
Goals: League 168, FA Cup 17
Debut: League, 16 February 1901 v Notts County (a) lost 2-0

Also played for: Bewdley Victoria, Stourbridge, Notts County (guest), Mid-Rhondda (player-manager), Grimsby Town (player-coach), Mannheim FC (Germany), England (7 full caps)

Black Country-born Joe Bache was a cultured inside-forward who occasionally played on the left wing. He had few equals in the art of dribbling, although, at times, he could be somewhat selfish, holding onto the ball far too long – much to the annoyance of his colleagues and, indeed, his manager!

Well mannered and easy going both on and off the field, Joe was certainly an intelligent footballer who displayed a masterly technique. He gave Aston Villa 15 years' excellent service, during which time he made 474 senior appearances – only three other players have made more: Charlie Aitken (660), Billy Walker (531) and Gordon Cowans (528). He also netted 185 goals, and is again currently lying in fourth place in the list of the club's all-time champion marksmen.

A youngster with Bewdley Victoria, Joe joined Villa two months before his 21st birthday, having served with his home-town club Stourbridge for three years prior to that.

His first start for Villa was in a friendly against Berlin a few days before making his League debut in place of the injured Billy Garraty, in a 2-0 defeat at Notts County. He played in a further six games that season, netting his first goal in a 3-1 reverse at Nottingham Forest in April 1901.

An ever present in 1901-02 when he linked up well with Scottish international Bobby Templeton on the left flank, Joe was injured when scoring on his international debut for England versus Wales in March 1903 and, as a result, missed the last nine League games as Villa finished runners-up to Sheffield Wednesday in the First Division, pipped to the post by a single point. Back to full fitness the following season, he top scored with 16 goals and added two more caps to his tally versus Wales and Ireland, finding the net in both games. Over the next few years he played in another four internationals, appeared in several England trials, represented the Football League on seven occasions, played for the Birmingham County FA and appeared for Birmingham in the annual challenge matches versus London in 1909 and 1913.

Retaining his form and fitness, Joe was quite brilliant in 1904-05 when he was joined by Albert Hall, both players helping Villa claim fourth spot in the League and lift the FA Cup, defeating Newcastle United 2-0 in the Final in front of 101,117 fans at The Crystal Palace. Joe, in fact, set up the opening goal after just two minutes. Following a corner, his low shot was blocked but the alert Harry Hampton pounced to drive the ball home.

Joe and Hall remained Villa's regular left-wing pairing for quite a while, and they scored 40 goals between them as Villa once more took second place in the League, this time behind Manchester United.

Leading scorer again in 1908-09 with 11 goals, Joe, who was now Villa's captain, bagged 22 the following term as Villa won the League Championship for the sixth time, and he was on target 16 times in 1910-11 when Villa achieved second place.

Continuing to impress all and sundry, Joe steadily upped his total of both appearances and goals and in 1912-13 saw Villa come agonisingly close to winning the double for the second time. They finished runners-up in the League to Sunderland despite having beaten the Wearsiders 1-0 in the FA Cup Final, when Joe occupied the outside-left position with Clem Stephenson as his inside partner.

In the last two pre-World War One seasons Joe helped Villa finish second and 13th in the First Division table, and during the hostilities he assisted Notts County as a guest while playing in four games for Villa, two in the Midland Victory League.

In July 1919 he became player-manager of Mid-Rhondda, and after a spell with Grimsby Town he spent six years in Germany, coaching Rot-Weiss (Frankfurt) and playing for Mannheim FC. He returned to Villa Park as reserve-team coach in 1927, had further spells with Mannheim and Rot-Weiss and then worked as a clerk in a Birmingham hospital before becoming mine host of the Traveller's Rest on Aston Cross and the Coaching House in Evesham. He later ran a gentleman's outfitters in Northfield.

Gareth Barry

Date of birth: 23 February 1981, Hastings, Sussex

Aston Villa record:
Appearances: League (Premiership) 278+12, FA Cup 17+2, League Cup 25, European 0+1, others 17+1
Goals: League (Premiership) 27, FA Cup 3, League Cup 4
Debut: Premiership, 2 May 1998, substitute v Sheffield Wednesday (a) won 3-1

Also played for: England (8 full and 27 Under-21 caps)

A naturally left-footed player, strong, mobile, workmanlike, aggressive (when he has to be) and totally committed, Gareth Barry has given his heart and soul on the park for Aston Villa over the last six years, producing some exquisite performances while occupying a variety of positions.

Although preferring a midfield role, he has also starred as a full-back, as an emergency central-defender and even as an out-and-out attacker, and never fails to deliver the goods.

Born in deepest Sussex, he joined the apprentice ranks at Villa Park at the age of 16 and turned professional in February 1998 under manager John Gregory, who, after seeing him produce some very impressive displays in the second team, handed him his senior debut three months later in front of more than 34,000 fans at Hillsborough when he came on as a second-half substitute for Ian Taylor in a 3–1 win.

Eight days later he started a Premiership game for the first time, helping Villa beat the champions Arsenal 1–0.

Inserted into the team at the start of the 1998–99 campaign on the left side of midfield, alongside Taylor, Lee Hendrie and Alan Thompson, he played in 32 games, and the following season he filled in at left-back for the injured Alan Wright. Later on he deputised very efficiently for Republic of Ireland international Steve Staunton, and he also successfully accompanied Gareth Southgate and Ugo Ehiogu in the heart of the defence.

After a niggling injury problem (a tweaked Achilles tendon), he came back in midfield where he really impressed, so much so that he was handed a five-year contract to celebrate his 18th birthday.

Barry scored his first Villa goal to seal a 2–0 win over Nottingham Forest in April 1999, and a fortnight later he netted in a 4–3 defeat by Charlton. Although goalscoring is not his forte, he had his best season in terms of goals in 2005–06 when he struck six times, including home and away strikes against Sunderland and a brace in an 8–3 League Cup win at Wycombe. Over the last two years he has also taken over as Villa's penalty taker, and although he has missed from the spot thankfully no real damage was done!

One of Barry's major strengths is his stamina. He is also very comfortable on the ball, strong and competitive and can certainly produce a powerful shot, mainly left footed, although he did score a spectacular goal with his right foot in the home Premiership game against Tottenham Hotspur early in the 2006–07 season.

Honoured by England as a Youth-team player, he was upgraded to the Under-21 ranks in 1999 as he continued to make progress and was eventually awarded his first full cap as a substitute against Ukraine in the run up to Euro 2000, quickly adding a second cap to his tally versus Malta. And, as time progressed, he became a key member of the Under-21 side and pushed his senior international appearances up to eight.

Niggling injuries have certainly affected his game over the last four years or so, especially in 2004–05 when his left knee caused him considerable grief. However, he is a born fighter and was quickly back in the fray, driving forward from midfield and showing his versatility with some brilliant performances, which resulted in many soccer reporters up and down the country asking the question 'Why isn't Barry in the England squad? We are crying out for a left-sided player to assist Ashley Cole.'

Seemingly the cornerstone of Villa's long-term plans, Barry, without doubt, is now a vital part of Martin O'Neill's team and, with his appearance record increasing by the minute, it is more than likely that Barry will figure in a claret-and-blue shirt for many years to come.

Frank Barson

Date of birth: 10 April 1891, Grimethorpe, Sheffield
Died: 13 September 1968, Winson Green, Birmingham

Aston Villa record:
Appearances: League 92, FA Cup 16
Goals: League 10
Debut: League, 19 October 1919 v Middlesbrough (a) won 4–1

Also played for: Albion FC (Sheffield), Cammell Laird (Sheffield), Barnsley, Burnley (guest), Manchester United, Watford, Hartlepools United (player-coach), Wigan Borough, Rhyl Athletic (player-manager), England (1 full cap)
Managed: Stourbridge

Although he played in only 108 matches for Aston Villa, Frank Barson gets into this book of legends simply because he was a brilliant centre-half and one of the most controversial footballers of his day.

His career began in 1905 when, aged 14, and after six years playing in local junior football, he signed for Barnsley in August 1911. The Tykes won the FA Cup in his first season at Oakwell, although Frank wasn't in the team.

During the war he served in the army and played as a guest for Burnley in 1916-17, but six weeks into the 1919-20 campaign Frank was an Aston Villa player, signed for £2,850 - the highest fee in the game at the time.

Taking over from Jimmy Harrop, who switched to left-half, Frank settled into the team splendidly and performed solidly at the heart of the defence as Villa raced through to the FA Cup Final, where they met and defeated Huddersfield Town 1-0 at Stamford Bridge. Frank had a great game, completely marshalling Terriers' centre-forward Sammy Taylor, who had already scored 40 goals that season.

Frank also played for England versus Wales in March 1920, lining up with his teammates Sam Hardy and Andy Ducat in a 2-1 defeat by Wales at Highbury. Frank didn't play well and was never chosen again.

On Boxing Day 1920, so determined to play for Villa, Frank trudged seven miles through heavy snow after a train derailment to make sure he arrived in time for the game at Old Trafford. Performing like a Trojan, he helped Villa win 3-1 in front of a then record crowd of 70,504.

A year later, Frank scored the winning goal for Villa, against Sheffield United at Bramall Lane - with a stunning 35-yard header!

Frank enjoyed his three-year association with Villa, but with young Tommy Ball ready to step forward he was sold to Manchester United in August 1922. He spent six seasons at Old Trafford, making 152 first-class appearances.

In the 1924-25 season, Frank was promised a pub if he skippered United back into the top flight. This duly happened, and he was handed the keys to a hotel in Ardwick Green. When he opened up for the first time, several admirers went along to celebrate. Most of them were so full of flattery that Frank, after just a quarter of an hour behind the bar, was so fed up he handed his keys to the head waiter and walked out of the door, never to return. He then telegraphed his wife, telling her to cancel the furniture delivery.

When he left United for Watford in May 1928 at the age of 38, Frank received scores of glowing reports from his teammates, club officials and supporters alike.

In May 1929 he was appointed player-coach of Hartlepools United, but after just five months in office he signed for Wigan Borough. After that he had a four-year spell as player-manager of Rhyl Athletic (June 1931-June 1935), managed Stourbridge briefly before returning to Villa Park as a youth-team coach in July 1935, taking over as senior coach and trainer three months later. After the war he acted as trainer with Swansea Town (July 1947-February 1954) and ended his career in football as trainer at Lye Town (July 1954-May 1956).

A blacksmith by trade, Frank's only failing as a defender was that he hardly knew his own strength and, on several occasions, tended to be rather impetuous with his challenges. Barrel-chested, with a broken, twisted nose to boot, he was, nevertheless, a bastion in defence with boundless enthusiasm. He was an outstanding captain who led by example, being an inspiration to all of his teammates.

Garth Dykes wrote in his 1994 book on Manchester United, *The United Alphabet*, 'His desire to always be in the thick of the fray brought him into many conflicts with the game's authorities.'

It is believed he was sent off the field at least 12 times in his career (twice with Aston Villa) and was once banned for six months during his Watford days. He was also suspended following an unsavoury incident during the Manchester United versus Manchester City FA Cup semi-final at Sheffield in March 1926. It was alleged that Frank had knocked out Sam Cowan, City's centre-half, in a scuffle. Although not dismissed by the referee, Frank was later suspended by the Football Association for two months.

Joe Beresford

Date of birth: 26 February 1906, Chesterfield
Died: 26 February 1978, Birmingham

Aston Villa record:
Appearances: League 224, FA Cup 27
Goals: League 66, FA Cup 7
Debut: League, 3 September 1927 v Liverpool (a) drew 0-0

Also played for: Askern Road Working Men's Club (Doncaster), Bentley New Village Old Boys, Bartley Colliery, Mexborough Athletic, Mansfield Town, Swansea Town, Stourbridge, Sutton Town, Hartlepools United (guest), England (1 full cap)

Joe Beresford was an old-fashioned inside-forward *par excellence*, who preferred to play on the right. Quite stocky in build, he was a fine close dribbler, expert passer of the ball and fast over the ground with a terrific shot, often choosing to have a crack at goal from distances of 20 to 30 yards.

He had played in all five positions on the forward-line prior to scoring 60 goals in two seasons for Mexborough Athletic, from where he switched to Mansfield Town in May 1926.

Described in the local press as a 'real bundle of tricks', Joe was always a potential match winner and very much a crowd pleaser, and he went on to net 18 goals in 35 appearances for the Stags, helping them win both the Midland Combination Cup and the Notts FA Senior Cup, among others, before joining Villa in May 1927 in somewhat unusual circumstances.

A club representative had been sent along to Edgeley Park to watch the Stockport County goalkeeper John Turner in action against Mansfield in a Combination match, but everyone seemed to be admiring the skills of a young player called Beresford. Villa, obviously impressed with the glowing reports they received, stepped in with an offer the deal was done and Joe, then aged 21, signed on the dotted line for a fee of £750 – a record for Mansfield at that time.

Meanwhile, County's goalkeeper Turner joined Wolves and later played for Watford and Rotherham United.

Joe went virtually straight into Villa's first team, making a sound debut in front of 35,000 fans against Liverpool at Anfield, and over the next eight years he appeared in more than 250 senior matches and scored 73 goals. He starred for the Football League XI in 1931 and again in 1934, the same year he was also capped by England, along with his Villa Park teammate Tom Gardner, against Czechoslovakia in Prague. Unfortunately, the Czechs won 2-1.

Linking up superbly down Villa's right flank with first Dicky York, then Jackie Mandley and later with Eric Houghton, Joe scored 11 goals in his first season, 14 in his second (when Villa finished third in Division One and lost to Portsmouth in the FA Cup semi-final at Highbury), 11 again in 1929-30 and 14 in 1930-31 when rampant Villa chased Arsenal home in the race for the League Championship, scoring a club record 128 goals in the process.

He was now enjoying his football immensely and reached double figures once more in 1931-32 (10 goals), followed by six in 1932-33 when, unfortunately, he was troubled by an ankle injury. Now being hard pressed for the inside-right berth by Welshman Dai Astley, he only managed five goals in 1933-34 and once again figured in a losing semi-final, Villa going out of the FA Cup to Manchester City at Leeds Road, Huddersfield.

At this juncture, Villa had several quality forwards on their books, and after a quiet 1934-35 season Joe opted for a change of scenery, transferring to Preston North End in September 1935 for £1,000. Two years later he was successful in his third FA Cup semi-final against West Bromwich Albion, and then at Wembley he gleefully helped North End beat Huddersfield Town to lift the trophy for the first time since their double-winning season of 1888-89.

Joe remained at Deepdale until December 1937, when he switched his allegiance to Swansea Town, with whom he won the Welsh Cup, before ending his career in May 1941 after brief spells with Stourbridge (being re-united with his former Villa colleague Alex Talbot) and Sutton Town, although he did come back for one game with Hartlepools United as a guest in 1943, at the age of 37. He had opened a fish shop in Stourbridge prior to the war and was later employed at ICI Witton for 11 years.

Danny Blanchflower

Date of birth: 10 February 1926, Belfast, Northern Ireland
Died: 9 December 1993, Surrey

Aston Villa record:
Appearances: League 148, FA Cup 7
Goals: League 10
Debut: League, 17 March 1951 v Burnley (h) won 3-2

Also played for: Bloomfield United, Glentoran, Swindon Town (guest), Barnsley, Tottenham Hotspur, Northern Ireland (56 full caps), Great Britain (1 app)
Managed: Chelsea, Northern Ireland

Danny Blanchflower was a wonderfully-consistent attacking wing-half of medium height (5ft 10in), slim build and trained down to a wiry strength.

On whatever surface, muddy, dry, dusty or lush, his deftness, poise, balance, thoughtful positioning and careful kicking were there for all to see and admire. His all-round play was technically sound, his tackle strong and his commitment on the field of play was nothing less than 100 percent.

He was masterful when in possession and hard to shake off the ball; his correctness and his refusal to be rushed gave his play an air of certainty and security. He passed with pin-point accuracy and authority and was an inspiration to those around him – his teammates that is, not his opponents!

Former Olympic footballer and well-known sports reporter Maurice Edeleston always spoke highly of Danny and once wrote 'Neatness, coolness and precision characterised his football.'

A great theorist and tactician, and a pretty efficient after-dinner speaker (when he was associated with Villa), Danny accumulated a wonderful set of statistics: he played in 720 club and international matches, scored more than 40 goals and skippered one of his clubs, Spurs, to the League and FA Cup double to a second FA Cup Final victory and also won the European Cup-winners' Cup, all within the space of three seasons.

He played Gaelic football as a youngster (for Connsbrook) as well as trying his luck at cricket, field hockey, squash, table tennis and badminton. He served in the RAF in Scotland during the war and played one game as a guest for Swindon Town before joining Glentoran in December 1945, turning professional a month later.

After three excellent years playing in the Irish league, Danny was transferred to Barnsley for £6,000 in April 1949 and from Oakwell he switched to Villa Park in March 1951, signed for £15,000.

Taking over at right-half from Larry Canning, and appropriately making his debut on St Patrick's Day, he served Villa superbly well for three and a half years, making 155 appearances and netting 10 goals. The team itself wasn't brilliant, far from it, but Danny stood out like a sore thumb, performing head and shoulders above the majority of his teammates. Nothing against the rest of the lads, but he was one hell of a player – so much so that in October 1954 Tottenham Hotspur moved in and paid £30,000 to take him to London. He got even better at White Hart Lane, becoming a member of one of the finest midfield trios in world football – along with the Scottish duo of John 'The Ghost' White and hard man Dave Mackay.

Voted FWA Footballer of the Year in 1958 and 1961, Danny gained 56 caps at senior level for Northern Ireland, winning four with Barnsley, nine with Villa and 43 with Spurs, and appeared in the 1958 World Cup Finals. He also represented the Irish League (as a Glentoran player) on five occasions, played for the Northern Ireland Regional League XI, starred for Great Britain against the Rest of Europe in 1955 and turned out for the Football League against the Irish League in 1960, while also touring Canada with the Irish FA in 1953, playing in eight of the 10 games. Danny also had the pleasure of captaining London versus Basle and Barcelona in the semi-final and Final of the 1958 Inter Cities Fairs Cup competition.

A troublesome knee injury, which lingered on for quite some time, eventually forced Danny to retire in June 1964. He then made a career in journalism, displaying in his writing the same innovative, forceful and, at times, controversial attributes that had marked his playing career.

Such was his high standing in the world of football, and despite an absence for several years, he had spells as manager of both Chelsea (December 1978–September 1979) and the Northern Ireland national team, and in May 1990 Danny received an honour never open to him during his playing days when Spurs met an Irish XI in a benefit match for one of the true all-time greats of football.

Danny's brother, Jackie, was badly injured in the 1958 Munich air crash when registered with Manchester United.

Des Bremner

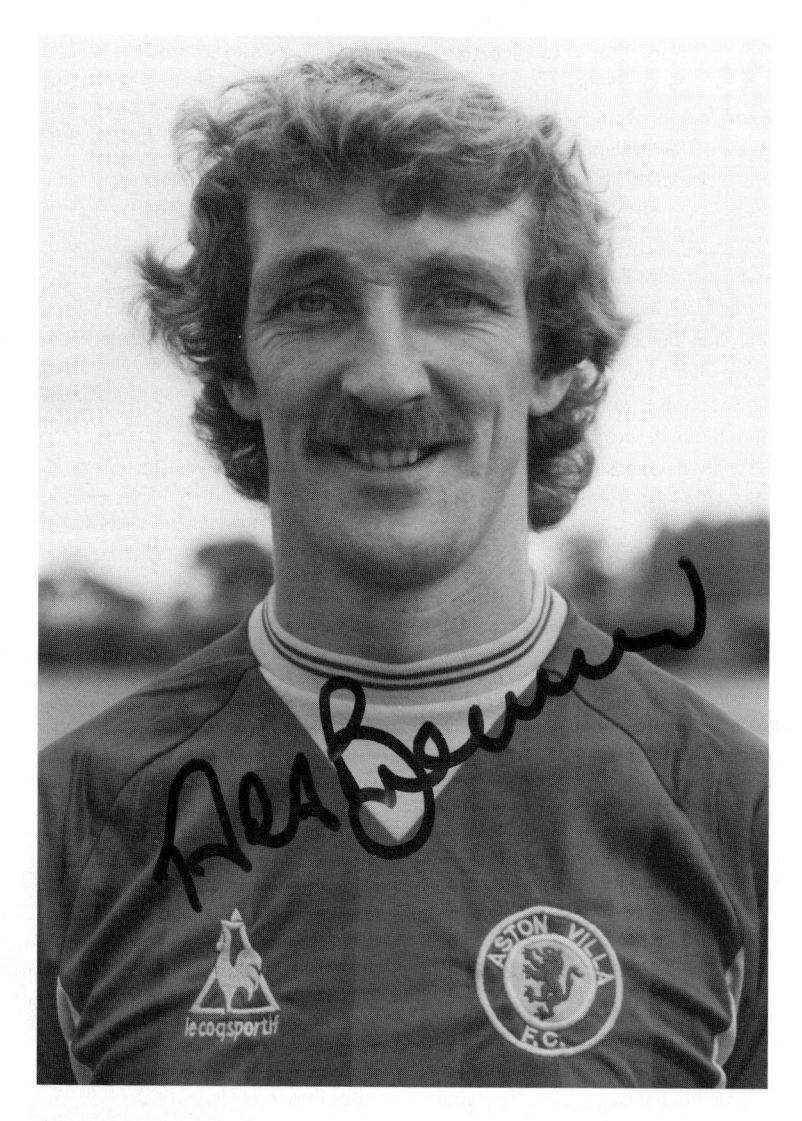

Date of birth: 7 September 1962, Aberchirder

Aston Villa record:
Appearances: League 170+4, FA Cup 14, League Cup 17+1, Europe 20, FA Charity Shield 1
Goals: League 9, League Cup 1
Debut: League, 22 September 1979 v Arsenal (h) drew 0–0

Also played for: Banks O'Dee 'A', Deveronvale, Hibernian, Birmingham City, Fulham, Walsall, Stafford Rangers, Scotland (1 full and 9 Under-21 caps)

When Des Bremner arrived at his first professional club, Hibernian, from the Highland League side Deveronvale, he did so faced with the truly daunting prospect of acting as understudy to Scottish international right-back John Brownlie.

Luck as well as misfortune, however, often play big parts in the careers of footballers, but Des would probably never have anticipated that he'd be taking over the number-two shirt after just a couple of weeks at Easter Road, after Brownlie suffered a double leg break in a clash with East Fife's Ian Printy in January 1973.

Des quickly established himself as a firm favourite with the Hibs fans, working hard, being tenacious in the tackle and doing the simple things well, which he continued to do throughout the rest of his career.

He made over 200 appearances in eight years at Easter Road, scoring 18 goals in the process and playing his part in some titanic European battles against Leeds United in 1975, for whom Des's namesake Billy pretty well single-handedly put paid to what would and should have been a famous victory for Hibs.

Des was, at this time, being watched by English scouts due to his consistent performances and, like most players, was keen to try his luck in England. Hibs required hard cash and agreed to transfer Des to Aston Villa after boss Ron Saunders came in with a £275,000 offer, plus former Clyde striker Joe Ward. Saunders later said of his new signing 'He was the most underrated footballer I ever purchased.'

Des was used as a defensive midfielder at Villa, a role he had filled latterly during his career with Hibs. Most Villa fans would agree that his greatest period in the claret-and-blue strip came during the club's League Championship-winning season of 1980–81 and their victorious European Cup run the following year, when many of Bayern Munich's moves in the De Kuip Stadium in Rotterdam faltered on the back of a crunching tackle from Villa's midfield powerhouse.

There is no doubt that Des played out of his skin throughout those two campaigns, but, perhaps harshly, most of the praise for Villa's triumphs in 1981 and 1982 was directed at other players around him.

The typically-modest Scotsman, though, merely said 'Villa won both the League title and the European Cup as a team. I didn't win it by myself, nor did any other individual.'

Des, who scored 10 goals in 227 senior appearances for Villa over a five-year period, became one of only a handful of players to cross the second city divide when he joined arch-rivals Birmingham in October 1984.

He appeared in 168 games for Blues and later assisted Fulham (from August 1989), Walsall (for three months, then being the oldest player ever to appear in a League game for the Saddlers, aged 37 years and 240 days versus Bristol City in May 1990) and non-League side Stafford Rangers before retiring in May 1992.

Besides his club activity, Des also represented his country, winning nine Under-21 caps and playing in one full international for Scotland as a second-half substitute for Kenny Dalglish in a 1–0 win over Switzerland at Hampden Park in April 1976.

In later years, Des returned to Villa Park as the club's academy coach, and he also held a position as an adviser with the Professional Football Association. He is still associated with the PFA as Managing Director of their Financial Services Division, based in Birmingham.

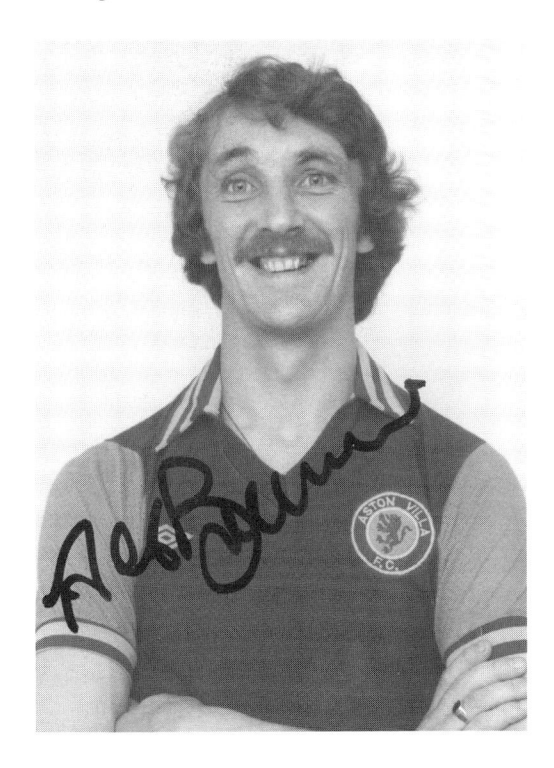

Frank Broome

Date of birth: 11 June 1915, Berkhamstead, Hertfordshire
Died: 10 September 1994, Bournemouth, Hampshire

Aston Villa record:
Appearances: League 133, FA Cup 18, Wartime 135
Goals: League 77, FA Cup 13, Wartime 91
Debut: League, 6 April 1935 v Portsmouth (a) won 1-0

Also played for: Boxmoor United Juniors, Boxmoor United, Berkhamstead Town, (wartime guest for Aldershot, Birmingham, Charlton Athletic, Chelmsford City, Chesterfield, Northampton Town, Nottingham Forest, Notts County, Revo Electric, Watford, Wolverhampton Wanderers, Worcester City), Derby County, Notts County, Brentford, Crewe Alexandra, Shelbourne (Ireland), England (7 full and 1 Wartime caps)

Managed: Notts County (acting manager), Exeter City (2 spells), Southend United, Bankstown (NSW, Australia), Corinthians (Sydney, Australia)

Frank Broome was Aston Villa's leading scorer three seasons running, 1936 to 1939, and he was also top marksman for the club in 1943–44.

A small, frail yet thrustful player, who could perform equally well anywhere along the forward line but admitted that he 'preferred to lead the attack', Frank was adept at switching positions during the course of a game and often caused defenders all sorts of problems. A prolific, dangerous goalscorer, he was quick over the ground, had two good feet and packed a powerful shot, being perhaps a little stronger with his right than his left; he was, without doubt, one of the game's finest marksmen inside (and outside) the penalty area during the latter part of the 1930s.

He was 19 years of age when he joined a then struggling Villa side, having scored plenty of goals in local non-League football. He netted three times in his first seven outings at the end of the 1934–35 season and 11 in 17 the following term, before making the centre-forward position his own in 1936–37 after Villa had been relegated to the Second Division for the first time in the club's history.

Playing in a spirited front line that regularly included Welshman Dai Astley, South African international Gordon Hodgson, wingers Eric Houghton and Jackie Maund, plus Freddie Haycock and latterly Ronnie Starling, Frank cracked in 29 goals as Villa finished a disappointing ninth in the table.

Maintaining his form throughout 1937–38, when he was joined in the attack at times by Charlie Phillips and Frank Shell, his goal tally this time round was 26, including 20 in the League, as Villa clinched the Second Division title, finishing four points clear of Manchester United.

Frank's form promptly earned him a place in the England squad to tour Germany, Switzerland and France that summer – and he celebrated with a goal on his international debut when the Germans were whipped 6-3 in front of 120,000 spectators and Heir Hitler in the Olympic Stadium, Berlin, in mid-May 1938. Frank and the rest of the England players reluctantly complied with the British Ambassador's wish to give the Nazi salute prior to the kick-off, and then went out and gained revenge on the pitch!

Frank added six more full caps to his total (occupying four different positions) and netted two more goals before the fighting broke out in Europe. During the hostilities, he represented his country in one wartime international versus Scotland at Hampden Park in May 1939 and in 1944 played for the FA XI. He also toured Australia with the FA party in 1951, played for an international XI against a District XI in 1940 and helped Wolves win the Football League (North) Cup in 1942 as a guest versus Sunderland.

Frank took his overall record with Villa to 286 appearances and 181 goals, before transferring to Derby County in September 1946. He spent three seasons with the Rams, netted a further 45 goals in 119 games, and then assisted Notts County from October 1949 to July 1953 by scoring 41 goals in 114 outings for the Magpies, whom he helped win the Third Division (South) Championship in 1950.

After that Frank served Brentford from July 1953, Crewe Alexandra from October 1953 and Shelbourne from February 1955, retiring as a player in June 1955 on his 40th birthday. He continued in football for the next 18 years, his duties being as follows: Notts County (initially assistant trainer, then caretaker manager from January-May 1957, assistant to manager Tommy Lawton until December 1957), Exeter City (manager-coach, January 1958-May 1960), Southend United (manager, May-December 1960), Bankstown of Sydney, Australia (manager-coach, July 1961-September 1962), Corinthians of Sydney (manager-coach, October 1962 for four years), Melita Eagles of Sydney (part-time coach, January-March 1967), Exeter City (manager, April 1967-February 1969) and finally coach in the Middle East (May 1970-April 1973).

Ernie Callaghan, BEM

Date of birth: 29 July 1907, Newtown, Birmingham
Died: 13 March 1972, Castle Vale, Birmingham

Aston Villa record:
Appearances: League 125, FA Cup 17, Wartime 151
Goal: Wartime 1
Debut: FA Cup third-round replay, 18 January 1933 v Bradford City (h) won 2-1

Also played for: Barton Arms, Rose Villa, Walmer Athletic, Hinckley Athletic, Atherstone Town, Cradley Heath, West Bromwich Albion (trial), Birmingham (trial), Solihull Town (guest)

Ernie Callaghan served Aston Villa as a player and then odd-job man for 41 years.

Born within walking distance of Villa Park, he surprisingly played for two clubs quite a distance from Birmingham – Hinckley Athletic and Atherstone Town – before having a brief spell with Cradley Heath. After unsuccessful trials at The Hawthorns and St Andrew's, which he applied for in person, he signed for Aston Villa as a full-time professional in September 1930 at the age of 23, after being recommended to the club by former player Jack Devey, who had seen him in action several times playing for Atherstone.

Already a seasoned defender, tough and reliable, having made well over 200 appearances at various levels covering a period of eight years since leaving Dartmouth County School in Birmingham, 'Mush', as he was known, had to wait until January 1933 before making his senior debut, lining up at centre-half in place of Alex Talbot in a 2-1 home win over Bradford City in a third-round FA Cup replay in front of 35,000 fans at Villa Park.

His League bow followed in early February when he starred in a 4-1 home defeat of Portsmouth. He was handed just five starts that season, two in 1933-34, only one in 1934-35 and 13 in 1935-36 when Villa were relegated to the Second Division for the first time in the club's history.

Now approaching his 29th birthday, Ernie was, at this juncture, seriously considering his future as a Villa player, but he was persuaded to stay on at the club, and although he played in only 14 League games in 1936-37, he never once let the side down as Villa struggled to keep in touch with the promotion contenders.

Having played all his previous games in the centre-half and wing-half positions, Ernie was then switched by his manager Jimmy Hogan to right-back for the start of the 1937-38 campaign, where he replaced Tom Griffiths. As partner to George Cummings, he helped Villa win the Second Division title and regain their top-flight status after just two seasons away, while also appearing in the FA Cup semi-final defeat by Preston North End at Bramall Lane, Sheffield.

During an interview for the club's match-day programme some years later, Ernie admitted 'We should never have lost that semi-final. We were by far the better team on the day; we had a goal disallowed when it was valid and one of their goals came totally against the run of play. I was obviously disappointed, as were the rest of the lads, but we quickly put that defeat behind us and set about clinching the Second Division title, which we did in some style, winning our last four matches.'

Ernie was an ever present in the last full season before World War Two, as Villa consolidated their position back with the big boys. But then competitive League football was postponed for the duration of the conflict, and, like so many other professional footballers up and down the country, he lost a good seven years of his career.

Ernie signed up with the police reserve and continued to play regularly between 1939 and 1946, amassing over 150 appearances for Villa, guesting for Solihull Town and representing the National Police against the RAF at Wembley in May 1943. He kept a tight rein on Arsenal's Ted Drake that day, but still ended up on the losing side. He also played for the Police Reserve XI and the Civil Defence at various times.

Ernie was on duty with the police force when Birmingham suffered a bombing blitz in September 1942, and for his conspicuous bravery he was duly awarded the British Empire Medal. Three years later he helped Villa win the Wartime League Cup, beating Blackpool 5-4 over two legs.

Ernie was heading towards his 40th birthday when League football resumed in August 1946, and although he was regarded as a senior reserve for that season he was called into action on 10 occasions and made his farewell appearance for the club at the ripe old age of 39 years and 257 days against Grimsby Town at Villa Park in April 1947, making him the oldest footballer ever to appear in a competitive match for the club. A crowd of around 34,000 saw Villa held to a 3-3 draw.

When the curtain came down on that campaign, Ernie retired as a player and was immediately appointed to the groundstaff, where he would work as the club's odd-job man for the next 24 years, until old age and poor health caught up with him in 1971.

Ernie 'Mush' Callaghan was a household name among Villa supporters and it was a fitting tribute when the club awarded him a long overdue testimonial in 1972, when a team comprising several members of Villa's 1957 FA Cup-winning team entertained a Midlands XI.

Len Capewell

Date of birth: 8 June 1895, Bordesley Green, Birmingham
Died: 12 November 1978, Evesham, Worcestershire

Aston Villa record:
Appearances: League 143, FA Cup 13
Goals: League 88, FA Cup 12
Debut: League, 1 April 1922 v Blackburn Rovers (a) won 2–1

Also played for: Saltley Baptists (Birmingham), Wolseley Athletic Works FC, Wellington Town (2 spells), Walsall, Small Heath Baptists

Len Capewell served as a soldier with the Royal Engineers in Belgium during World War One and played very little competitive football. However, once the hostilities had ended he made up for lost time by joining Wellington Town before signing as a semi-professional for Aston Villa in January 1921 for a fee of £700, moving up to the professional ranks in August 1922. He had already appeared in five League games and scored three goals, including one on his debut at Blackburn Rovers when he was introduced in place of the injured Billy Kirton, with Scotsman Bill Dickson switching to the inside-right position to allow him to lead the attack.

In fact, Villa beat neighbours Birmingham for Len's signature after assistant secretary Wally Strange, along with senior director Howard Spencer, a former player, had negotiated the transfer at Wellington's home ground earlier in the season, just before the team coach left for an away game at Wrexham.

Known as 'King' and 'Nobby' around Villa Park, Len had 17 outings in the first team the following season, netting another five goals while occupying both inside-forward positions as well as his normal centre-forward berth. He also played one game as an emergency centre-half in place of Tommy Ball in a 4-0 home win over Nottingham Forest.

In 1923–24 Len finally established himself as a regular in the team. He had a wonderful first full season, his best so far, helping Villa reach the FA Cup Final and finish sixth in Division One. During the first half of the campaign he played at inside-left with Arthur Dorrell on the wing, and after that he led the attack with the two Billys, Kirton and Walker, either side.

Smart and energetic with two good feet, Len could, so the *Sports Argus* reporter said, 'Slice his way through the tightest of defences...with all the defiance of a pint-sized battleship.'

He was a tough competitor and he certainly thrilled the crowds with his all-action performances. He scored 26 goals that season, including his first hat-trick in a 3-2 home League win over Tottenham Hotspur and six in six Cup ties, but unfortunately he couldn't find the net in the Final as Villa went down 2-0 to Newcastle United in the first all-ticket game at Wembley.

Injuries affected Len's performances in 1924–25 when he managed only 19 appearances, yet he still struck nine goals, four coming in the 7-2 FA Cup win over Port Vale.

Back to full fitness the following season when the current offside law was first introduced, he top scored with 34 goals, bagging a brilliant five-timer in a 10-0 home win over Burnley and cracking in another treble versus Huddersfield Town (won 3-0) as well as claiming five twos. He also found the net in eight successive League games during September and October.

Leading marksman again in 1926–27 with 16 goals, three coming in a 5-3 home victory over Everton while suffering from a dislocated shoulder, Len was now being made to work overtime to retain his position ahead of new signing George Cook from Huddersfield. In fact, Cook replaced him at the end of that season and held onto the centre-forward spot in 1927–28, with Joe Beresford and Billy Walker occupying the inside-forward positions and Len acting as reserve.

After making only 11 senior appearances in two and a half years and notching his 100th Villa goal versus Leicester City in April 1929 (plus having to cope with another centre-forward in George Brown, also from Huddersfield), Len left and joined forces with Walsall in February 1930 in an exchange deal that brought goalkeeper Fred Biddlestone to Villa Park. He spent only six months with the Saddlers, rejoining his former club Wellington Town in August 1930 and finally retiring in May 1939, a month short of his 44th birthday.

After World War Two, he occasionally turned out for Small Heath Baptists in the local Sunday League (1947) before quitting the game for good and taking over a coffee tavern. He was then employed in the press experimental department of BSA for 22 years, eventually retiring in 1970 to live out the rest of his life in Droitwich, Worcestershire.

A keen golfer, billiards and snooker player and club cricketer, Len was 82 when he died in 1978.

James Cowan

Date of birth: 17 October 1868, Bonhill, Renton, Dunbartonshire
Died: 12 December 1915, Glasgow

Aston Villa record:
Appearances: League 316, FA Cup 38, Charity Shield 2
Goals: League 21, FA Cup 5
Debut: League, 7 September 1889 v Burnley (h) drew 2-2

Also played for: Jamestown, Vale of Leven, Scotland (3 full caps)

Although he stood at only 5ft 7in tall and weighed around 11st, James Cowan was the rock at the heart of the Aston Villa defence during the 1890s. Apart from height and weight, he had everything else a footballer needs – pace, being extremely quick over short distances, a strong tackle, expert positional sense, sound heading and passing abilities, shrewd tactics and a direct and powerful shot.

He was a brilliant footballer, one of the best of his era, and he served Aston Villa superbly for 13 years as a player, and after retiring he coached the youngsters at the club for another season.

Known as the 'Prince of half-backs', 'Jas', as he was always referred to by friends and colleagues alike, never complained before, during or after a game, and he was hardly ever in trouble with the referee. Indeed, there is no record of him ever being cautioned and certainly never sent off.

He joined Villa at the age of 20, signing as a full-time professional in August 1889 from Scotland's prolific Vale of Leven club. Villa, in fact, possibly pipped near neighbours Warwick County to his signature. Club secretary George Ramsay had overheard a conversation at a local game indicating that County were prepared to ask 'Jas' down to Birmingham for a trial, so he sneaked in there first – and what a signing it was!

'Jas' went straight into the team, made a sound debut against Burnley and was an ever present in his first season of English League football. Thereafter, he remained Villa's first-choice centre-half, occasionally performing as an emergency inside-right, until 1901 when, at the age of 33, he was replaced by Alf Wood.

In March 1892 he gained an FA Cup runners'-up medal when Villa lost 3-0 to arch-rivals West Bromwich Albion, and in 1893-94, when he again appeared in every match, he was quite brilliant, helping Villa win their first League title.

However, after gaining a Cup-winners' medal he was in trouble with the club in December 1895 when he chose to train away from the ground in Scotland, preparing himself for the famous Powderhall Sprint. He won that race, pocketed £80, but on his return to Villa he was fined four weeks' wages and suspended for seven days by a furious committee, who actually thought he was at home (in Bonhill) recovering from injury. In all, he missed seven League games on the trot, and Villa lost two of them but still managed to go on and win their second League title that season.

The following term (1896-97), James played out of his skin as Villa emulated Preston North End's 1888-89 feat by claiming the League and FA Cup double, with 'Jas' scoring once (in a 3-3 draw at Liverpool) in a total of 37 games.

In April 1896 he won the first of three senior caps for Scotland, lining up against England at Parkhead, Glasgow. His other two international outings were also against the English, at Crystal Palace in April 1897 and at Parkhead in April 1898 when he captained the side. However, one feels that if he had been registered with one of the two Glasgow clubs, then he would surely have won more caps than he did, but we shall never know.

Before he retired as a player in the summer of 1902, James collected two more League Championship-winning medals – in 1898-99 and 1899-1900 – and he also played in the first game of the 1901 FA Cup semi-final but not in the replay, when Villa lost to Sheffield United.

A teacher by vocation, he remained at Villa Park for two years coaching the youngsters. He was then mine host of The Grand Turks' Head, High Street, Aston (May 1904-December 1906), and returned to football in July 1907 as Queen's Park Rangers' first-ever manager, a position he held for six years. Rangers won the Southern League title and held Manchester United to a 1-1 draw in the annual FA Charity Shield game in his first season, winning the League Championship for a second time in 1912.

Returning to Scotland in November 1913, he was suddenly taken ill and within three months he died at the age of 47.

* John Cowan, his younger brother by two years, also played for Villa between 1895 and 1899, and he also assisted Vale of Leven, Preston North End, Glasgow Rangers and Dundee Harp. In fact, he too helped Villa win the League title in 1895-96 and complete the double the following season.

Gordon Cowans

Date of birth: 27 October 1958, West Cornforth, County Durham

Aston Villa record:
Appearances: League 399+15, FA Cup 28+1, League Cup 40+4, European 26+1, FA Charity Shield 1, others 12+1
Goals: League 49, FA Cup 3, League Cup 5, European 2, others 1
Debut: League, 7 February 1976, substitute v Manchester City (a) lost 2-1

Also played for: Bari (Italy), Blackburn Rovers, Derby County, Wolverhampton Wanderers, Sheffield United, Bradford City, Stockport County, Burnley, England (4 Youth, 2 B, 5 Under-21 and 10 full caps)

Gordon Cowans joined Aston Villa as an apprentice in July 1974 and was a member of the club's successful youth team before turning professional in August 1976, having made his first-team debut as 17-year-old in between times.

It was only a matter of time before he established himself in the first team on a regular basis, doing so during the 1976–77 season when Villa won the League Cup.

Gordon's brilliant control in midfield helped Villa finish seventh in the First Division in 1979–80, the two-footed midfielder being rewarded for his efforts with the PFA Young Player of the Year award for that season.

At the start of 1980–81 manager Ron Saunders had assembled a splendid side, Gordon being an integral part in midfield, where he linked up with workhorse Des Bremner and skipper Dennis Mortimer. Able to spray precision passes wide and long, short and narrow to strikers Garry Shaw and Peter Withe or out to his left-winger Tony Morley, he developed into a brilliant schemer.

In what was a thrilling Championship-winning campaign, Villa saw off second-placed Ipswich Town to win the title for the first time since 1910.

After Saunders's departure, Tony Barton took over as manager, and although Villa finished a disappointing 11th in the League Gordon was still in great form, helping his colleagues win the European Cup by beating Bayern Munich 1–0 in Rotterdam.

The following season, 1982–83, Villa bravely defended their European title and reached the quarter-final stage but lost over two legs to Italian giants Juventus, Gordon having scored in the first game.

Villa and Gordon, however, tasted glory again by winning the European Super Cup, beating Barcelona 3–1 on aggregate having lost the first leg 1–0, with Gordon scoring a penalty in the second leg at Villa Park.

By the time of England's home match against Wales in February 1983, Gordon's form earned him his first full cap under manager Bobby Robson. He impressed alongside Bryan Robson in midfield, but just when everything was running smoothly Gordon broke his leg in a pre-season friendly in Spain, forcing him to miss the entire 1983–84 campaign and lose his place in the team.

Thankfully, he regained full fitness and was back at Villa Park under new boss Graham Turner for the following season, but in June 1985 he was sold, along with Paul Rideout, to Italian Serie A side Bari. This came as a shock, as both players, especially 'Sid' Cowans, were huge hits with the supporters. Indeed, the club's fanzine *Missing Sid* was named after him.

Having reaching the top flight of Italian football for the first time in 15 years, Bari were confident they had a chance of staying up, especially with the addition of the two English imports.

Under manager Bruno Bolchi, however, things didn't go according to plan. Bari won only five matches, finished next to bottom and were relegated back to Serie B, only to return to the top flight 12 months later under new boss Enrico Catuzzi.

Quickly demoted again, Gordon, now aged 29, agreed to stay in Italy for another year, but Bari made only a slight improvement and finished in seventh place.

At this juncture, Gordon returned to England and Villa took up their option of first refusal, manager Graham Taylor re-signing him on a free transfer. After a season of consolidation, having been promoted in the summer of 1987, Villa challenged for the Championship in 1989–90 but finished runners-up to Liverpool.

When Taylor took over the England job, he recalled Gordon, 33, to the team for his 10th and final cap against the Republic of Ireland in a Euro '92 qualifier. He scored two goals for his country.

Sold to Blackburn by Ron Atkinson in November 1991, Gordon returned to Villa Park for a third spell in July 1993 before seeing out his playing days with Derby, Wolves, Sheffield United, Bradford City, Stockport and Burnley, the latter as reserve-team player-coach. In August 1998 he was back at Villa Park as assistant manager-coach.

With 526 games under his belt, Gordon is third in Villa's all-time appearance list.

Jimmy Crabtree

Date of birth: 23 December 1871, Burnley
Died: 31 May 1908, Birmingham

Aston Villa record:
Appearances: League 178, FA Cup 22, Charity Shield 2
Goals: League 6, FA Cup 1
Debut: League, 2 September 1895 v West Bromwich Albion (h) won 1–0

Also played for: Burnley Royal Swifts, Burnley (2 spells), Rossendale, Heywood Central, Oreston Rovers (2 spells), Plymouth Argyle, England (14 full caps)

Jimmy Crabtree was a naturally-gifted footballer who rose rapidly through the ranks at his first League club, Burnley, to win England recognition at the age of 22.

His first cap came in a 2-2 draw with Ireland in March 1894, and he went on to appear in another 13 internationals up to March 1902, nine of which were won, including those of 9-0 and 13-2 against the Irish and 9-0, 6-0 and 4-0 versus Wales. Jimmy also represented the Football League as a Burnley player, competing against the Scottish League twice and the Irish League once in the early 1890s.

Playing non-League football in and around Burnley, he was, in fact, an amateur at Turf moor in 1889-90 when he made his League debut but was told nicely to 'return when older and try again'. He did just that, signed as a professional in August 1892 and never looked back.

Jimmy scored nine goals in 77 games for the Clarets before a contractual dispute led to him joining Villa for £250 in August 1895. At that time, the transfer was thought to be the first involving that amount of money anywhere in the world.

At 5ft 10in tall and weighing almost 14st, Jimmy was ideally built to become a powerful defender. Rated as one of the finest players in the left-half position during the 1890s, he was a hard but fair tackler, clever at close quarters and equally reliable in open play where his cool, resourceful and intelligent style made him a class above the rest.

He also excelled in the finer points of the game and was one of the most versatile players in the country, able to defend, create and attack down both sides of the pitch while occupying either of the two full-back positions or that of centre-half. He also deputised at centre-forward for George Johnson in the League game against Sunderland in January 1901, setting up Billy Garraty's goal in a 2-2 draw.

One of the best paid professionals of his time, Jimmy, who had captained Burnley on several occasions and went on to do likewise with Villa, quickly settled down in his new surrounding. He made 28 League appearances in his first season with the club, gaining a Championship-winners' medal for his efforts. He was then outstanding in 1896-97 when Villa completed the coveted League and Cup double, Jimmy playing in 31 of the 37 matches and having the pleasure of heading home the winning goal in the Cup Final against Everton.

Very sensitive to criticism, Jimmy would often storm off in a temper, although not from the pitch, but whenever someone told him or hinted that he was not performing up to standard or was not obeying orders. He was, in effect, his own man and there is no doubt whatsoever that deep down he loved his football.

He gave Villa excellent service for eight and a half years, appeared in exactly 200 first-class matches (the last against Grimsby Town, away, in April 1902) and he also added two more League Championship-winning medals to his collection before teaming up with Devon non-League side Oreston Rovers, eventually joining Plymouth Argyle in January 1904.

Jimmy stayed at Home Park for just six months. He made only five senior appearances before returning to Oreston, and after holding several coaching positions with schools and junior clubs based in Devon Gloucestershire and Birmingham he quit football for good in 1908 and became licensee of the Royal Victoria Cross pub in William Street, Lozells, where he remained for two years.

Unfortunately Jimmy died in 1908 and Villa supporters (and indeed Burnley fans) were stunned to learn of his death at just 36 years old.

A relative, also named Jimmy Crabtree, born in Clitheroe in 1895, kept goal for Blackburn Rovers, Rochdale and Accrington Stanley between 1913 and 1924.

Vic Crowe

Date of birth: 31 January 1932, Abercynon, Glamorgan

Aston Villa record:
Appearances: League 294, FA Cup 34, League Cup 23
Goals: League 10, FA Cup 1, League Cup 1
Debut: League, 16 October 1954 v Manchester City (a) won 4-2

Also played for: Handsworth Wood Boys School, Erdington Albion (West Bromwich Albion's nursery team), Stirling Albion (amateur), Peterborough United, Wales (16 full caps)
Managed: Aston Villa, Portland Timbers (NASL, 2 spells)

Flamed-haired wing-half Vic Crowe had a trial with Aston Villa in 1951. He then completed his National Service and also assisted Stirling Albion before returning to Villa Park to sign professional forms in June 1952.

He gained experience by playing alongside and against some quality footballers in Villa's reserve team. He finally got a game in the first XI when Irish international Danny Blanchflower moved to Tottenham Hotspur in 1954, making his League debut against Manchester city at Maine Road.

He made 28 senior appearances that season, occupying both wing-half positions. In 1955–56 he played in 36 matches and scored his first senior goal, in a 3–0 home victory over Newcastle United in late October.

He was sidelined through injury for most of the 1956–57 campaign, appearing in only one League game and, as a result, missed the FA Cup Final win over Manchester United, his place going to Stan Crowther who later joined United.

Thankfully, Vic regained full fitness and also returned to first-team duty on a regular basis halfway through the 1957–58 season and, thereafter, until his transfer to Peterborough United as player-coach in July 1964. He produced some exquisite performances, captaining the side that won the Second Division in 1960 (missing only one match) and to a League Cup Final success a year later. He also played in two FA Cup semi-final defeats, in 1959 versus Nottingham Forest and in 1960 versus Wolves.

A member of the Wales squad at the 1958 World Cup Finals in Sweden, but not called into action, he went on to gain 16 caps for his country at senior level over a period of four years, the first against England in the autumn of 1959 when he replaced Con Sullivan, and the last against Hungary in 1963.

A player of spirit and determination, Vic was an important element in the Villa side for many years. His performances were greatly appreciated by the fans and players alike, and, above all, he was a honest-to-goodness competitor who never gave less than 100 percent out on the pitch, no matter what the circumstances were.

After amassing over 350 appearances for Villa, Vic spent three years with Peterborough, leading them to the League Cup semi-finals in 1966 when they lost over two legs to West Brom.

From July 1967 to May 1969 he was assistant manager (to his former playing colleague Phil Woosnam) with the NASL club Atlanta Chiefs. He then returned to Villa Park as assistant coach in September 1969 before taking over as manager from Tommy Docherty in January 1970.

Unfortunately, Vic was unable to save Villa from relegation. However, the following season he led his Third Division team to the League Cup Final against Tottenham Hotspur, which Villa lost 2–0. He then saw his side finish top of Division Three in 1972, breaking many records along the way. He was sacked in 1974 after Villa had slumped to 14th in Division Two.

In the summer of 1975 Vic returned to the United States, accepting the position of manager of Portland Timbers. He brought a cast of English players with him, many of them youngsters from the Midlands area, and they went on to win the Western Division Championship while also reaching the NASL Final, losing 2–0 to Tampa Bay Rowdies.

The success forced the club to add temporary seating to accommodate fans for their two home Play-off games, and the Timbers twice played in front of record crowds that topped 30,000, unheard of in US soccer at the time.

Vic stayed in Portland until May 1976 when he returned to England. However, the Timbers beckoned again in 1980 and he returned there for another three years. Although his teams never captured the success of that first year, he left an indelible mark on soccer in the Pacific north west by introducing thousands of Portland area residents to the joys of the game.

Today, Portland is a soccer hotbed. The Timbers are still members of the professional USL First Division and play in the same stadium where Vic and the boys excelled back in 1975.

After scouting for several Midland-based clubs and acting as advisory manager to non-League outfit Bilston Town, Vic retired from football in 1997. He now lives in Sutton Coldfield.

George Cummings

Date of birth: 5 June 1913, Thornbridge near Falkirk, Scotland
Died: 8 April 1987, Birmingham

Aston Villa record:
Appearances: League 210, FA Cup 22, Wartime 184
Goals: Wartime 5
Debut: League, 16 November 1935 v Chelsea (h) drew 2–2
Also played for: Thornbridge Waverley, Thornbridge Welfare, Grange Rovers, Partick Thistle, (wartime guest for Revo Electric, Solihull Borough, Birmingham, Falkirk, Nottingham Forest, Northampton Town), All-British XI (1 game), Scotland (9 full caps)
Managed: Hednesford Town

Scottish-born George Cummings, nicknamed 'Icicle', was a rock-solid full-back, as hard as rock, cool and composed, resilient and totally committed to defending. He kicked long and true, possessed a crunching, bone-shaking tackle and had one of the best shoulder charges in the game. His attitude on the field was second to none and his footballing brain never stopped working.

He captained Aston Villa for four years from 1945 to 1949 and made over 400 first-team appearances for the club either side of World War Two, spending almost 14 years as a registered player. Then, after retiring in May 1949, he was employed as third-team coach until July 1952.

After representing Scotland at junior international level in 1929-30, George was 19 years of age when he signed as a full-time professional for Partick Thistle in August 1932. He spent three years in the Scottish First Division, making over 70 appearances and winning the first three of nine full caps, in a 2-0 win over England in front of almost 130,000 spectators at Hampden Park in April 1935 and versus Wales (1-1) and Northern Ireland (won 2-1) later in the year. He also played twice for the Scottish League team and toured Canada and the US with the Scottish FA in the summer of 1935.

With Celtic, Newcastle United, Rangers, Motherwell and Stirling Albion all chasing his signature, in November 1935 George joined Aston Villa for £9,350 – a record incoming fee for Partick – actually putting pen to paper inside a café in Princess Street, Edinburgh, sitting alongside the Villa chairman Fred Normansell, who had travelled north by train to complete the deal in time for George to make his debut against Chelsea in place of the injured Danny Blair.

At the time Villa were struggling at the foot of the First Division table and leaking goals aplenty.

Partnering Tom Griffiths during the second half of that 1935-36 season, George quickly became a huge favourite with the Villa Park faithful, but his gallant efforts were to no avail as Villa were relegated from the top flight of English football for the first time in the club's history.

He struggled with a knee injury during the 1936-37 campaign but returned to full fitness for the next season and played his part in helping Villa win the Second Division Championship, along with his right-back colleague Ernie 'Mush' Callaghan. Indeed, Ernie and George were regarded by some as being the best pair of full-backs in League football around this time and they played exceedingly well in 1938-39 as Villa consolidated themselves in Division One. George also added his other six Scottish caps to his collection (1936-39), appearing twice more versus England as well as Germany, Wales, Northern Ireland and Czechoslovakia.

During the war George served as a guest with several clubs, played for a British XI against the Football League and starred in one Victory international, still finding time and energy to make over 180 appearances for Villa and gain a League North Cup-winners' tankard in 1944 when Blackpool were defeated 5-4 on aggregate in the two-leg Final, with George nullifying the threat of England wing wizard Stanley Matthews.

The recipient of a Football League South runners'-up medal in 1946, George retained his place at left-back until the end of the 1948-49 season when he officially handed over the number-three shirt to Dicky Dorsett.

Remaining at Villa Park for a few years to coach the youngsters, George then moved into management with Hednesford Town in May 1953, holding office until May 1954 when he went into scouting, accepting appointments with Burnley and Wolverhampton Wanderers before pulling out of football altogether to take employment at the Dunlop Rubber Company. He was approaching his 74th birthday when he died in 1987.

Tony Daley

Date of birth: 18 October 1967, Lozells, Birmingham

Aston Villa record:

Appearances: League 189+44, FA Cup 15+1, League Cup 22+2, European 6, others 9+2
Goals: League 31, FA Cup 2, League Cup 4, others 1
Debut: League, 20 April 1985 v Southampton (a) lost 2-0

Also played for: Wolverhampton Wanderers, Watford, Walsall, FC Madeira (Portugal), Hapoel Haifa (Israel), Nailsworth FC, Forest Green Rovers, Aston Villa Old Stars, England (4 Youth, 1 B and 7 full caps)

After representing Aston Manor, Holte Comprehensive School and Birmingham Boys, Tony Daley began his footballing career in earnest as an apprentice with Aston Villa, signing in June 1983 and turning professional in May 1985.

Playing mainly as an out-and-out winger, he spent 10 seasons at Villa Park before leaving to sign for Wolverhampton Wanderers, later assisting Watford, Walsall and two non-League sides, Nailsworth and Forest Green Rovers, while also playing in Portugal and Israel before retiring to become a fitness coach, firstly with Sheffield United.

Tony accumulated a total of 339 senior appearances for his four major English League clubs (scoring 45 goals). He gained a League Cup-winners' medal with Villa in 1994 – his only senior club prize for several years' hard work.

He was also capped by England at both Youth and Under-21 levels before playing in seven full England internationals during the early 1990s under his former manager Graham Taylor, appearing in the Euro '92 Championship in Sweden.

Always showing plenty of endeavour and commitment, and blessed with terrific pace and a powerful right-foot shot (when he chose to let fly), Tony brought a slice of fresh air to Villa's attack once he had bedded himself into the first team on a regular basis (1986).

It was, indeed, a pleasure to see a touchline winger grace the First Division at a time when the game, on the whole, was somewhat defence orientated.

He made only five senior appearances in 1984–85 and 26 the following season, but after that he produced many outstanding performances, giving quite a few experienced defenders plenty to think about. A real old-fashioned winger, direct with strength and purpose, Tony had an excellent season at Villa Park in 1986–87, making 40 appearances. However, he was then troubled by a spate of injuries and started only 11 games in 1987–88 before regaining full fitness, as well as his technique and form in 1988–89, when he played in 38 games, following up with a best return of 44 in 1989–90.

After Josef Venglos had taken over from Graham Taylor as manager for the next campaign, Villa struggled at the wrong end of the First Division table and only just avoided relegation, but Tony continued to impress, turning in some excellent performances. He maintained his form in 1991–92, making 41 appearances and helping Villa push up to seventh place in the table. He also won his first full cap versus Poland.

Unfortunately, in the first season of Premiership football in 1992–93, under new manager Ron Atkinson, injuries saw Tony manage only 13 outings for Villa, but he was impressive again in 1993–94 as Villa reached Wembley, where they beat Manchester United 3-1 in the League Cup Final.

Surprisingly, certainly to a lot of Villa fans, Tony – after 290 games in the claret-and-blue strip – was transferred to Midland neighbours Wolves for £1.25m at the end of that season, teaming up again with former Villa Park colleagues Paul Birch, Gordon Cowans and Stephen Froggatt, as well as his old boss Graham Taylor.

He spent four seasons at Molineux but was plagued by injuries for most of his time at the club and made only 27 senior appearances before joining up (yet again) with his ex-manager Taylor at Watford in July 1998.

He switched to Walsall in June 1999 but made only eight competitive appearances for the Saddlers (three of them as a substitute) before slipping out of Football League action after just three months at a lower level.

In 1995 Tony was the subject of a half-hour documentary. The series – called *Respect* – filmed for Carlton TV, was produced and directed by Pogus Caesar and featured the likes of Dwight Yorke, John Barnes and Ron Atkinson all paying tribute to the remarkable skills of the Birmingham-born footballing hero. Tony is now a fitness coach with Sheffield United.

Alan Deakin

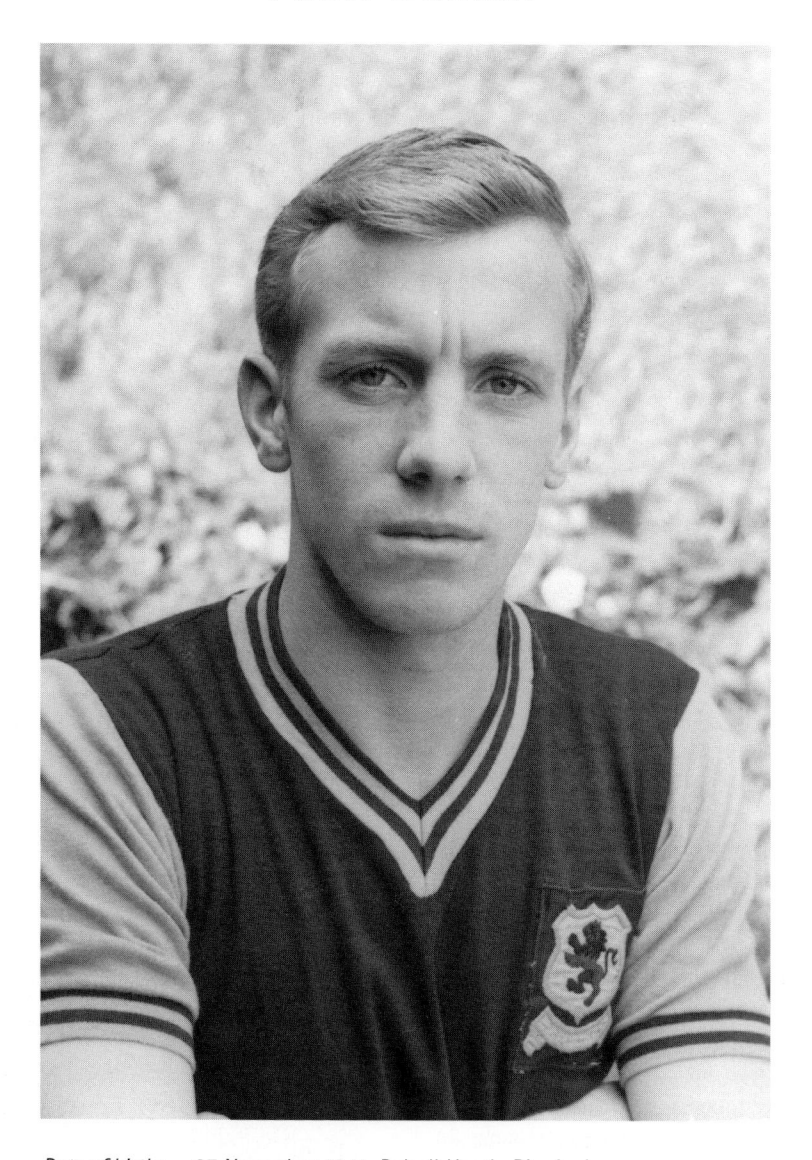

Date of birth: 27 November 1941, Balsall Heath, Birmingham

Aston Villa record:
Appearances: League 230+1, FA Cup 17, League Cup 22
Goals: League 9
Debut: League, 5 December 1959 v Rotherham United (a) lost 2–1

Also played for: Cannon Hill Rovers, Walsall, Tamworth, Metropolitan Cammell FC, Aston Villa Old Stars, England (6 Under-21 caps)

Alan Deakin represented South Birmingham Boys before being spotted by eagle-eyed Aston Villa scout Dave Manship. He was persuaded to join the groundstaff at Villa Park as a 15-year-old in November 1956, did very well and was offered a professional contract two years later by manager Joe Mercer.

Formerly an inside-forward, Alan was switched to the wing-half position with great success and, after making his League debut shortly after his 18th birthday, he never looked back, going on to accumulate an excellent record with Aston Villa of 270 senior appearances and nine goals. He was also honoured by England, playing in six Under-23 internationals during the early 1960s.

He was certainly in terrific form around that time but, unfortunately, when in line for a full cap he broke an ankle, then a leg and also a toe during the 1964–65 campaign, which knocked him back considerably.

Strong-willed, determined and a never-say-die competitor, Alan bounced back and continued to give Villa wonderful service until moving to nearby Walsall in October 1969.

At the end of Alan's debut season of 1959–60, Villa celebrated by winning the Second Division Championship. Twelve months on and re-established in the top flight, Villa reached the League Cup Final, Alan starring in every round. The Final itself, however, was held over until the start of the next campaign when a confident side took on and defeated Rotherham United 3-2 on aggregate in the first of the two-leg Finals.

Along with several other talented youngsters who were at the club around that time, among them Norman Ashe, Charlie Aitken, Mike Tindall and Alan Baker, Alan became a valuable member of the first-team squad and the fans started to talk in excited anticipation as the boss duly christened his youngsters 'Mercer's Minnows'.

Under the inspiring captaincy of Vic Crowe, Villa produced some splendid performances in the League with Alan manning midfield superbly. He was outstanding when Bolton Wanderers and Sheffield Wednesday were whipped 4-0 and 4-1 respectively. In 1961-62, when he was absent just twice, he had a hand in three of the five goals that flew into the Blackpool net in September, worked his socks off in a terrific 5-4 victory over Arsenal at Highbury in March 1962, and then teased and tormented Leicester City when Villa won 8-3 at home the following month.

In 1963 Villa reached the League Cup Final for the second time in three years, but on this occasion they went down 3-1 on aggregate to rivals Birmingham City. Alan missed those two Final clashes through injury, but he was back to his best the following season before injury struck him hard in 1964–65, causing him to miss half of the scheduled 53 League and Cup games as Villa struggled to stay clear of the relegation zone.

Manager Mercer was replaced by Dick Taylor for the 1965–66 season when Alan missed several more games, although he did play well in a wonderfully-exciting 5-5 draw with Spurs at White Hart Lane, scoring one of Villa's goals while Tony Hateley bagged the other four.

Sadly, after Villa had slipped out of the top flight at the end of 1966–67, fresh faces were introduced by new boss Tommy Cummings including a couple of midfielders. After an indifferent 1968–69 campaign, when the team never looked liked regaining their First Division status, Third Division football was looming when Alan moved to Fellows Park in October 1969. He later spent a few years playing non-League football and appeared regularly in charity games with the ex-Villa players. On retiring he became a welder with the Gamwell Engineering Company based in Witton, near to Villa Park.

His brother, Mike, played for Crystal Palace, Aldershot and Northampton Town.

THE LEGENDS OF ASTON VILLA

Jack Devey

Date of birth: 26 December 1866, Newtown, Birmingham
Died: 11 October 1940, Moseley, Birmingham

Aston Villa record:
Appearances: League 268, FA Cup 38, others 2
Goals: League 168, FA Cup 18
Debut: League, 5 September 1891 v Blackburn Rovers (h) won 5-1

Also played for: Aston Brook School, Montrose Youth Club (Aston), Wellington Road FC (Perry Barr), Excelsior FC (Birmingham), Aston Manor, Aston Unity, West Bromwich Albion (amateur), Mitchell St George's, England (2 full caps)

Jack Devey was associated with Aston Villa football club for 43 years – as a player, coach and director.

After learning the in and outs of the game with several well-established local clubs and having a brief spell with West Bromwich Albion, he signed for Villa as a full-time professional in March 1891, making his League debut against Blackburn Rovers six months later when he scored twice in a 5-1 win.

He had a terrific first season, top scoring with 34 goals in 30 games, including a hat-trick against Burnley (won 6-3) and four versus Accrington, which they won 12-2 – the club's biggest-ever League win.

Maintaining his form, he was leading marksman for the next three seasons and became one of the club's greatest-ever captains, holding office for eight years.

He went on to appear in over 300 first-class matches for Villa, scoring a total of 186 goals. He gained five League Championship-winners' medals (1894, 1896, 1897, 1899 and 1900), two FA Cup-winners' medals (1895 and 1897), played in the 1892 losing FA Cup Final, won two full caps for England – both against Ireland in March 1892 (with teammates Charlie Athersmith and Dennis Hodgetts) and March 1894 (again with Hodgetts when he scored in a 2-2 draw), and participated in five England trials between 1891 and 1894, as well as representing the Football League on four occasions in the mid-1890s.

A decidedly-skilful inside-right or centre-forward, he was exceptionally clever with his head and both feet and was lethal in front of goal, scoring from all angles given a chance.

He was quite brilliant when the double was won in 1897, netting 17 times in 29 League games, including a well-taken hat-trick in a 4-3 victory at Burnley. He also scored vital goals in games against Nottingham Forest, Preston North End, Stoke and Sunderland at home, and Everton and Nottingham Forest away.

He had many exciting partners in the Villa attack, among them Albert Brown, John Campbell, Bob Chatt, Dennis Hodgetts and Freddie Wheldon, and for several seasons he played with flying winger Athersmith on the right flank. In fact, some considered this pairing to be the finest duo in the Football League, and if it hadn't been for the likes of Derby County's John Goodall and Steve Bloomer, and Gilbert Smith of Oxford University and the Old Carthusians, Jack would have played for England many more times.

Jack continued as a player until April 1901 – his position in the Villa attack going, technically, to Joe Bache, with Billy Garraty also in the line up.

By now a shareholder, he coached the senior players at Villa Park during the 1901–02 season before being elected to the Board of Directors, a position he held for 32 years from June 1902 to September 1934, although he continued to coach for a further year.

In 1890 he opened a sports-outfitters shop in Lozells, which he ran, successfully, for several years. He also played cricket for Warwickshire for 13 years, from April 1894 to September 1907. An opening or middle-order right-hand batsman, and occasional right-arm medium-pace bowler, he appeared in 154 matches for the Bears. With the bat, he accumulated 6,550 runs in 253 innings for an average of 28.11. His highest score was 246 against Derbyshire at Edgbaston in 1900. With the ball, he claimed 16 wickets at an average of 40.93 with a best return of 3-65. He also claimed 70 catches, mainly close to the wicket.

One interesting point is that it has been said that Jack's first 'game' for Villa was as a guest in a charity-organised baseball match in March 1890.

Two of Jack's brothers – Harry and Will – were also registered players with Aston Villa in 1892-93. Will also played for Small Heath, Wolves, Notts County, Walsall and Burton Wanderers.

Johnny Dixon

Date of birth: 10 December 1923, Hebburn-on-Tyne, County Durham

Aston Villa record:
Appearances: League 392, FA Cup 38, Wartime 5
Goals: League 132, FA Cup 12, Wartime 3
Debut: League, 31 August 1946 v Middlesbrough (h) lost 1-0

Also played for: Spennymoor United, Newcastle United (trial), (wartime guest for Hull City, Middlesbrough, Newcastle United, Sunderland), Aston Villa Old Stars

When League football resumed after World War Two Villa were top-heavy with ageing players – 17 who had been engaged by the club before 1939 when still signed up as professionals. In fact, there had been little effort on the part of the directors to bring in some fresh, young talent.

One player new to the supporters, however, was inside-forward Johnny Dixon, who had arrived at Villa Park in August 1944 from the North East after writing in for a trial rather than being spotted by a scout.

He quickly bedded into his new surroundings, having played in a handful of Regional League South fixtures at the end of the 1945–46 campaign and scoring on his debut against Derby County.

He was given 17 outings during the 1946–47 campaign, scoring six goals, and played in 12 matches the following season, adding a further five goals to his tally before gaining a permanent place in the side halfway through 1948–49 when he took over at inside-left from George Edwards, having England international Les Smith as his wing-partner.

Dark haired, strong and with two good feet, Johnny was quick-witted and was able to evade and elude defenders with ease and balance. He also possessed enough speed over short distances to get free of his marker and was a smart passer as well as being able to pack a decent shot, mainly right-footed.

He was hardly ever spoken to by a referee, certainly never sent off, and without doubt he was one of the finest sportsmen ever to pull on the claret-and-blue strip.

He reached double figures in the goalscoring stakes for the first time in 1949–50 (netting 11 times) and was top scorer in each of the next three seasons, bagging 16 goals in 1950–51, notching a personal best of 28 in 1951–52 when he was an ever present, helping Villa finish sixth in the First Division, and scoring 14 in 1952–53 when he was joined in the attack by Irish international centre-forward Dave Walsh.

Always preferring the inside-left berth, Johnny had a new winger with him in 1953–54, Peter McParland, and between them they hit 15 goals, creating another dozen at least. Johnny was also named reserve for England versus Wales.

During 1954–55 Johnny took over the captaincy at Villa Park from Danny Blanchflower, and he retained the honour for four years. He led by example, as always, and although Villa didn't pull up too many trees over the next two seasons – they only just scraped clear of relegation at the end of 1955–56 – Johnny's form never waned, his determination and commitment showing through week after week.

The proudest moment of his career came in May 1957 when he led Villa to FA Cup glory over Manchester United at Wembley. He scored five goals en-route to that Final, including a couple against Luton Town in a third-round replay and an important opener in the quarter-final victory over Burnley. He was then at his best against United, driving his players forward at every opportunity while getting back to cover his defenders when required.

Over the next four seasons Johnny made 53 appearances, playing in four games when Villa won the Second Division Championship in 1959–60 after being relegated the season before, and his last and 435th first-team outing was against Sheffield Wednesday at Villa Park in April 1961 when he scored in a 4–1 victory and also suffered a broken nose.

Only five players have made more League appearances for Villa than Johnny, and he is currently in eighth position in the list of the club's all-time appearance makers at senior level. He is also in sixth place in the club's all-time scoring charts with a total of 144 League and FA Cup goals to his credit.

On his retirement at the end of the 1960–61 season, Johnny remained at Villa Park as a coach, mainly looking after the younger players, for six years, helping in the development of future stars like Charlie Aitken, Alan Baker, Alan Deakin, John Sleeuwenhoek, Mike Tindall and Mick Wright.

A teetotaller and non-smoker, Johnny played in local charity matches for the Aston Villa old stars until he was well over 60 years of age, and he also ran an ironmongery on the Erdington–Sutton Coldfield border until he retired in September 1985.

The name of Johnny Dixon was revered at Villa park for more than 20 years as a player and coach, and he will go down in history as being one of the club's greatest post-World War Two footballers.

Arthur Dorrell

Date of birth: 30 March 1896, Small Heath, Birmingham
Died: 13 September 1942, Alum Rock, Birmingham

Aston Villa record:
Appearances: League 355, FA Cup 35
Goals: League 60, FA Cup 5
Debut: League, 8 September 1919 v Derby County (a) lost 1-0

Also played for: Carey Hall Sunday School, Port Vale, England (4 full caps), England XI (1 cap)

Arthur Reginald Dorrell was the son of a former Leicester Fosse, Aston Villa and Burslem Port Vale player. Although a 'Brummie', born within walking distance of Birmingham City's former ground at Muntz Street, Arthur was educated in Leicester and developed his football with Carey Hall Sunday School before joining the army. He served during World War One and played football for his unit as well as competing regularly as a track sprinter, winning the 100 metres title in the 1916 French Athletics Championships.

After returning to England he was recommended to Villa by his father and signed as a full-time professional in May 1919, at the age of 23. After only a handful of reserve-team games he made his League debut on the left wing in place of Harold Edgley against Derby County at the Baseball Ground in front of 12,000 fans in early September, scoring his first goal five weeks later against Preston North End.

He and Edgley shared the wing duties during the remainder of the season, although Arthur never appeared in the FA Cup competition – that is until the Final itself against Huddersfield Town. The unfortunate Edgley broke his leg in a League game against Chelsea three weeks before the Final, allowing Arthur to step forward and collect a winners' medal after Villa's 1-0 victory at, ironically, Stamford Bridge, the ground where Edgely was injured.

He played in 34 League games in 1920-21 with Clem Stephenson as his inside partner and was an ever present the following season when Billy Walker took over from Stephenson. The pair were made for each other, and they gave several defences a tough time, especially the over-worked player occupying the right-back position.

In 1922-23 Arthur was absent just once and missed three League games in 1923-24 when, once again, Villa reached the FA Cup Final. Unfortunately, this time round they failed to lift the trophy, losing 2-0 to Crystal Palace in the first all-ticket game at Wembley.

Fast over the ground, with two good feet and terrific dribbling skills, Arthur frequently combined style with brilliance and served as a superb partner to Walker, then later Len Capewell and Dicky York, and then Walker again as he wound down his career at Villa Park.

He held down the left-wing position, virtually unchallenged, right through to 1929 when Frank Chester arrived on the scene. Arthur had his best scoring seasons in 1927-28 and 1928-29 when he netted nine goals in each campaign, and in the mid-1920s he was selected to play for England in four internationals against Belgium, versus Wales at Swansea, versus France (when he scored in a 3-2 win in Paris) and against Ireland in Belfast – and his inside-left colleague in each match was his buddy from Villa, Billy Walker, who skippered the side against France.

Arthur also represented the football League on two occasions against the Irish League in 1922-23 and 1924-25. He played in three internationals trials between 1924 and 1926 and also appeared for an England XI.

Ice cool in his approach to the game, hardly anything ruffled or disturbed Arthur, and overall he spent 12 wonderful years at Villa Park (up to May 1931), scoring 65 goals in almost 400 appearances. In fact, only one other winger – Eric Houghton – has played in more games for the club than Arthur and Houghton is the only winger to have scored more goals.

On leaving Villa Park he signed for Port Vale, staying just over a season with the club before retiring to take over as mine host of the Pelham Arms on Washwood Heath Road, Alum Rock, not far from where he was born.

Arthur's brother, Billy, played for Hinckley Athletic and Leicester City, and a cousin was also an amateur footballer in Leicester.

Dion Dublin

Date of birth: 22 April 1969, Leicester

Aston Villa record:
Appearances: League 120+35, FA Cup 6+1, League Cup 14+1, European 2, others 8+2
Goals: League 48, FA Cup 1, League Cup 9, others 2
Debut: League, 7 November 1998 v Tottenham Hotspur (h) won 3-2

Also played for: Wigston Fields, Oakham United, Norwich City (2 spells), Cambridge United, Manchester United, Coventry City, Millwall, Leicester City, Celtic, England (4 full caps)

As a youngster, Dion Dublin played intermediate football for two local junior clubs before moving to Norwich City at the age of 16, turning professional in March 1988. He failed to make the Canaries first team and within five months had signed for Cambridge United on a free transfer.

His goals helped the Abbey Stadium club gain promotion from the Fourth to the Second Division in successive seasons of 1989–90 and 1990–91, and in 1991–92 he played a massive part in helping Cambridge finish fifth in the last-ever season of the old Second Division. However, when the team failed to win promotion via the Play-offs he was surprisingly snapped up by Manchester United, Alex Ferguson signing him for £1million in August 1992.

He scored on his full Premiership debut for the Reds at Southampton, but on his first start at Old Trafford versus Nottingham Forest nine days later he suffered a broken leg and damaged ankle ligaments, which kept him out of action for five months. He returned with a flurry of goals for the reserves.

In 1993–94 his chances of first-team football were restricted due to the excellent form of Eric Cantona, and after being left out of United's FA Cup-winning team he left at the end of the season and signed for Coventry City for £2 million.

In four and a half years at Highfield Road, Dion was regarded as one of the Premiership's top strikers, and in 1997 he won the first of his four full England caps. That season he shared status as the Premier League's top marksman with Blackburn's Chris Sutton and Liverpool's Michael Owen with 18 League goals.

Despite being left out of England's 1998 World Cup squad, his exploits at club level attracted the attention of Aston Villa, and in November 1998 the shaven-haired striker moved to Villa Park for £5.75 million, linking up with Stan Collymore.

He started off superbly well, scoring twice on his debut against Spurs, and, in fact, he netted seven goals in his first three outings, cracking in a hat-trick in his second outing at Southampton.

Unfortunately, during a League game against Sheffield Wednesday in December 1999, Dion sustained a life-threatening broken neck. Doctors monitored the situation closely and decided that he would have to have a permanent titanium plate inserted to hold three neck vertebrae together. In April 2000, a week after returning to the team, Dion helped Villa reach their first FA Cup Final in 43 years (which they lost 1–0 to Chelsea), after scoring his penalty in the semi-final shoot-out with Bolton Wanderers at Wembley.

An awkward looking player, hard working and exceptionally good in the air, Dion was a handful for most defenders and became a huge favourite with the fans. However, he came under pressure for a place in the first team with the arrivals of Juan Pablo Ángel, Darius Vassell and Peter Crouch, and as a result he was loaned out to First Division Millwall towards the end of the 2001–02 season. On his return to Villa Park he regained his position as leader of the attack as strike-partner to Vassell and took his tally of goals to 60 (in 189 appearances) before his contract expired in the summer of 2004.

At that juncture, Dion signed for Leicester City, who had just been relegated from the Premiership, but in his first season with the Foxes he scored only four times in 38 matches. Then, after losing his place to Mark de Vries, he was successfully switched into defence before having his contract terminated by mutual consent in January 2006. He immediately signed for Celtic on a short-term deal until the end of the season and achieved double success, gaining Scottish League Cup and Scottish Premier League winners' medals and coming on as a substitute to score the clinching goal in the League Cup Final versus Dunfermline Athletic.

In September 2006 Dion returned to Norwich City on a season-long contract and took his career record in senior football to almost 700 appearances and close to 220 goals.

Andy Ducat

Date of birth: 16 February 1886, Brixton, London
Died: 23 July 1942, Middlesex, London

Aston Villa record:
Appearances: League 74, FA Cup 4
Goals: League 4
Debut: League, 2 September 1912 v Chelsea (h) won 1–0
Also played for: Westcliff Athletic (Essex), Woolwich Arsenal, Birmingham (guest), Bellis & Morcom (guest), Grimsby Town (guest), Alexander Pontorium FC (guest), Fulham, Corinthian Casuals, England (6 full caps) and cricket for Surrey CCC, England (6 Tests)
Managed: Fulham

Andrew Ducat played international football and cricket for England – being one of an elite group to have represented their country in both sports.

He is best known for being the only man to have died during a game at the Lord's cricket ground. He apparently suffered a heart attack after lunch, while playing in a wartime match between teams from his unit of the Home Guard from Surrey against another from Sussex. The match was abandoned.

Andy was born in London but grew up in Southend, and he had successful careers in both football and cricket. As a footballer, he started out playing for non-League Southend United before joining First Division Woolwich Arsenal in 1905. He made his Gunners debut in February 1905 against Blackburn Rovers, playing at centre-forward. After losing his place in 1906–07 he was switched to right-half and became a regular in seasons 1907–08 and 1908–09.

During his time at Arsenal, Andy won three caps for England, the first against Ireland in Belfast in February 1910 when he starred in a convincing 6–1 win. On his second appearance for England, against Wales the following month, he scored the only goal of the game to earn his team victory.

Andy's ability and success with England brought attention from bigger clubs than Arsenal, who were, at the time, going through a financial crisis. Eventually he was sold to Aston Villa for £1,000 in June 1912, having appeared in 235 first-team matches (including wartime fixtures) and scored 24 goals for the Gunners.

After suffering a broken leg in his fourth match for Villa in a 1–0 League defeat at Manchester City, he was unfortunately sidelined for the FA Cup Final that season when Villa beat Sunderland. He also missed out on a League runners'-up medal that same season but thankfully recovered to become a stalwart in the side, captaining Villa to their sixth FA Cup triumph in 1920 when Huddersfield Town were defeated 1–0. Andy also regained his England place having not played since 1910 and gained three more caps during 1920, the last in a 2–0 win over Ireland at Roker Park in late October, bringing his total number of England appearances to six.

After serving Villa for nine years and guesting for Birmingham, Grimsby Town and two non-league clubs during the war, Andy switched his allegiance to Fulham in May 1921. He remained at Craven Cottage until announcing his retirement as a player in May 1924.

At that point, he succeeded Phil Kelso (his former boss at Arsenal) as Fulham's manager. However, the Cottagers struggled with Andy in charge and, with results going against him, he was sacked in July 1926. A month later he was reinstated as an amateur and signed for Corinthian Casuals, finally taking off his soccer boots in 1928 to concentrate on playing cricket, which he did admirably until 1931.

Perhaps keener on cricket than he was on football, Andy first joined the Surrey ground staff at The Oval in 1906 and soon became a regular member of the county team, playing with the great Jack Hobbs and Ernie Hayes.

Standing 5ft 10in high, he was a powerful, forcing batsman who appeared in 428 first-class matches and scored 23,373 runs, including 52 centuries for his adopted county. His highest innings score was 306 not out against Oxford University in 1919 and his overall average was an impressive 38.63. He actually scored 994 runs in less than six weeks in 1928, including a century in four successive matches

As an occasional bowler, Andy took 21 wickets for 903 runs and he also held 205 catches. He was voted one of Wisden's Cricketers of the Year in 1920, but unfortunately he missed many matches due to injury during his career and was absent for the whole of the 1924 season after breaking his arm in the nets.

Andy played in only one Test Match, the third against Australia at Headingly in 1921 when he was unlucky to make only three in his first innings and two in his second. He was declared doubly out in the first innings when a piece of wood flew off his bat as he played a swinging ball bowled by Ted McDonald. The ball itself looped to slip where it was caught, while at the same time that small piece of wood from his bat dislodged a bail, but he was subsequently given out caught rather than hit wicket.

After ending his cricketing activities on the field, Andy became a cricket coach off it, being employed at Eton College for five years. He also worked as a sports reporter and publican, and he ran a sports shop until his sudden death in 1942.

Jimmy Dugdale

Date of birth: 15 January 1932, Liverpool

Aston Villa record:
Appearances: League 215, FA Cup 27, League Cup 12, Charity Shield 1
Goals: League 3

Also played for: Harrowby (Liverpool), West Bromwich Albion, Queen's Park Rangers, England (3 B caps)

There haven't been too many footballers who have won the FA Cup with two different clubs in the space of three seasons. Some 50 years ago, Jimmy Dugdale did just that – helping West Bromwich Albion beat Preston 3-2 in the 1954 Final and Aston Villa defeat Manchester United 2-1 in the 1957 Final.

The Liverpool-born centre-half established himself in Albion's team during the latter stages of his first season as a professional at The Hawthorns, taking over from the impeccable Joe Kennedy.

An accident to Joe in mid-December 1952 let in Jimmy for his debut against Bolton Wanderers, whose centre-forward was England's 'Lion of Vienna' Nat Lofthouse. Although on the losing side, Jimmy coped very well with the experienced Lofthouse, who said afterwards 'This lad's going to be a good 'un.'

Jimmy – a lance corporal in the army during his national service – signed as a full-time player on his demob in May 1952. He appeared in 15 League games that season, helping Albion finish fourth in the table, four points behind the champions Arsenal. The following season he played in 32 senior matches as the Baggies pressed Wolves hard and long for the title, which eventually went to Molineux, while Albion lifted the Cup at Wembley with Jimmy playing his part in a superb team performance.

He made 75 senior appearances at the heart of Albion's defence as well as starring in three B internationals for England and representing the Football League versus the Scottish League in 1953-54 before Kennedy returned. Jimmy was relegated to the reserves, at which point he opted for a change of scenery by switching to Villa Park for £25,000 in February 1956.

Dubbed the 'Laughing Cavalier', Jimmy, with his mop of black hair, replaced Con Martin at centre-half and had an impressive first outing against Arsenal. He never scored a goal for Albion, but he quickly put that right by netting in his 11th game for Villa, sadly to no avail, in a 4-3 defeat at Tottenham.

With first Bill Baxter and Pat Saward, and then Stan Crowther and Saward lining up alongside him in the middle line, Jimmy and the team had an excellent 1956-57 season, which ended in more Wembley glory as Villa beat Matt Busby's double-chasing team to lift the trophy for the first time since 1920. Jimmy had a terrific game, boldly and bravely battling it out with Tommy Taylor and generally coming out on top.

In the semi-final Jimmy played against his former employers, Albion, and had to mark one of his great pals, Ronnie Allen. After a 2-2 draw at Molineux, Villa won the replay 1-0 at St Andrew's but the game was marred by a clash between Jimmy and Allen, which resulted in the Baggies centre-forward going off with a head injury.

Jimmy recalled at a gathering of former players to mark Albion's Centenary in 1979 'I genuinely went for the ball, but will admit I did go in hard and some referees would have given a foul. I apologised to Ronnie in hospital the following day and we shook hands.'

Jimmy continued as a regular in the Villa side for the next four seasons, missing only 16 games (mainly through injury) out of a possible 200.

He was terrific when Villa won the Second Division Championship at the first attempt following relegation in 1960, and just over a year later he helped Villa win the first-ever League Cup Final, beating Rotherham 3-2 over two legs.

Injuries troubled Jimmy early in the 1961-62 campaign, and manager Joe Mercer replaced him with a talented youngster, John Sleeuwenhoek. For Jimmy, that marked the end of his Villa career. After 255 appearances for the club he joined Queen's Park Rangers in October 1962, but a serious knee injury caused him to retire seven months later.

Quitting football completely, Jimmy entered the licensing trade, and became a Witton publican, later acting as steward at the Lion's Club (a branch of the Villa supporters club), the Hasbury Conservative Club near Halesowen and the Reddings, home of the Moseley rugby club.

In 1990 Jimmy had a leg amputated, confining him to a wheelchair. Three years later a testimonial match was arranged on his behalf when Villa entertained Birmingham City.

Now a resident in Acocks Green, Jimmy still enjoys his football, albeit via TV and radio, and loves to attend the ex-player's functions held at The Hawthorns and Villa Park.

George Edwards

Date of birth: 1 April 1918, Great Yarmouth, Norfolk
Died: 21 January 1993, Lapworth, Warwickshire

Aston Villa record:
Appearances: League 138, FA Cup 14, Wartime 125
Goals: League 34, FA Cup 7, Wartime 94
Debut: League, 5 November 1938 v Manchester United (h) lost 2-0

Also played for: Yarmouth Caledonians, Norfolk County, Yarmouth Town (2 spells), Norwich City (2 spells), (wartime guest for Birmingham City, Chelmsford City, Coventry City, Leicester City, Northampton Town, Nottingham Forest, Notts County, Walsall, West Bromwich Albion, Worcester City, Wrexham), Bilston United

Signed as an amateur by Norwich City at the age of 16, George Edwards turned professional at Carrow Road in April 1936 but made only a handful of first-team appearances for the Canaries before transferring to Aston Villa in June 1938.

Unfortunately, due to a training-ground accident when he chipped a bone in his ankle when challenged by defender Bob Iverson, his debut in the claret-and-blue was delayed for five months – until November – and after that he never took to the field without having heavy strapping around his suspect ankle!

After three League outings for Villa, World War Two broke out, but George continued to play football during the hostilities, gaining experience with several Midland clubs including Birmingham, Coventry, West Bromwich Albion and Walsall, and, thankfully, that damaged ankle didn't affect his performances one little bit. Indeed, at the end of the 1943–44 season George helped Villa beat Blackpool in the Wartime League North Cup Final and in the transitional campaign of 1945–46 he scored 39 goals in 35 games as Villa finished runners-up (to Blues) in the Football League South Championship. He was actually Villa's leading marksman during the war with 94 goals.

Returning to Football League action in August 1946, George went on to serve Villa for a total of 13 years, eventually moving into non-League football with Bilston United in August 1951.

A fine, purposeful outside-right with a lot of pace, good skill and a powerful shot, George could also occupy the centre-forward position, but it was as a winger that he made his name.

He appeared in only three games before World War Two, but after the hostilities he was virtually an ever present in the forward line for the first two seasons, missing only two games and scoring 21 goals including one of the fastest ever seen at Villa Park – netting after just 13.5 seconds of the third-round FA Cup clash with Manchester United in January 1948, a game Villa lost 6–4 in front of almost 59,000 spectators.

During those two first post-war campaigns, George occupied four of the five forward-line positions, failing to line up at outside-left. He started off leading the attack in 1946–47 before Trevor Ford arrived on the scene, and after that he deputised for the Welsh international when required, always doing an efficient job.

George was injured in the 5–2 home defeat by Blackpool on New Year's Day 1949 and was out of the team for 14 weeks, during which time Villa lost only one match. But as soon as he was fit, he was back into the groove and finished the campaign with 13 goals to his credit, one less than top marksman Ford.

George made only 13 appearances in 1949–50 as manager Alex Massie looked at different options on the right wing, using Miller Craddock and even Johnny Dixon.

The following season he was certainly undecided who to play there, choosing seven different players to wear the number-seven shirt, George being one of them. In the end, after George Martin had taken over as manager, the job went to Herbert Smith, thus allowing George to move to pastures new, namely Bilston United.

He eventually called it a day in September 1955, after a brief spell with Yarmouth Town, and on his return to Birmingham he took over a newsagents/sub-post office and also became an Aston Villa shareholder.

George, who, in his early days, was a sprint champion and later in life enjoyed a game of billiards and snooker, was approaching his 75th birthday when he died in 1993.

Ugo Ehiogu

Date of birth: 6 October 1972, Hackney, London

Aston Villa record:
Appearances: League 223+14, FA Cup 22+2, League Cup 22+1, Europe 18
Goals: League 12, FA Cup 1, League Cup 1, Europe 1
Debut: League, 24 August 1991 v Arsenal (h) won 3–1

Also played for: West Bromwich Albion, Middlesbrough, Glasgow Rangers, England (1 B, 15 Under-21 and 4 full caps)

Versatile defender Ugochuku Ehiogu started his career as an apprentice with West Bromwich Albion under manager Ron Atkinson in April 1988.

Nurtured through the intermediate and reserve teams, he turned professional in July 1989 and made his League debut for the Baggies as a second-half substitute in the away game with Hull City in September 1990 – the first of only two senior appearances for the Black Country club.

Albion suffered relegation to the Third Division at the end of that season. They were struggling desperately, and although they wanted to keep hold of their best players, in July 1991 Ugo was allowed to leave The Hawthorns, signed again by Ron Atkinson who, by now, was in charge of Aston Villa. He paid just £40,000 for the 6ft 2in, 14st 10lb Londoner and as time progressed, Ugo proved to be one of Atkinson's finest-ever captures for the club.

Able to play in any defensive position, he made his first appearance for Villa at right-back before developing into an excellent centre-half, being strong, mobile and forceful on the ground, powerful and confident in the air and, above all, unflustered and totally committed to playing competitive League and Cup football.

He established himself as a regular in the Villa side halfway through the 1993-94 season when he was brought in to partner Shaun Teale in the absence of Paul McGrath, but he missed the League Cup Final win over Manchester United, sitting on the bench as a substitute.

The following term, when relegation threatened, he and McGrath played superbly well together, and it was much of the same in 1995-96 when he was joined at the back by Gareth Southgate as Villa finished a creditable fourth in the Premiership and won the League Cup for the fifth time in the club's history by beating Leeds United 3-0 in the Final.

Ugo had a storming game at the heart of the defence that afternoon, and he and Southgate completely bottled up the threat of strikers Tomas Brolin, Brian Deane and Tony Yeboah.

In May 1996 Ugo was called up for his first full England cap, coming on as a second-half substitute for Tony Adams in the 3-0 win over China in Beijing. Three more caps followed, and he also represented his country in one B and 15 Under-21 internationals.

An ever present in 1996-97, he continued to give Villa great service, and the following season he reached the milestone of 200 senior appearances for the club, eventually going on to reach an overall tally of 303 before transferring to Middlesbrough in November 2000 for a club-record fee at that time of £8 million. His former club, Albion, received an agreed sell-on fee of around £3 million.

Unfortunately, Ugo didn't have the greatest of starts to his career with Boro, limping off just four minutes into his debut with a hamstring injury that kept him out of action for several months. It would be fair to say that Ugo was by now becoming rather injury prone and, in fact, since 2000 he has had a string of muscle pulls and strains and a twisted knee.

Ugo was soon joined at the Riverside Stadium by two more Villa players, defensive colleague Gareth Southgate arriving in July 2001 and midfielder George Boateng in August 2002. Prior to the 2006-07 Premiership campaign, Southgate became Ugo's boss after taking over the managerial duties from Steve McClaren.

Ugo, despite his niggling injury problems, became the mainstay of the Middlesbrough central defence and played his part in Boro's League Cup Final victory over Bolton Wanderers in 2004 before he suffered a serious knee injury, which forced him to miss several important games during the 2004-05 season.

After agreeing to move back to West Bromwich Albion during the January transfer window of 2006, the deal was suddenly cancelled when a number of Middlesbrough players became injured.

Ugo remained at the Riverside Stadium and went on to take his appearance tally with the Teesside club past the 150 mark, before assisting Glasgow Rangers in 2006-07.

Albert Evans

Date of birth: 18 March 1874, Barnard Castle, County Durham
Died: 24 March 1966, Warwick

Aston Villa record:
Appearances: League 179, FA Cup 24
Debut: League, 7 November 1896 v Bury (h) drew 1–1
Also played for: Stornforth & West Auckland Schools, Egglestone Abbey Boys, Barnard Castle, West Bromwich Albion
Managed: Coventry City

Albert Evans was an excellent full-back, clean-tackling, a precise kicker, strong in body and limb, and a defender who gave Aston Villa terrific service for more than 11 years.

After doing well in the north-east of England with his home-town club Barnard Castle, Evans was signed by Villa as a full-time professional in August 1896, initially acting as reserve to Howard Spencer and Jimmy Welford.

Halfway through the season, having made his senior debut at right-back in place of Spencer in the home League game with Bury, he was given two more outings before gaining a regular place in the side as Spencer's partner at a time when Villa's charge towards the League and FA Cup double was gathering momentum.

Remaining undefeated in the last 10 First Division games and powering their way through to the FA Cup Final, with Evans in fine form, Villa duly completed the double, finishing 11 points in front of runners-up Sheffield United in the League and beating Everton 3–2 in the Cup Final at Crystal Palace when Evans was outstanding.

Indeed, Evans received high praise from two Everton players after the Final. Scottish international right-winger Jack Taylor said 'I never had such a quiet game...Evans marked me so closely that I asked if I could switch wings.'

Taylor's inside-partner and fellow countryman John Bell admitted that Evans was 'Exceptional – one of the best players on the pitch.'

Evans appeared in 15 League and seven Cup games in 1896–97 and duly collected his two winners' medals. The following season he was an ever present when partnering Spencer and also Tom Bowman, and missed just five matches in 1898–99 when his right-back colleagues included Charlie Aston and Bert Sharp and eight in 1899–1900 when he and Spencer were quite brilliant as Villa won back-to-back League Championships.

Still fit and in good form, Evans continued to play with aggression, commitment and consistency, but after another fine season (1900–01,) when he represented the Football League and came close to gaining a full England cap, he broke his leg against Sheffield United in the fourth game of the 1901–02 campaign, this the first of five such injuries he was to suffer in his career.

He was out of action for a year, returning at the start of the 1902–03 season, but ironically he fractured the same leg against another Sheffield side, Wednesday, on New Year's Day 1903 and once more was sidelined for a considerable period, until the following October.

He came back for a handful of games after that but sadly suffered a third leg fracture, which forced him to miss the 1905 FA Cup Final against Newcastle United.

By now Villa's full-back pairing comprised Spencer and Freddie Miles, and, not getting any younger, Evans regained his fitness and played regularly for the second XI before transferring to nearby West Bromwich Albion in October 1907, having accumulated over 200 first-class appearances for the club.

He appeared in 37 League games for the Baggies (as partner to Jesse Pennington) before tragedy struck again, Evans breaking his left leg for a fourth time on Christmas Day 1908 in the League game against Gainsborough Trinity at The Hawthorns.

At that point he called it a day, retiring in May 1909 to become Albion's trainer, a position he held until 1915, having broken his leg again while playing in a charity match.

In May 1919 Evans accepted a coaching position with Sarpsborg FC in Norway but spent only a few months there before taking over as manager of Coventry City in June 1920 (the third at the club in three months). He inherited a poor side at Highfield Road and was lucky to stave off relegation, but he stuck in there, and although cash was tight he got the club on a sound footing before leaving in November 1924.

Thereafter he travelled the world, doing several jobs including gold prospecting in the Yukon and sheep farming in Canada. He returned to England in 1950 and for a while acted as a scout for Villa, spotting a few fine players in the process.

When he died at the age of 92, Evans was the last survivor of Villa's double-winning side from 1897.

Allan Evans

Date of birth:	12 October 1956, West Calder, Polbeath, Edinburgh, West Lothian

Aston Villa record:

Appearances:	League 374+6, FA Cup 26, League Cup 42+1, European 19+1, FA Charity Shield 1, others 4
Goals:	League 51, FA Cup 3, League Cup 6, others 2
Debut:	League, 4 March 1978 v Leicester City (h) drew 0-0
Also played for:	Dunfermline Athletic, Leicester City, Brisbane United (Australia), Darlington, Scotland (4 full caps)
Managed:	Greenock Morton

Aston Villa's defence in the club's Championship and European Cup-winning campaigns of 1980–81 and 1981–82 was superb, and right at the heart was rugged Scotsman Allan Evans, who formed a terrific partnership with fellow countryman Ken McNaught.

Evans was the backbone of the team for almost a decade, and in his 12-year association with the club he accumulated well over 450 senior appearances – only Charlie Aitken, Billy Walker, Gordon Cowans and Joe Bache have played in more first-class games for the club.

As a teenager, Evans spent four years in Malta and Cyprus before spending five years with Dunfermline Athletic, playing as a professional from October 1973. Unluckily, he broke his right leg when making his Scottish League debut against Rangers, but he recovered within three months and in his last season north of the border (1976–77) scored 15 goals from the centre-forward position, including two hat-tricks for the Pars against Clyde and Stranraer.

He was signed by Aston Villa manager Ron Saunders from Dunfermline Athletic for just £30,000 in July 1977 (about the same time that Ken McNaught arrived from Everton) and, after bagging six goals in a 10-0 home Central League win over Sheffield United, he made his debut in the Football League (wearing the unfamiliar number-seven shirt) against his future club Leicester City. He made 10 senior appearances that season before establishing himself in the team in 1978–79 (alongside McNaught) as Villa finished eighth in the First Division.

Solid in everything he did – tackling, heading, kicking and defending – Evans missed very few games over the next seven years, and in 1980–81 he was, as mentioned earlier, quite outstanding, as Villa's defence conceded only 40 goals in 42 matches to win the League title for the first time in 71 years. Evans scored seven goals during that campaign, including three against Sunderland, two in a 4-0 home win and one in a 2-1 victory at Roker Park.

In 1981–82, when Villa triumphed again by beating the German champions Bayern Munich 1-0 in the European Cup Final, Evans was like a rock, especially in the earlier away games against Dynamo Berlin, Dynamo Kiev and Anderlecht. And then, with his co-defender McNaught, he completely blotted out the goal threat of the Bayern strike duo of Ule Hoeness and Karl-Heinz Rummenigge.

Evans, a huge favourite with the fans, then starred once more in 1982–83 as Villa lifted the European Super Cup after beating Barcelona over two legs, coming back from 1-0 down to win the return game at Villa Park by 3-0.

Evans's performances during the 1981–82 season earned him four full caps for Scotland, the first against Holland, followed by two others against Northern Ireland and England (at Hampden Park) and his last versus New Zealand in the World Cup Finals in Spain when he played alongside Liverpool's Alan Hansen in a 5-2 win.

During his last five years at Villa Park, Evans had several 'new' central-defensive partners, including Paul Elliott, Steve Foster, Brendan Ormsby, Steve Sims, Martin Keown and David Mountfield – and after relegation had been suffered at the end of the 1986–87 season, Evans, Sims and Keown helped the club regain their top-flight status at the first attempt (as runners-up behind Millwall).

In August 1989 Evans left Villa Park on a free transfer to join Leicester City, moving to the Australian club Brisbane United in 1990 before teaming up with his former Villa playing colleague Brian Little, who was boss at Darlington (March 1991). After helping the Quakers climb out of the Conference, he then moved back to Filbert Street as assistant to Little in June 1991, to his old hunting ground Villa Park in November 1994, to Stoke City in February 1998 and to West Bromwich Albion in September 1999. In June 2000 he was appointed manager of the Scottish club Greenock Morton, where he remained for two years.

Trevor Ford

Date of birth: 1 October 1923, Swansea
Died: 29 May 2003, Swansea

Aston Villa record:
Appearances: League 120, FA Cup 8
Goals: League 60, FA Cup 1
Debut: League, 18 January 1947 v Arsenal (a) won 2-0

Also played for: Powys Avenue School, Swansea Boys, Tower United (Swansea), Swansea Town, Clapton Orient (guest), Sunderland, Cardiff City, PSV Eindhoven (Holland), Newport County, Romford, Wales (1 Victory and 38 full caps)

In October 1950 a 27-year-old Trevor Ford was the subject of a British football transfer record when he signed for 'Bank of England' club Sunderland for a fee of £30,000 from Aston Villa, this after he had turned down lucrative offers from clubs in Colombia and Portugal.

He was a footballing celebrity at the time due to his prolific scoring record – having netted 61 goals and made 128 appearances for the Birmingham-based club over a period of three and a half years from January 1947. Prior to that, he had notched nine goals in 16 League games while playing for Swansea Town.

At Sunderland, Trevor failed to gel on the pitch with several of his teammates, one being former record-breaking signing Len Shackleton – although his goalscoring record was still impressive.

After striking 70 goals in 117 outings for Sunderland, he signed for Cardiff City in December 1953 for £29,500 and spent three years at Ninian Park before joining the Dutch club PSV Eindhoven in August 1956. He later had decent spells with Newport County (July 1960-April 1961) and Romford, finally taking off his shooting boots in May 1962, although he did continue to play in various charity matches over the next 12 years (fitness permitting). He also ran a garage business in Swansea – having taken an interest in this line of work while playing for Sunderland.

Capped 38 times by Wales at senior level between 1946 and 1957 (14 coming as a Villa player), Trevor became the Principality's all-time joint aggregate goal scorer with 23 goals, later equalled by Ivor Allchurch and then beaten by Ian Rush.

Unfortunately, he was not included in the Welsh squad for the 1958 World Cup following his suspension from the game. He also played in one Victory international against Ireland in February 1946, having served in the Royal Artillery during the war, during which time he scored five goals in nine games as a guest for Clapton Orient.

During his time with Villa – which lasted from January 1947 when he was part of a £9,500 player-exchange deal involving Tommy Dodds, who moved in the opposite direction to Swansea Town until his departure to Roker Park – Trevor gave the fans plenty to cheer about.

Described as being 'a terrorist in the penalty area in an era when centre-forwards reigned supreme and goalkeepers were cannon fodder' his no-nonsense, hard-hitting, bustling style saw him finish as the club's leading scorer three seasons running – claiming 18 goals in 1947-48, 14 in 1948-49 (which included a rasping four goals in a 5-1 win over Wolves) and another 18 in 1949-50, and all this after he had netted nine times in nine starts at the end of the 1946-47 campaign following his transfer from the Vetch Field.

He was the fifth Villa player to wear the number-nine shirt during the 1946-47 season and immediately drew up a fine understanding with Dicky Dorsett and Jack Martin. He was soon joined in the attack by 'Sailor' Brown and later by Johnny Dixon and Billy Goffin.

Trevor had a mind of his own. Sometimes he would train alone, even return to the ground during the afternoon to put in some extra work. He loved his football, and although he was a controversial character the fans loved him.

When his controversial autobiography *I Lead the Attack* was published in the early 1950s, he exposed 'under the counter' payments, and when it was serialised in a Sunday newspaper he upset the whole soccer hierarchy and found himself suspended. He was subsequently reinstated, only to be banned once more when Football League secretary Alan Hardaker uncovered an illegal payment of £100 by Sunderland to Trevor himself.

When I spoke to Trevor in 1976 he told me that his greatest claim to fame was not as a footballer but on the cricket pitch; he was substitute fielder for Glamorgan against Nottinghamshire in a county Championship match at St Helens, Swansea, when Malcolm Nash was clubbed for a world-record six sixes in one over by the West Indian Test batsman Garry Sobers.

Billy Garraty

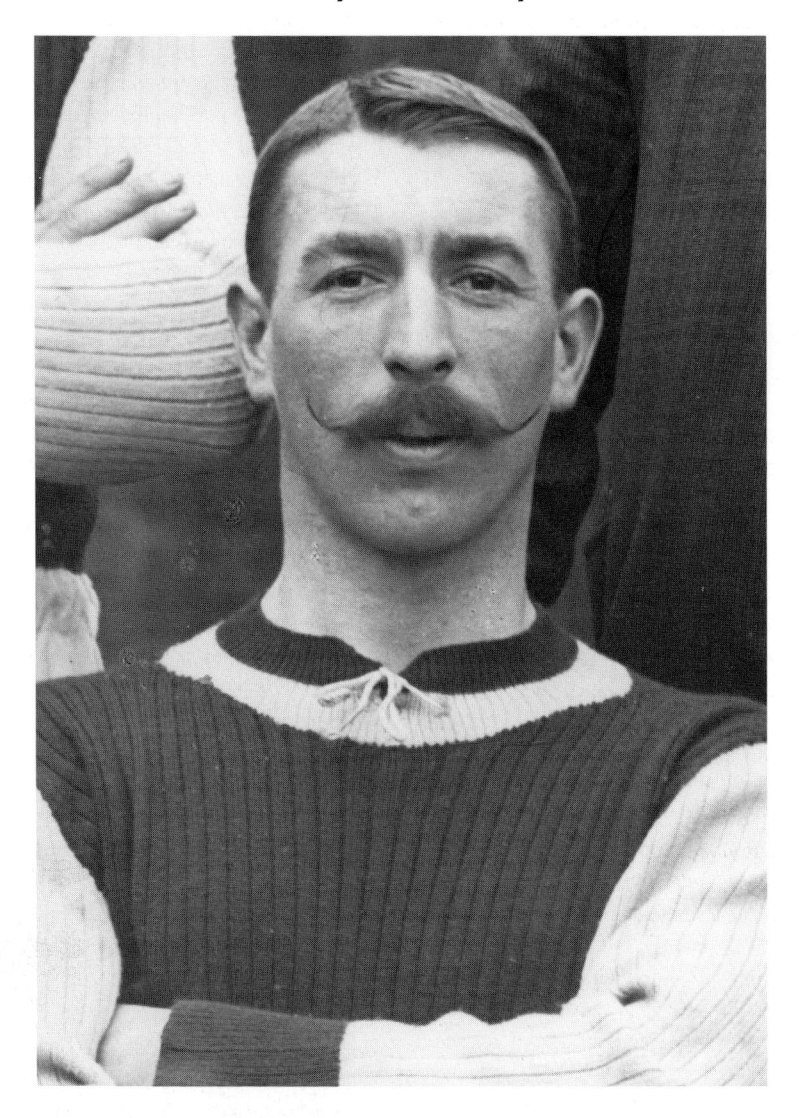

Date of birth: 6 October 1878, Saltley, Birmingham
Died: 6 May 1931, Perry Barr, Birmingham

Aston Villa record:
Appearances: League 223, FA Cup 31, Other 1
Goals: League 96, FA Cup 15
Debut: League, 2 April 1898 v Stoke (h) drew 1–1

Also played for: Church Road & Saltley St Saviour's Schools (Birmingham), Ashted Swifts, St Saviour's FC, Highfield Villa, Lozells FC, Aston Shakespeare, Leicester Fosse, West Bromwich Albion, Lincoln City

Billy Garraty had an excellent goalscoring record throughout his career. With subtle skills, good pace, powerful shooting and excellent mobility, he was the country's leading marksman in season 1899-1900 when his 27 goals in only 33 matches helped Villa win the League title for the fifth time.

He later added an FA Cup-winners' medal to his collection in 1905 and also played in one full international match for England, lining up against Wales at Portsmouth in March 1903 when his forward partner was club-mate Joe Bache, who scored in a 2-1 win.

A positive forward, always looking to get in a shot on goal, Garraty - with a dashing moustache - was only 18 when he joined Villa as a full-time professional in August 1897, having just won a junior international cap with the Birmingham FA. He played twice on the left wing towards the end of his first season and had to wait until March 1899 before establishing himself in the first team, joining Jack Devey and Fred Wheldon in the central-forward positions following an injury to George Johnson.

Garraty never looked back after that. He scored six goals in nine games that season, including a superb hat-trick in a 7-1 home win over his future club West Bromwich Albion, as Villa roared on towards the League title.

The following season he was brilliant, and besides his tally of League goals, which included two more hat-tricks versus Sunderland (won 4-3) and Notts County (won 6-2), he also netted three times in the FA Cup.

His goals dried up somewhat in 1900-01, managing only 11 as Villa struggled in the League and lost in the FA Cup semi-final to Sheffield United in a replay, and it was much of the same in 1901-02 when he netted only seven times. But you can never keep a good goalscorer down for long, and in 1902-03 Garraty was back to his brilliant best, finding the back of the net on 15 occasions as Villa missed out on two fronts – finishing runners-up in the League behind Sheffield Wednesday (beaten by a point) and losing again in the Cup semi-final, this time to Bury.

Joint second top scorer with McLuckie in 1903-04, Garraty suffered a few niggling injury problems and was being pressed for a place in the first team by several players, but he regained full fitness, held his position and in 1904-05 helped Villa win the FA Cup, beating Newcastle United 2-0 before more than 101,000 fans at the Crystal Palace when he and Harry Hampton caused plenty of problems for the defenders.

After one more fine season, top scoring again with 21 goals in 1905-06, Garraty lost his place in the team early in 1906-07, and after netting 112 times in 259 senior appearances for Villa he moved to Leicester Fosse in September 1908.

He spent only a month at Filbert Street, returning to the West Midlands to sign for West Bromwich Albion for £270 in October 1908. Made captain at The Hawthorns, he spent two years with the Baggies before switching his allegiance to Lincoln City for £100, and he finally announced his retirement in May 1911.

He was out of football for a short while before returning as Villa's trainer for two months at the end of the 1912-13 season, when he saw the team win the FA Cup. However, he was then taken seriously ill with pneumonia but thankfully made a good recovery, and from 1923 until his death at the age of 52 he worked as a beer delivery driver for Ansells brewery in Aston, attending home games at Villa Park whenever possible.

Billy George

Date of birth: 29 June 1874, Shrewsbury
Died: 4 December 1933, Birmingham

Aston Villa record:
Appearances: League 358, FA Cup 40, others 3
Debut: League, 9 October 1897 v West Bromwich Albion (a) drew 1–1

Also played for: Woolwich Ramblers, Trowbridge Town, Birmingham (player/trainer), England (3 full caps)

Said, and confirmed by many, to have been the greatest goalkeeper ever to play for Aston Villa, Billy George was first choice at Villa Park for 10 and a half years, from October 1898 until March 1909, only missing matches through injury, illness and international duty.

A regular soldier stationed at Trowbridge, having earlier played for Woolwich Ramblers in London, he was persuaded to travel to the Midlands for a trial, did exceptionally well and was asked to leave the army and sign as a full-time professional. He had no hesitation and put pen to paper in front of committee member Fred Rinder and secretary George Ramsay.

However, Villa had infringed the FA rules in arranging and completing the deal, and were found guilty. The club was severely censored and fined £50 while George, along with Messrs Rinder and Ramsay were all suspended from taking part in any football activities for a month. But that sort of money meant nothing in terms of what George was to give back to the club over the course of time.

In October 1897, when the transfer papers were officially completed and accepted, and he was free from suspension, George made an impressive League debut in a 1–1 draw away to West Bromwich Albion, and, acting initially as deputy to Jack Whitehouse, he was called into action seven times that season before taking over on a regular basis five games into the 1898-99 campaign, which culminated in him gaining a Championship-winners' medal.

The following season he added a second League-winners' prize to his collection and later, in 1901 and 1903, he helped Villa reach the semi-final stage of the FA Cup before going one better in 1905 and gaining a winners' medal when Newcastle United were defeated 2-0 in the Final at Crystal Palace in front of 101,117 spectators. He was outstanding in that game and pulled off three superb saves as Villa clung on to a one-goal lead before Harry Hampton netted his second to clinch victory.

A huge man, standing almost 6ft 2in tall and tipping the scales at 21st 7lb, he was capped three times at full international level by England, lining up against Wales (0–0), Ireland (won 1–0) and Scotland (drew 2–2) at the end of the 1901–02 season, the later game being staged at his home ground, Villa Park, before a crowd of 15,000.

He participated in the abandoned international at Ibrox Park against Scotland in April 1902 when 26 fans were killed and almost 450 injured. He also represented the FA, appeared in two international trials and played once for the Football League against the Irish League in 1901. And if it hadn't been for the form of Bolton's John Sutcliffe and Tom Baddeley of Wolves, then one feels that George would surely have gained more recognition on the international scene than he managed.

Described in various matchday programmes as having 'a keen eye who disposed of the ball to the best advantage', George had tremendous reflexes for a big man. He was agile, had a good fist when punching the ball and was courageous in 50–50 situations, although he hardly ever dived at an opponent's feet, choosing to throw his legs in the way of any shot that might be driven towards him and his goal.

After an exceptionally-fine run he lost his place in the Villa goal to Arthur Cartlidge but remained at the club as a reserve and as assistant trainer until moving across the city to join neighbours Birmingham as player-trainer in July 1911. In fact, he was pressed into action by Blues against Barnsley two months after joining in an emergency, after Horace Bailey had cried off at the 11th hour.

Remaining in the game until World War One, he later took employment at the Austin Rover car plant at Longbridge, Birmingham (retiring in 1958) and played second XI cricket for Warwickshire between 1901 and 1907; he also assisted Wiltshire and Shropshire in the Minor Counties League. He scored a century for Warwickshire in 47 minutes in 1902.

Colin Gibson

Date of birth: 6 April 1960, Bridport, Dorset

Aston Villa record:
Appearances: League 181+4, FA Cup 12, League Cup 26, European 13+1, Other 1
Goals: League 10, European 2
Debut: League, 18 November 1978, substitute v Bristol City (h) won 2-0

Also played for: West Sussex Schools, Portsmouth (amateur), Manchester United, Port Vale, Leicester City, Blackpool, Walsall, England (4 Youth, 1 B and 1 Under-21 caps)

Colin Gibson's professional career spanned 20 years, and in that time he appeared in 378 club games and scored 34 goals.

A stylish full-back who could also play in midfield, Gibson was an exponent of the overlap and, when given the chance, he could send in a powerful shot, normally left footed.

After being rejected by Portsmouth he joined Aston Villa as an apprentice in the summer of 1976 and turned professional in April 1978, making his League debut seven months later as a second-half substitute for the injured Allan Evans in a 2-0 home win over Bristol City.

With Gary Williams and Gordon Smith initially ahead of him in the pecking order for the left-back position, Gibson finally gained a regular place in the first team during the last quarter of that 1978-79 season, retaining it with confidence throughout the next campaign when he scored his first two goals for the club, in a 2-1 home League win over Everton and a 2-1 victory at Coventry.

However, during the 1980-81 campaign, as Villa strove on towards their first League Championship triumph for over 70 years, Gibson was pressed hard and long for the number-three shirt by Williams and Eamonn Deacy, but he remained confident and, despite a few injury worries, played his part and duly collected a winners' medal after making 21 appearances as Kenny Swain's full-back partner.

He remained a regular in the side until early February 1982 and was capped by England at Under-21 level versus Norway, before another injury let in Williams. This proved to be a body blow for Gibson, who subsequently missed out on Villa's European Cup glory, although he was in the squad for the Final in Rotterdam and early in 1982-83, albeit small consolation, he helped Villa lift the European Super Cup at Barcelona's expense.

Returning to the side on a permanent basis halfway through that season, Gibson remained first choice at left-back until December 1984 when he was switched into midfield to accommodate Tony Dorigo. Teaming up with Gordon Cowans, Steve McMahon and Paul Birch, he produced some excellent displays, so much so that in November 1985 Manchester United boss Ron Atkinson moved in with a £275,000 bid and whisked Gibson off to Old Trafford, where he performed reasonably well for three seasons as a hard-working utility player who filled in whenever and wherever he was needed – possibly to the detriment of his overall career – until a severe knee-ligament injury intervened.

He was hurt in a pre-season friendly in Sweden in August 1988 and for the next two years underwent a series of operations and hopeful comebacks, which usually resulted in further breakdowns. After a loan spell with Port Vale, and almost 100 senior outings for United, he was transferred to Leicester City for £100,000 in December 1990, where he was re-united with the former Aston Villa forward Brian Little, then in charge at Filbert Street. Unfortunately, Gibson continued to suffer injury problems which restricted his appearances for the Foxes, although he did assist Leicester in their run-in to victory in the 1994 Play-off Final at Wembley. However, the following day he was given a free transfer and after that played out his career in the lower Divisions with Blackpool (four games) and Walsall (40 games), eventually quitting competitive football in the summer of in 1995.

Jimmy Gibson

Date of birth: 12 June 1901, Larkhall, Lanarkshire
Died: 1 January 1978, Erdington, Birmingham

Aston Villa record:
Appearances: League 213, FA Cup 12
Goals: League 10
Debut: League, 7 May 1927 v Huddersfield Town (a) drew 0-0

Also played for: Morning Star FC, Larkhall Thistle, Kirkintilloch Rob Roy, Glasgow Ashfield, Partick Thistle, Scotland (10 full caps)

'Jimmy Gibson was a darn good player, one of the most competent footballers ever, a terrific motivator, whose bravery, stamina, stealth and a flair for the unexpected highlighted a wonderful career' are the words of former Aston Villa defender Alec Talbot during a conversation I had with him after a charity game in Cradley Heath in the late 1960s.

Yes, indeed, James Davidson Gibson was a wonderfully-cultured half-back. He could occupy all three middle-line positions, doing so with authority and consistency. Standing 6ft 2in tall and weighing around 12st, he was long striding, a tireless performer and a solid and fair tackler who loved to drive forward into the opposing half of the field to give his forwards a helping hand and then, when required, race back to assist his defenders when danger threatened at the other end of the pitch. He once struck the bar with a header from a Villa corner and, seconds later, booted the ball off his own goal line, having sprinted 100 yards downfield as the opposition counter-attacked.

He was approaching his 20th birthday when he joined Partick Thistle as a professional in April 1921. Making his debut almost immediately, he went on to appear in nearly 200 competitive games for the Firhill Park club, 171 coming in the League when he also netted 43 goals – a surprisingly high scoring record for a half-back. He also represented Scotland in four full internationals – against England twice, Wales and Northern Ireland – and appeared in two inter-League matches for the Scottish League before transferring to Aston Villa for a then record fee of £7,500 in April 1927.

Over the next nine years or so he gave the Villa supporters plenty to cheer about with his forthright approach to the game, his never-say-die attitude making him a firm favourite with the Holte Enders.

After his debut on the last day of the 1926-27 season, Gibson made 24 appearances the following season and in March 1928, he had the pleasure of helping his country thrash England 5-1 when the Scots were dubbed the 'Wembley Wizards'.

A knee injury sidelined him for long periods during the 1928-29 campaign, but he was back to his best in 1929-30 when he became part of a wonderful half-back line comprising of himself, Alec Talbot and Joe Tate, the trio being affectionately known as 'Wind, Sleet and Rain.'

Villa went goal crazy in 1930-31, scoring 131 League and Cup goals. Gibson netted only twice – one a real beauty in a 6-1 win at Huddersfield – but he did have a hand in at least 25 others as he produced some great link-up play and delivered pin-point passes through to the likes of strikers 'Pongo' Waring, Eric Houghton and Billy Walker.

Adding further international honours to his tally, Gibson eventually ended his Scotland career with 10 caps to his name, as he continued to perform splendidly for Villa until 1934-35 when Tom Gardner took over at right-half on a regular basis, with Jimmy Allen in the centre and Billy 'Gypo' Kingdom on the left.

In May 1936 Gibson decided to retire from competitive football, having appeared in almost 450 senior games for clubs and country. In 1940 he came out of retirement to play as a guest for an international XI against a District XI, and after World War Two he took employment as a welfare officer at the ICI works in Witton, a position he held until 1962.

Gibson was 76 years of age when he died in 1978, having seen Villa win the League Cup the previous season.

His father, Neil, also played professional football, representing Scotland (1895-1905) as well as serving with Glasgow Rangers and Partick Thistle.

Andy Gray

Date of birth: 30 November 1955, Gorbals, Glasgow

Aston Villa record:
Appearances: League 165+2, FA Cup 10+2, League Cup 25, European 5, others 1
Goals: League 59, FA Cup 3, League Cup 14, European 2
Debut: League, 4 October 1975 v Middlesbrough (a) drew 0-0

Also played for: Clydebank Strollers, Dundee United, Wolverhampton Wanderers, Everton, Notts County, West Bromwich Albion, Glasgow Rangers, Cheltenham Town, Scotland (4 Under-23 and 20 full caps)

Glaswegian Andy Gray supported Hibernian as a lad, but he also enjoyed watching Rangers! Before leaving school he was registered as an amateur with Dundee United, who rewarded him with a professional contract in May 1973.

He made rapid progress and went on to score 45 goals in 86 appearances for the Tannadice club, gaining a Scottish Cup runners'-up medal in 1974 before transferring to Aston Villa for £110,000 in September 1975, signed to replace the injured Keith Leonard.

He spent just over two seasons at Villa Park, linking up well with Brian Little in his second. He collected a League Cup-winners' prize in 1977 after playing in the first two of three encounters with Everton in the Final and at the same time was voted PFA Footballer of the Year and also Young Player of the Year.

A colourful character in more ways than one both on and off the field, Andy was a brave, strong and confident striker, a tremendous header of the ball, who led the line with great determination. He was a never-say-die sort of player, totally committed to playing football; he was one of the great old-fashioned centre-forwards to emerge since World War Two, and he certainly made defenders earn their keep with his powerful and courageous displays inside the penalty area – which caused him several injuries, mainly to his head.

He was certainly robust and enthusiastic, and could score the most unlikely goals – which he did frequently.

In September 1979, after netting 69 times in 144 games for Villa, Andy became the most expensive footballer in Great Britain when Wolves boss John Barnwell paid £1.15m (£1.46m with VAT and various levy charges added on) for his signature, the transfer forms being completed on the Molineux pitch with manager John Barnwell before Wolves' home League game with Crystal Palace.

Andy went on to score 45 goals in 162 first-class matches for Wolves, one of his strikes winning the League Cup Final of 1980 versus Nottingham Forest, a simple tap in from two yards. He also went down with Wolves but was happy to stay and helped them regain top-flight status at the first attempt.

By this time Andy was already an established Scottish international, having won the first of his 20 full caps against Romania in December 1975 as a Villa player. He scored six goals for his country, having earlier represented Scotland as a youth-team player and in four Under-23 matches. His last senior appearance came against Iceland in 1985 as a player with Everton, whom he joined for £250,000 in November 1983.

During his time at Goodison Park he gained winners' medals in three major competitions: the Football League, FA Cup (scoring against Watford in the 1984 Final) and European Cup-winners' Cup (netting in the Final against Rapid Vienna). His strike partners on Merseyside were Adrian Heath (later with Aston Villa) and Graeme Sharpe.

Villa re-signed him as a stop-gap in July 1985 for £150,000. He did well in a struggling side, scoring seven times in 46 starts, but he was not getting any younger and, after another full season and a loan spell with Notts County, he moved to neighbours West Bromwich Albion (signed by his former boss Ron Saunders).

In September 1988 Andy fulfilled a lifetime ambition by joining Glasgow Rangers, whom he helped win the Scottish Premier League and reach the League Cup Final in his only season at Ibrox.

Job done, he then played briefly for non-League side Cheltenham Town before retiring in May 1991, having amassed a career record at club and international level of 215 goals in 614 games.

Andy returned to Villa Park for a third time as assistant to manager Ron Atkinson in the summer of 1991 and quit the game at the end of that season to concentrate on his role as an analyst and pundit for soccer on Sky Sports.

Ray Graydon

Date of birth: 21 July 1947, Bristol

Aston Villa record:

Appearances: League 188+4, FA Cup 10, League Cup 25+1, Europe 2, Charity Shield 1
Goals: League 68, FA Cup 3, League Cup 9, Europe 1
Debut: League, 14 August 1971 v Plymouth Argyle (h) won 3–1

Also played for: Bristol Rovers, Coventry City, Washington Diplomats (NASL), Oxford United, England (amateur and Youth caps)
Managed: Walsall, Bristol Rovers

Right-winger Ray Graydon began his career with Bristol Rovers, for whom he made his League debut in September 1965.

In June 1971 – after scoring 38 goals in 157 senior games for Rovers – he moved to First Division Aston Villa, signed by manager and ex-player Vic Crowe, for £50,000 plus Brian Godfrey.

Ray spent six seasons at Villa Park, twice winning promotion and gaining a League Cup-winners' medal when he scored from a late penalty rebound in the 1975 Final against Norwich City. His first effort was saved by former Villa 'keeper Kevin Keelan, but Ray reacted quickly to fire the ball home to clinch Villa's first domestic Cup win since 1961.

Ray loved to hug the touchline. Fast and direct, he possessed good, close ball control and could deliver the perfect cross, given time and space.

He was in exceptional form in 1971–72, helping Villa win the Third Division title when he netted 14 goals in 45 League games as part of an exciting forward line comprising himself, Geoff Vowden or Pat McMahon, Andy Lochhead, Chico Hamilton and Willie Anderson.

With Bruce Rioch feeding him passes, Ray continued to impress in 1972–73 as Villa just missed out on promotion to the top flight, but in 1973–74 he was plagued by injury problems and missed half of Villa's 48 games.

Back to full fitness the following season, he scored in the opening day draw at York and went on to finish up as the leading marksman with 27 goals, three more than Brian Little, who was now his inside-partner, as Villa completed a 'mini' double by winning the League Cup for the second time and gaining promotion to the First Division under manager Ron Saunders.

In September 1975 Villa played their first-ever game in Europe against the Belgian side Antwerp in the UEFA Cup, and Ray had the pleasure of scoring the club's first goal at this level. Unfortunately, Villa lost 4–1 and they also went down 1–0 in the second leg.

Ray again topped the scoring charts with 14 goals as Villa just managed to avoid relegation, and in his last season at the club (1976–77) he netted seven times in 22 matches but missed out on League Cup glory after the boss (Saunders) had made changes to the team.

In July 1977 Ray was transferred to Coventry City for £50,000. He then had a short spell with Washington Diplomats before joining Oxford United for £35,000 in November 1978. Announcing his retirement as a player in May 1981, he remained at The Manor Ground as a senior coach.

He became highly respected in this field, and after assisting Watford he did particularly well at Southampton before taking a similar position at Queen's Park Rangers.

Ray eventually moved into management with Walsall in the summer of 1998, replacing the Dane, Jan Sorenson. He introduced an element of professionalism to the club and in his first season led the Saddlers to promotion – this after the Saddlers had been marked down as favourites for relegation!

Walsall's team cost around £80,000 and they went up with perhaps the smallest operating budget of any club in the League. And for his efforts, Ray was voted just behind Sir Alex Ferguson, Kevin Keegan and the other League-winning chiefs in the poll for Manager of the Season.

Unfortunately, relegation followed in 2000, but after re-assessing the situation and bringing in a few more players, Walsall beat Reading in the Play-off Final to win back their place in Division Three within 12 months.

After losing the local derby to West Bromwich Albion in January 2002, Ray was sacked, the decision meeting with derision among the local press. However, the same batch of reporters expected he would walk straight into another job in football within days, and he did, taking over as boss of his first club Bristol Rovers, with whom he stayed for two years, twice steering Rovers clear of relegation before his dismissal in January 2004.

Ray then accompanied Howard Wilkinson as coach to China (mid-2004), but this arrangement lasted only a matter of months, and in February 2005 he became coach at Leicester City under manager Rob Kelly.

THE LEGENDS OF ASTON VILLA

Albert Hall

Date of birth: 21 January 1882, Wordsley, Stourbridge
Died: 17 October 1957, Stourbridge

Aston Villa record:
Appearances: League 195, FA Cup 19, FA Charity Shield 1
Goals: League 51, FA Cup 10
Debut: League, 19 December 1903 v Nottingham Forest (a) won 7-3

Also played for: Brierley Hill Wanderers, Wall Heath, Stourbridge (2 spells), Millwall, England (1 full cap)

Albert Hall was an exceptionally-talented goalscoring outside-left, a real box of tricks, lightning quick with a cracking right-foot shot.

He was 21 years of age when he joined Aston Villa in July 1903 from Stourbridge, whom he had been registered with for three seasons as an inside-forward

In fact, he continued in that position with Villa and scored six goals in 11 games in his first season, including one terrific effort on his debut in a stunning 7-3 win at Nottingham Forest.

He was successfully switched to the left flank halfway through the 1904-05 campaign following an injury to Arthur Lockett, linking up splendidly with Joe Bache.

Albert never looked back after that. Eager and committed, he played his part in helping Villa win the FA Cup in April 1905, beating Newcastle United 2-0 in the Final in front of almost 102,000 spectators at Crystal Palace. He delivered crosses for both goals scored by Harry Hampton, the first on two minutes and the second on 76, and he also came close to finding the net himself, hitting the outside of the post in the first half and firing just over the bar from 18 yards soon after the restart.

A niggling knee injury (initially suffered during the second city derby against arch-rivals Birmingham) caused him to miss a handful of games in both the 1905-06 and 1906-07 campaigns; he also switched wings when Villa were seeking to find a permanent replacement for Billy Brawn on the right flank.

He was then quite outstanding in 1907-08, scoring 13 League goals as Villa took the runners'-up spot in the First Division. He also appeared for the Football League against the Scottish League and was twice named as reserve for the full England team.

Unfortunately, Albert's goals dried up the following season, although he did manage another game for the Football League side against the Scots before bouncing back to net six times in 1909-10, including two fine strikes in a 5-2 home victory over Sheffield Wednesday, as Villa powered on towards their sixth League title in 16 years.

After a successful international trial, Albert was subsequently capped for the first and only time by England in February 1911. Selected to play on the left wing against Ireland in Belfast after injuries had ruled out Sunderland's Arthur Bridgett and George Wall of Manchester United, he produced a fine performance as England battled to earn a 1-1 draw.

One felt that Albert deserved to gain more representative honours, but with so many other talented left-wingers in the game at the same time he knew, deep down, he was fortunate to get one outing for his country.

Surprisingly Albert was in and out of the Villa team during the next four seasons, accumulating only 23 appearances and missing out on an FA Cup-winners' medal in 1913, having lost his place to Joe Bache who was switched to the left wing to accommodate the influential Clem Stephenson.

A loyal servant, Albert remained at Villa Park until December 1913 when he moved, somewhat reluctantly I gather, to London to sign for Southern League side Millwall for a fee of £1,500, having scored 61 goals in 214 senior appearances during his 10 and a half years with the Villa.

He did reasonably well with the Lions during his two seasons at The Den before World War One halted his senior career. He returned to the Midlands to sign for his former club Stourbridge but was forced to retire with a knee injury in August 1916. He remained in the town and in later years took employment as an enamelware manufacturer. He was 75 when he died.

Harry Hampton

Date of birth: 21 April 1885, Wellington, Shropshire
Died: 15 March 1963, Wrexham, North Wales

Aston Villa record:
Appearances: League 339, FA Cup 34, Wartime 3
Goals: League 215, FA Cup 27, Wartime 5
Debut: League, 19 November 1904 v Manchester City (a) lost 2–1

Also played for: Potters Bank (Salop), Lilleshall Ironworks, Shifnal Juniors, Hadley FC, Wellington Town (two spells), Birmingham, Newport County, Lilleshall Town, (wartime guest for Bellis & Morcom FC, Blackpool, Derby County, Fulham, Nottingham Forest, Reading, Stoke), England (4 full caps)

Harry Hampton is one of Aston Villa's true household legends. His shoulder charges on goalkeepers made him an idol among the home supporters in the days when such tactics were allowed. He was certainly robust to the extreme and once knocked over Willie 'Fatty' Foulke, the giant 22-stone Sheffield United custodian, and quite regularly a defender had to pick himself up, gather his breath and dust himself down after being on the receiving end of one of Harry's crunching charges!

His direct, all-action approach and, indeed, his bravery inside the penalty area when boots were flying in all directions and his devil-may-care attitude brought him a staggering 247 goals, including a record 215 in League matches alone for Aston Villa.

Known affectionately as ''Appy 'Arry' Hampton', he was a real terror to opposing goalkeepers and defenders alike and during the decade leading up to World War One, he was rated as one of the finest marksmen in Britain.

Signed from Wellington Town where he was known as the 'Wellington Whirlwind', Harry served Aston Villa for almost 16 years, from August 1904 until February 1920 when he moved across the city to neighbours Birmingham on a free transfer.

He helped Villa twice win the FA Cup, firstly in 1905 when he scored twice in the Final against Newcastle United (2-0) and secondly in 1913 versus Sunderland (1-0). He also gained a League Championship-winners' medal in 1910 when he top-scored with 26 First Division goals, including four hat-tricks. But he was disappointed in 1913 when Sunderland took the title, thus preventing Villa from completing the League and Cup double for the second time in their history. In fact, Harry returned a personal best tally of 30 goals that season, including a club record five in a 10-0 home win over Sheffield Wednesday.

He represented England in four senior internationals, scoring on his debut in a 4-3 win over Wales in March 1913. He later appeared against the Welsh for a second time and also starred in two internationals against Scotland, striking the winning goal in a 1-0 victory at Chelsea in April 1914.

Harry also represented the Football League on three occasions and played in the annual challenge match for Birmingham against London in 1909, 1911 and 1913. He was badly gassed during World War One but recovered and played as a guest for several top clubs, having one outing for Blues in December 1916.

Recruited by Birmingham to bolster their attack, he scored 11 goals in his first 10 League games, including four in an 8-0 home win over Nottingham Forest. He also netted twice on his debut in an emphatic 5-0 win at Barnsley.

In his second season he struck 16 goals in 34 games, helping Blues win the Second Division Championship. In 1921-22 he was used as a right-half for a few games and eventually moved on after Joe Bradford had established himself in the side.

Not getting any younger but still alert, Harry moved to Newport County in September 1922. He returned to Wellington Town for a second spell in January 1924 and later acted as coach at Preston North End (June 1925-January 1926). He spent two years playing in the Birmingham Works League and also assisted Lilleshall Town before coaching Birmingham's colts side from October 1934 to May 1937.

Harry later ran the Carlton café in Queen Street, Rhyl, and quite regularly during the summer season he was visited by scores of Villa and Blues supporters!

He remained in North Wales and was almost 78 years of age when he died in 1963.

His elder brother George played for Glossop, Aston Villa and Shrewsbury Town before World War One.

Sam Hardy

Date of birth: 26 August 1883, Newbold Verdom, Derbyshire
Died: 24 October 1966, Chesterfield

Aston Villa record:
Appearances: League 159, FA Cup 24, Wartime 2
Debut: League, 1 September 1912 v Chelsea (h) won 1–0

Also played for: Newbold White Star, Chesterfield, Liverpool, Plymouth Argyle (guest), Nottingham Forest (two spells). England (21 full caps)

'Sam "Chuffer" Hardy was one of the greatest goalkeepers I ever saw play' said Jesse Pennington, the former West Bromwich Albion and England left-back who was in the game for 19 years (1903–22). Indeed, Sam was quite a player and during a wonderful career amassed well over 600 appearances at club and international level. He made goalkeeping look easy and would have been considered a world-class player in any era.

With masterly anticipation, he was universally regarded as the best in his position in England until the emergence of Birmingham's Harry Hibbs.

Commanding the number-one spot in the England team either side of World War One, ahead of such greats as Burnley's Jerry Dawson and Tim Williamson of Middlesbrough, he won 21 caps over a period of 14 years between February 1907 and April 1920, played in three Victory internationals, represented the Football League against the Scottish League on two occasions, starred for Birmingham against London and lined up in two England international trials, the first against the South of England in 1913 and the second against the North of England in 1914.

The recipient of a First Division Championship-winning medal with Liverpool in 1906, when he conceded only 26 goals in 30 games, he went on to collect a Second Division winners' medal with Nottingham Forest in 1922 and was also presented with two FA Cup-winners' medals, both with Aston Villa, the first in 1913 against Sunderland (1-0) and the second in 1920 against Huddersfield Town (1-0). During World War One he twice helped Nottingham Forest win the Midland Principal Section Championship and win the Victory Shield after a two-leg victory over Everton.

Known also as 'safe and steady Sam', Hardy made his League debut for Chesterfield in 1903, and after his £500 move to Anfield he remained first-choice 'keeper for Liverpool for seven years from 1905, making a total of 239 appearances before signing for Aston Villa for just £600 in May 1912.

Taking over between the posts from Brendel Anstey, Sam missed only five games in an excellent first season with the club. He produced some wonderful displays as Villa came mightily close to claiming their second double by winning the FA Cup and finishing runners-up behind Sunderland in the League.

In 1913-14 he was absent from eight League games as Villa once again finished second in the League, this time behind Blackburn Rovers, and then, in 1914-15, he missed just one match, at home to Sheffield United, when the team ended up in 13th position – their lowest placing since 1900-01.

During the latter stages of World War One, Sam played in two Victory League games, and he was up and running again when peacetime football resumed after a break of four years, by which time Villa had several new faces at the club – among them an up-and-coming young goalkeeper by the name of Tommy Jackson.

Retaining his place unchallenged, Sam made 40 senior appearances in 1919-20 and 30 the following season before being replaced by the promising Jackson.

Having played as a guest for Nottingham Forest (and also for Plymouth Argyle) during the war, he was recruited as a full-time professional at The City Ground for £1,000 in August 1921. He spent four seasons with Forest, for whom he made his last League appearance in October 1924 at the age of 41.

On his retirement in May 1925, Sam returned to Chesterfield where he ran a hotel, and later he owned his own billiard and snooker hall in Alfreton, Derbyshire. He was 83 when he died in 1966 – having watched England win the World Cup three months earlier.

His nephew, Ted Worrell, a right-back, played for Aberdare, Fulham, New Brighton, Southport, Sheffield Wednesday and Watford between 1910 and 1929.

Jimmy Harrop

Date of birth: 9 September 1884, Heeley, Sheffield
Died: 1958, Derbyshire

Aston Villa record:
Appearances: League 153, FA Cup 18, Wartime 6
Goals: League 4
Debut: League, 2 September 1912 v Chelsea (h) won 1–0

Also played for: St Wilfred's and Heeley County Schools, Kent Road Mission, Ranmore Wesleyans, Sheffield Wednesday, Denaby United, Rotherham Town, Liverpool, Sheffield Wednesday (guest), Sheffield United, Burton All Saints

Signed from Liverpool for £600 in June 1912, Jimmy 'Head Up' Harrop served Aston Villa for almost nine years, during which time he appeared in 177 first-team matches and scored four goals.

The son of a Yorkshire farmer, he failed to make Sheffield Wednesday's first team and struggled at Rotherham before finally making a start with Liverpool, who handed him his League debut against Bolton Wanderers in January 1908.

Able to play in all three half-back positions but preferring the pivotal role, Jimmy was one of the cleverest defenders in the game, a player who brought intelligence to bear when tackling and then feeding passes through to his forwards.

He gave the Merseysiders four years' excellence service (making 139 appearances) before transferring to Villa Park – a month after goalkeeper Sam Hardy had taken the same road.

Taking over from Sam Whittaker at left-half, he partnered Bill Morris during the first part of the 1912–13 season before moving into the centre of the defence to accommodate Jimmy Leach. The season ended in glory as Villa won the FA Cup and finished runners-up to Sunderland (beaten Cup finalists) in the League. Jimmy also scored his first Villa goal, which earned a point from a 2–2 draw with near-neighbours West Bromwich Albion at The Hawthorns.

Cool and methodical, crafty at times, Jimmy missed only three senior games during the 1913–14 campaign; he netted his second goal for the club – and again it helped save a point from a 3–3 home draw with Tottenham Hotspur.

This same season saw Jimmy twice represent the Football League against the Southern League and Irish League. He also appeared in two international trials, starred for the Birmingham FA against the London FA and was named as a reserve for the senior England side against Wales at Cardiff in March, when three senior defenders were all struggling with injuries.

Many felt at the time that he was good enough to win a full cap, but Franklin Buckley (Derby County), Billy Watson (Burnley), Billy Wedlock (Bristol City), Joe McCall (Preston) and Bobby McNeal (West Bromwich Albion) were all ahead of him in the pecking order.

Two more goals came Jimmy's way in 1914–15, the first proving crucial – the winner at home to the Albion (2–1). His other came in a 5–0 home victory over Middlesbrough.

During World War One Jimmy worked in the manufacture of agricultural implements and played as a guest for Sheffield Wednesday, turning out for Villa towards the end of the hostilities, his six senior outings coming in the Midland Victory League.

When peacetime football resumed in August 1919 he was appointed team captain by Villa, but unfortunately he was forced to miss the 1920 FA Cup Final against Huddersfield Town through injury, his place going to Frank Moss. Bitterly disappointed, having played in the first four rounds, he sat in the stand at Stamford Bridge to watch his colleagues lift the trophy with a 1–0 victory after extra-time, his buddy Billy Kirton scoring the all-important goal.

He appeared in 23 competitive games the following season, but with Frank Barson now bedded in at centre-half and Frank Moss also staking a claim, Jimmy moved to Sheffield United in March 1921.

He spent just over a year at Bramall Lane before drifting into non-League football with Burton All Saints, finally retiring in May 1924 at the age of 40.

Tony Hateley

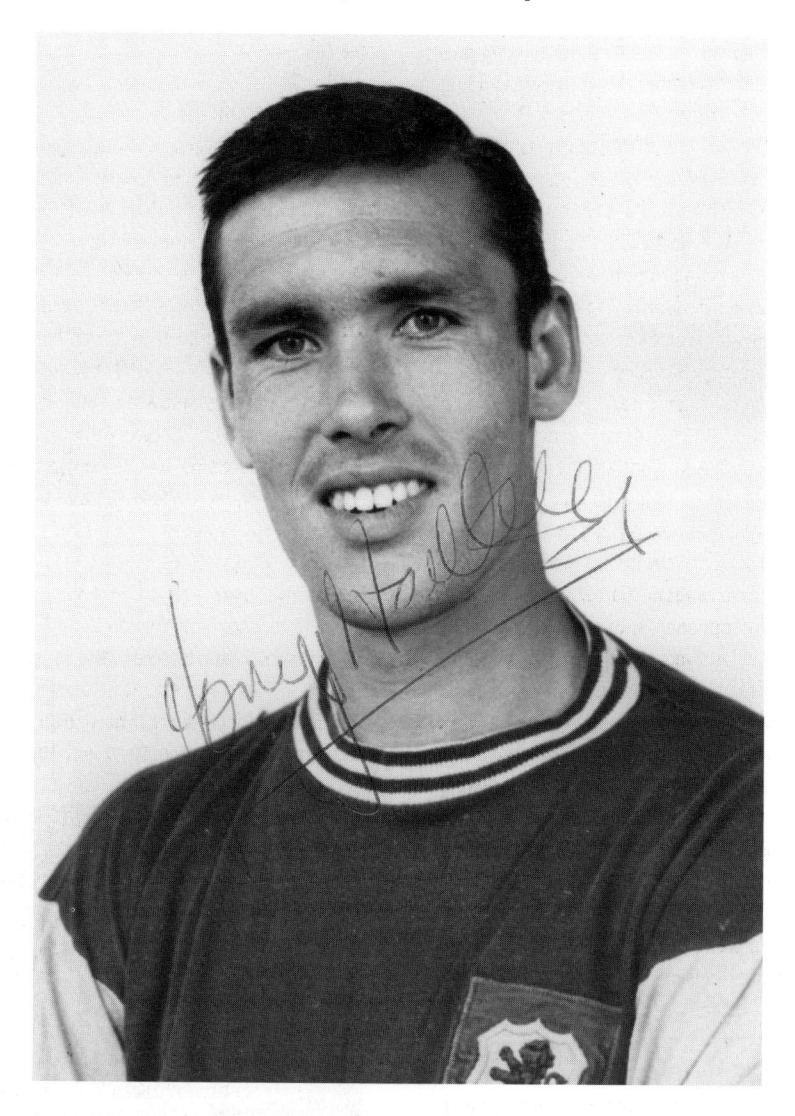

Date of birth: 13 June 1941, Derby

Aston Villa record:
Appearances: League 127, FA Cup 8, League Cup 13
Goals: League 68, FA Cup 5, League Cup 13
Debut: League, 24 August 1963 v Nottingham Forest (a) won 1-0

Also played for: Normanton Sports Club (Derby), Derby County (associated schoolboy, 1955), Notts County (2 spells), Chelsea, Liverpool, Coventry City, Birmingham City, Oldham Athletic, Bromsgrove Rovers, Prescot Town, Keyworth United

Tony Hateley

A footballing nomad who served with 10 different English clubs from the age of 15, striker Tony Hateley's playing career spanned some 20 years, during which time he scored 211 goals in 434 League appearances and over 300 goals in all competitive games (including his time at non-League level).

Starting his career with Notts County, his heading ability was reminiscent of the great Tommy Lawton and his footwork in and around the penalty area wasn't bad either. He netted 114 times in 207 outings for the Magpies, helping them gain promotion from the Fourth Division in 1960. Soon afterwards, in September 1960, he achieved the unusual feat of scoring a hat-trick of headers in a 5-1 win over Barnsley.

His form and marksmanship earned him a move to Aston Villa in August 1963, signed by manager Joe Mercer for just £20,000. And what an impact Tony had in his new surroundings, notching 19 goals in his first season, including the winner on his debut against Nottingham Forest and following up with a further strike when making his League Cup debut for the club against his 'favourite' opponents, Barnsley.

Thankfully, his efforts, along with those of Harry Burrows (who struck 16 League goals), helped Villa preserve their First Division status, and the following season Tony weighed in with another 34 goals, the highest by a Villa player for four years, since Gerry Hitchens's haul of 42 in 1960-61.

An out-and-out striker, tall and muscular, he bagged four goals in a 7-1 League Cup win over Bradford City and, in fact, scored 10 times in that competition as Villa went out at the semi-final stage to Tony's future club, Chelsea.

Adding a further 28 goals to his tally in 1965-66, including yet another four in a 5-5 League draw with Tottenham Hotspur at White Hart Lane, Tony played in only 12 senior games after that before transferring to Stamford Bridge, signed by manager Tommy Docherty as a replacement for broken leg victim Peter Osgood, for a club record £100,000 in October 1966. At that time he was only the second footballer to command a six-figure fee (the first was Alan Ball).

An FA Cup runner-up with Chelsea (against Spurs) in 1967, Tony spent only nine months at Stamford Bridge before switching north to Liverpool, signed by manager Bill Shankly.

He did well at Anfield, scoring a goal every two games, including a hat-trick in his third outing versus Newcastle United. He formed an excellent partnership up front with England World Cup winner Roger Hunt but lost his place to teenager Alun Evans (later to play for Aston Villa).

Tony, who was once dubbed the 'wealthy wanderer', admitted that he loved it at Anfield and was sorry to leave Liverpool, which he did in September 1968 when he teamed up with Coventry City for a fee of £80,000, linking up with Willie Carr, Dave Clements and Ernie Hunt at Highfield Road.

In August 1969 he moved again, this time to nearby Birmingham City for £72,000, returning to Meadow Lane for a second spell in November 1970. A member of Notts County's Fourth Division Championship-winning side the following year, he rounded off his League career with Oldham Athletic (July 1972 to May 1974) and thereafter played non-League football until retiring in August 1979 at the age of 38.

Tony later worked in Everton's lottery office at Goodison Park before taking employment with the Nottinghamshire-based brewery Thwaites, later working for a soft drinks company

His son, Mark Hateley, also a striker, played for Coventry City, Portsmouth, Queen's Park Rangers, Glasgow Rangers, Leeds United, Hull City and England (32 caps won) between 1978 and 1997.

Gerry Hitchens

Date of birth: 8 October 1934, Rawnsley, Staffordshire
Died: 24 April 1983, Hope, Clwyd, North Wales

Aston Villa record:
Appearances: League 132, FA Cup 18, League Cup 10
Goals: League 78, FA Cup 7, League Cup 11
Debut: League, 21 November 1957 v Birmingham City (h) lost 2-0

Also played for: Highley Council School, Highley Youth Club, Highley Village Boys, Highley Miners' Welfare, Kidderminster Harriers, Cardiff City, Inter Milan (Italy), Torino, Atalanta (Italy), Cagliari (Italy), Worcester City, Merthyr Tydfil, England (8 full caps)

Centre-forward Gerry Hitchens was the first Englishman to be capped when registered with a foreign club. He was an Inter Milan player when he scored in a 3-1 win over Switzerland at Wembley in May 1962. I had earlier seen him find the net with his first kick when making his England debut in an 8-0 home win over Mexico in May 1961. He then struck twice in a 3-2 win over Italy in Rome – shortly before his £80,000 transfer to the San Siro Stadium in Milan. Fellow strikers Jimmy Greaves, Denis Law and Joe Baker also moved to Italy that same season.

He played for England in the 1962 World Cup Finals in Chile and won a total of seven caps, scoring five goals. However, when Alf Ramsey took over as England's team manager, Gerry's international career came to an end – Ramsey preferring to pick only home-based players.

Nevertheless, Gerry chose to stay in Italy for a period of eight years, and besides serving with Inter Milan he also played – and scored – for Torino, Atalanta and Cagliari, all of whom were based in Serie 'A'.

Having notched plenty of goals in minor football, Gerry began his career as a semi-professional with Kidderminster Harriers in August 1953. He joined Cardiff City on a full-time contract for a modest fee of just £1,500 in January 1955 and grabbed a vital goal on his debut for the Bluebirds, who beat the reigning League champions Wolves to retain their First Division status (April 1955).

From an 'uncut diamond' he was polished into a 'precious jewel' at Cardiff, and he prospered greatly, forming a terrific partnership with the former Aston Villa and Welsh international star Trevor Ford at Ninian Park. Gerry was Cardiff's leading scorer two seasons running before moving to Villa Park for £22,500 in December 1957, having netted 57 times in 108 senior games for the Welsh club.

He also fired in 18 goals in 12 Test Matches when touring South Africa with the FA party in the summer of 1956.

Robust, with an awkward swashbuckling style, yet strong and energetic, Gerry could shoot with either foot. He was also very useful in the air, and he donned the famous claret-and-blue strip superbly for four seasons after replacing Derek Pace as leader of the attack, making his debut in front of almost 40,000 fans in the second city derby against Aston Villa.

He hit three goals in his next two matches and was Villa's leading scorer three seasons running: in 1958-59 with 18 goals, in 1959-60 with 25 and in 1960-61 with 42 – the most by a Villa player since 'Pongo' Waring's haul of 50 in 1930-31.

On average he scored a goal every 150 minutes for Villa – claiming 96 in 160 outings. He whipped in a brilliant five-timer in an emphatic 11-1 home win over Charlton Athletic in November 1959 as Villa surged towards the Second Division Championship. He also played his part in helping Villa reach the League Cup Final the following season, although by the time the two-leg Final against Rotherham United came he was playing in Italy, having been replaced at Villa Park by Derek Dougan.

On his return from Italy in November 1969, Gerry signed for non-League side Worcester City. He later assisted Merthyr Tydfil in the Welsh League (from September 1971) before announcing his retirement from competitive football in May 1972.

At that juncture he went into business in Pontypridd and participated in several charity matches when time allowed. Unfortunately, he died at the age of 48 while taking part in a charity game in Wales in 1983.

Dennis Hodgetts

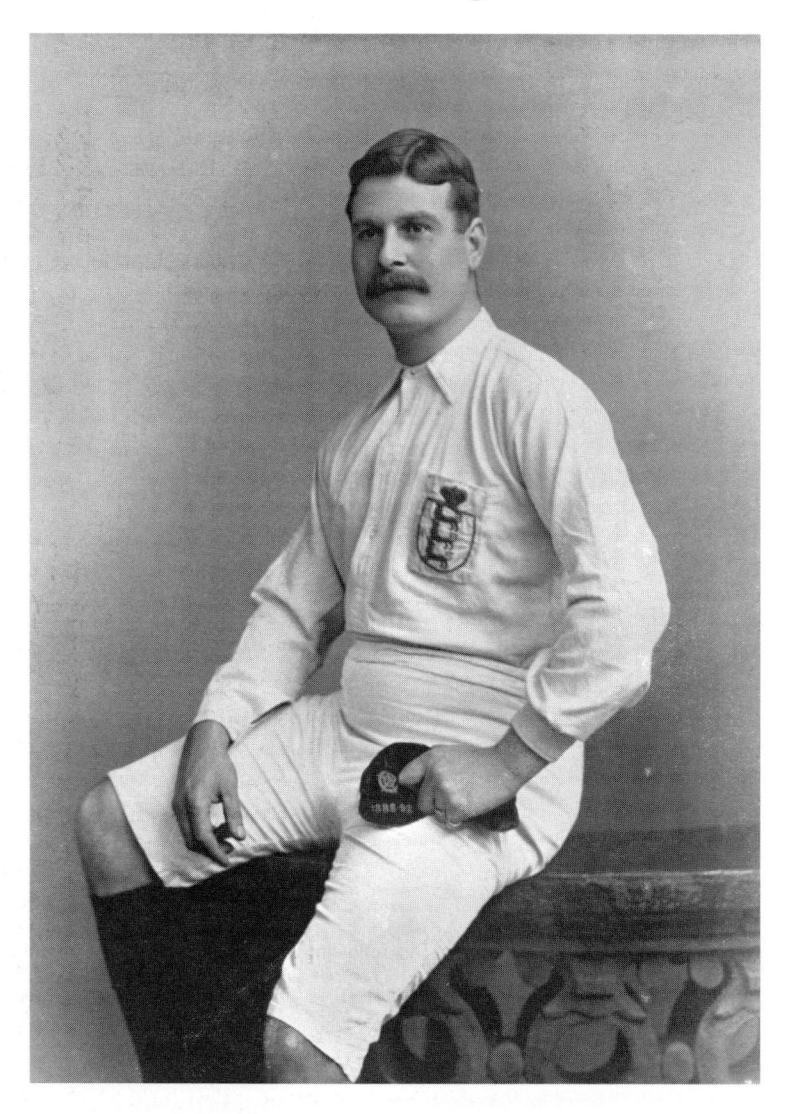

Date of birth: 28 November 1863, Edgbaston, Birmingham
Died: 25 March 1945, Perry Barr, Birmingham

Aston Villa record:
Appearances: League 181, FA Cup 37
Goals: League 61, FA Cup 27
Debut: FA Cup, 30 October 1886 v Wednesbury Old Athletic (h) won 13-0

Also played for: Mitchell's St George's, Birmingham St George's (2 spells), Great Lever (Bolton), Small Heath (Birmingham), England (6 full caps)

Able to play, and play exceedingly well, as an inside-left or left-winger, Dennis Hodgetts, tall and weighty, was difficult to dispossess and was rarely barged off the ball. With his waxed moustache and his hair neatly parted, he was certainly a star performer, being a sagacious passer, quick-witted and altogether an uncommonly-fine forward who gave Aston Villa wonderful service for over a decade.

Strong and decisive in his approach to the game, he was full of clever and inventive ideas, always coming up with something different when least expected, certainly to opposing defenders! He could use both feet but preferred his left and at times, when in full flight, he was unstoppable, and besides creating chances aplenty for his colleagues he scored some memorable goals himself.

He joined Aston Villa as a professional in February 1886, having earlier assisted two local clubs and Great Lever FC in Lancashire. He made a flying start to his career with the Villains, scoring a hat-trick on his debut against Wednesbury Old Athletic in a first round FA Cup-tie in October 1886. In fact, besides his treble that day, he also assisted in six other goals in a 13-0 win.

He scored again in the next round versus Derby Midland, did likewise against Wolves in the third round (first game), struck a decisive goal in the quarter-final win over Darwen and, after playing his part in the semi-final victory over Glasgow Rangers at Crewe, he scored the first goal in the Final against neighbours West Bromwich Albion, Villa going on to lift the trophy for the first time in the club's history.

The following season he scored regularly in local competitions, helping Villa win the Birmingham Senior Cup and share the Lord Mayor of Birmingham Charity Cup with Walsall Swifts. And then, in 1888-89, he played a major part as Villa finished runners-up to Preston North End in the first-ever League Championship.

In February 1888 he won the first of his six England caps, starring in a 6-1 win over Wales at Crewe. A month later he scored in a 2-1 win over Scotland at Hampden Park and then, with his Villa teammate Albert Allen (who scored a hat-trick), helped beat Ireland 5-1 in Belfast.

His other three international appearances followed later, against Ireland and Scotland at the end of the 1891-92 season and versus Ireland in March 1894. Hodgetts also appeared in five international trials and represented the Football League against the Scottish League in 1895.

He was the club's leading marksman in 1889-90 with 11 senior goals but thereafter concentrated on his wing play and creativity rather than his scoring ability, although he still managed his fair share of goals, weighing with eight in 1890-91, 15 in 1891-92 when Villa lost to West Bromwich Albion in the FA Cup Final, eight more in 1892-93 and 14 in 1893-94, 12 coming in the League as Villa lifted the Championship trophy for the very first time.

By now playing at inside-left, Hodgetts teamed up superbly well with his wing partner Steve Smith in the mid-1890s, and, after Villa had finished third in the League table in 1894-95 and triumphed in the FA Cup Final for a second time (beating Albion 1-0 at Crystal Palace), he gained a second Championship-winners' medal in 1895-96.

That was to be his last season in the claret-and-blue strip. In August 1896 Hodgetts was transferred, surprisingly, across the city to arch-rivals Small Heath (now Birmingham City). He spent two seasons with Blues, retiring in August 1898. In the summer of 1899 he returned to Villa as a senior coach but spent only a season in his new role before talking over as mine host of the Salvation Inn on Summer Lane, Aston, a few minutes walk from Villa Park.

In June 1910 Hodgetts, who couldn't keep away from the club, was elected vice-president, a position he held until his death.

Besides his footballing exploits, Hodgetts was also a fine billiards player who won a major tournament in 1899.

Eric Houghton

Date of birth: 29 June 1910, Billingborough, Lincolnshire
Died: 16 May 1996, Lincolnshire

Aston Villa record:
Appearances: League 361, FA Cup 31, Wartime 151
Goals: League 160, FA Cup 10, Wartime 87
Debut: League, 4 January 1930 v Leeds United (h) lost 4–3

Also played for: Boston Town, Billingborough Rovers, Billingborough FC, (wartime guest for Brentford, Coventry City, Hereford United, Kidderminster Harriers, Leicester City, Nottingham Forest, Notts County), Notts County, England (7 full caps)
Managed: Notts County, Rugby Town

It was said that when Eric Houghton kicked a football, it was sensible not to stand in its path. Between the two World Wars, the Aston Villa and England left-winger established a reputation for having one of the most powerful shots in the game and, in fact, some goalkeepers, years after retiring, still recalled the times when Eric's bullets flew past them from all angles.

On and off the pitch, Eric – the winger with dynamite in his boots – was a mild-mannered, quiet, unassuming and courteous fellow. He loved playing football and there is no record of him ever being cautioned – he was certainly never sent off. Even after retiring, he remained the quiet man of soccer.

Eric was destined for a life in soccer as soon as he started to bang in the goals as a prodigiously-prolific teenage centre-forward. Indeed, he simply loved his football, playing for his school team on a Saturday morning, for his village side in the afternoon and occasionally for another team on a Sunday.

After excelling in local non-League circles, notably with Boston Town, he was recommended to Aston Villa by his uncle, Cec Harris, a former player at the club.

After a successful trial, Eric gave up his job as a baker to turn professional in August 1927, earning £3 a week. He never looked back.

Successfully converted into a winger, preferring the left flank (although he did play on the right), Eric, two-footed and fast, served Villa magnificently for 19 years and in that time scored 170 goals in 392 League and FA Cup matches and another 87 in 151 Wartime games. In fact, in all levels of football for Villa, Eric netted 345 goals (79 penalties) in 707 appearances. He is the club's fifth highest scorer of all time and when asked what was the best goal he ever scored, Eric had no hesitation in saying 'The one I fired home from 40 yards against Derby County in December 1931.'

He actually cracked home a penalty in his last outing for Villa – in a reserve game against Huddersfield on Boxing Day 1946, a couple of days before he moved to Notts County.

Eric gained rapid promotion to the senior side, uncharacteristically missing a penalty on his League debut against Leeds in January 1930 but impressing generally with his dashing style, his slick manipulation of the ball and, above all, his shooting prowess.

He remained a regular in the side until he left in December 1946, teaming up with some brilliant forwards including Billy Walker and 'Pongo' Waring, George Brown and Ronnie Dix, and Dai Astley and Frank Broome.

With Walker as his partner on the left wing and Waring charging through the middle, Villa had a wonderful attacking side in the early 1930s. Twice they almost won the League title, missing out to Arsenal each time, and in the space of four years (August 1930-May 1934) they scored 402 League goals, Eric netting 85 of them, several from the penalty spot or from a free-kick.

At club level, Eric helped Aston Villa regain their First Division status in 1938 (after two years in the second sphere) and win the Wartime League Cup North in 1944 versus Blackpool. Capped seven times as a full international by England (1930-32), he played his part in six excellent wins: 5-1 versus Ireland (his debut), 4-0 versus Wales, 4-1 versus Belgium, 6-2 versus Ireland (again), 3-0 versus Scotland and 4-3 versus Austria. He also represented the Football League on four occasions, was an England trialist, played for the Birmingham County FA Juniors against Scotland in 1928 and had several games for the RAF and RAF XI.

After leaving Villa Park, Eric spent three years playing for Notts County before taking over as manager, leading the Magpies to the Third Division South Championship in 1950. He returned to Villa as team manager in September 1953 and four years later proudly led his team to victory in the FA Cup Final over double-chasing Manchester United.

He spent five years in charge before being dismissed in November 1958 as the team began to struggle. Later boss of Rugby Town, he then did some scouting for his former colleague Billy Walker when he was manager of Nottingham Forest, did likewise for Villa and Walsall before returning to Villa Park as a coach in 1970, moving up to the directors' box in 1972, and thereafter serving as club president until his death in 1986.

As a manager, Eric, who also played in a first-class cricket match for Warwickshire against India at Edgbaston in August 1946, ruled by a quiet strength of character which earned him widespread respect.

Archie Hunter

Date of birth: 23 September 1859, Joppa near Ayr, Scotland
Died: 29 November 1894, Birmingham

Aston Villa record:
Appearances: League 32, FA Cup 41
Goals: League 9, FA Cup 33
Debut: FA Cup, 13 December 1879 v Stafford Rangers (a) 1–1

Also played for: Third Lanark, Ayr Thistle

Archie Hunter was the first Aston Villa captain to lift the FA Cup, doing so in 1887 after West Bromwich Albion had been defeated 2-0 in the Final at the Oval. At the same time he became the first player to score in every round of the competition, hitting a hat-trick in the 13-0 win over Wednesbury Old Athletic in round one and then following up with strikes against Derby Midland (6-0), Wolves (in the first and last of four games, 2-2 and 2-0), Hornchurch (5-0), Darwen (3-2) and two against Glasgow Rangers in the semi-final at Crewe before sealing victory in the Final over the Baggies.

Arguably Villa's greatest-ever skipper, Archie was still a teenager when he joined Villa in August 1878 – 10 years before the commencement of League football.

In fact, legend has it that he originally travelled south to Birmingham, planning to go into business and play for the local Calthorpe club, but after failing to locate the ground he was persuaded to sign for Villa instead by the then club secretary and former player George Ramsay, who, two years earlier, had secured the services of William McGregor in roughly the same way. Archie quickly forgot about his business plans and became a brilliant footballer instead.

In fact, Ramsay took Archie under his wing and played Archie under a different name to hide his true identity, so that other clubs (mainly from Scotland) didn't get to know of his whereabouts.

A strong, well-built inside-forward with a powerful shot, Archie – known as the 'Old Warhorse' – was an individual with a commanding personality; he was robust yet decidedly fair and never committed a foul in anger. A mixture of toughness and cleverness, he loved to run the touchline, dragging defenders to him and then darting inside to link up with his centre-forward.

He was such an important member of the side that for one away game with Notts County in November 1889 Villa chartered a special train to get him to Meadow Lane in time for the kick-off.

He was a regular in the team from the word go and scored, on average, a goal every two games during his time with the club, contributing greatly during the 10 seasons from 1880-81 to 1889-90. In fact, he struck over 150 goals during that time, the majority coming in friendly matches and various local Cup competitions, although he did claim 33 in the FA Cup – the most by any player for the club.

In his Football League career, which covered only two seasons from September 1888 to March 1890, Archie made just 32 appearances, scoring nine goals. Unfortunately he missed Villa's first-ever game against Wolves on 8 September 1888 but played in 19 of the 22 that season, his first against Stoke (h) when he also struck his first League goal in the competition as Villa won 5-0.

After scoring twice in 13 starts during the first half of the following season, Archie tragically suffered a heart attack in the match against Everton at Goodison Park in January 1890. While he was being transferred to a Liverpool hospital, the game continued, but the Villa players were so shocked that they virtually gave up and lost 7-0.

Sadly Archie never recovered his health, and after an agonising four-year stay in Birmingham's General Hospital he died at the age of 35. It is said that on his death bed he asked to be lifted up one last time to see the crowd making its way to Perry Barr, then Villa's home.

Despite being one of the great footballers of the 19th-century game, Archie never fulfilled his dream of playing for Scotland against England because at the time, the Scottish Football Association had a policy of not selecting 'Anglo-Scots' (i.e. Scots who were registered with clubs in the English League).

In September 1895 Villa and West Bromwich Albion played a memorial match for Archie at the Aston Lower Grounds.

The headstone on Archie's grave in Birmingham reads:

'This monument is erected in loving memory of Archie Hunter, the famous captain of Aston Villa, by his football comrades and the club as a lasting tribute to his ability on the field and his sterling worth as a man.'

In 1998 Archie Hunter was inducted into the English Football League's list of 100 legends.

His brother Andy also played for Villa between August 1879 and May 1884 before emigrating to Australia. He too died from a heart attack, aged 23.

Billy Kirton

Date of birth: 2 December 1896, Newcastle-upon-Tyne
Died: 27 September 1970, Sutton Coldfield

Aston Villa record:
Appearances: League 229, FA Cup 32
Goals: League 53, FA Cup 6
Villa debut: League, 25 October 1919 v Middlesbrough (a) won 4–1

Also played for: Todds Nook School (North Shields), Pandon Temperance, Leeds City, Coventry City, Kidderminster Harriers, Leamington Town, England (1 full cap)

Billy Kirton was a wonderfully consistent inside-right, cheerful and clever with a wonderful first touch. He also packed a powerful shot with his right foot and could pass a ball with precision, short or long, from five yards up to 40, across or down the field.

He accumulated a creditable though not large goal tally, as his main value to the team was a splendid capacity to link up with his wing partner, which, for the first few years of his Villa Park career, was Charlie Wallace and afterwards it was the strong-running Dicky York.

His first professional club was Leeds City, whom he signed for in May 1919. But when the Yorkshire club went bust and its players were put up for sale, Billy was recruited by Villa for just £500 in October 1919.

He made an impressive debut against Middlesbrough, having a hand in two of the goals in a 4-1 win. Kirton ended his first season with an FA Cup-winners' medal in his hand after his deflected header from Arthur Dorrell's left-wing corner-kick defeated Huddersfield Town 1-0 after extra-time in a tightly-fought Final at Stamford Bridge.

Billy struck 16 goals in his first season with Villa (1919–20) but managed only 34 in the next four seasons, having his best return in 1921–22 (13 goals) as Villa finished fifth in the First Division table, their highest placing since 1914. Billy was also capped for England during this season, lining up against Ireland in Belfast in the October when he scored in a 1–1 draw. His Villa teammates Frank Moss and Billy Walker also starred against the Irish. This was Billy's only cap, although he was named as a reserve on three separate occasions and appeared in two internationals trials.

In April 1924 Billy played at Wembley for the first time, but it turned out to be a sad occasion as Villa lost 2-0 to Newcastle United in the FA Cup Final – the first all-ticket game at the stadium.

A knee injury prevented him from being an ever present in 1924–25 – he missed the last nine games – and he played in only half of Villa's competitive fixtures in 1925–26, sharing the inside-right position with Clem Stephenson.

Not getting any younger and with the odd injury creeping in here and there, Billy managed just eight appearances in 1926–27 and he scored his last Villa goal in a 3–1 defeat away to Leeds United.

The forward-line at Villa Park now comprised York, Stephenson, George Cook, Walker and Dorrell, and with Len Capewell, Frank Chester and a handful of up-and-coming youngsters seemingly ahead of Billy in the pecking order, he moved to pastures new, joining Coventry City in September 1928 for £1,500.

He spent two years at Highfield Road, appeared in 17 games and then had spells with Kidderminster Harriers and Leamington Town before retiring in July 1931 at the age of 34. In later life Billy ran a newsagents' shop in Kingstanding, Birmingham, and was often found deep in conversation with ardent supporters, most of whom still remembered him as a talented player who gave Aston Villa football club excellent service for nine years, averaging almost a goal every four games.

A teetotaller and non-smoker, besides being a fine footballer, Billy was also a pretty good golfer who once had a handicap of eight – and had the pleasure of holing in one at the Sutton golf course.

Alex Leake

Date of birth: 11 July 1871, Small Heath, Birmingham
Died: 29 March 1938, Birmingham

Aston Villa record:
Appearances: League 128, FA Cup 13
Goals: League 7, FA Cup 2
Debut: League, 13 September 1902 v Nottingham Forest (a) lost 2-0

Also played for: Jenkins Street and Little Green Lane Schools (Bordesley Green, Birmingham), Hoskins & Sewell FC (2 spells), Kings Heath Albion, Saltley Gas Works, Singers FC (Coventry), Old Hill Wanderers, Birmingham, Burnley, Wednesbury Old Athletic, England (5 full caps)

Centre-half Alex Leake was born within walking distance of Birmingham City's former ground at Muntz Street. He played for several local intermediate clubs before joining Blues as a full-time professional in July 1894, just 48 hours after his 23rd birthday.

Playing football was a pleasure for Alex. He would crack a joke with an opponent while robbing him of the ball, chunter and chit-chat to the opposition in a crowded penalty area when waiting for a corner kick to be taken and he even carried out a lengthy conversation with the referee and at times a linesman, when there was a pause in play.

A genuine 'Brummagem Button' with a dapper moustache and smartly-groomed hair, Alex was a good-tempered, honest defender, whose stamina was unsurpassed. He never played to the gallery but always battled well for his team, no matter what the circumstances.

He was safe in defence, never overdid the fancy stuff and was always hard to beat in 50:50 situations. As well as being an exceptionally fine tackler he was also superb at intercepting long passes, could head a ball hard and true and kicked long and straight. He was, on many occasions, the star performer and without doubt his sense of humour made him a great favourite with the fans and colleagues alike.

He made his League debut for Blues at left-half away at Preston in October 1895 and was switched to centre-half later in the season. He performed well but unfortunately his efforts were all in vain, as Blues slipped into the Second Division after losing two and drawing one of their four Test Matches at the end of the campaign.

Alex spent eight years with Blues, making a total of 221 senior appearances before transferring to Aston Villa in June 1902. Two years later he won the first of five full caps for England, lining up against Ireland. He was never on the losing side at international level and he also represented the Football League.

Alex partnered Alf Wood and also played alongside Albert Wilkes in his first two seasons at Villa Park, helping Villa reach the semi-finals of the FA Cup in 1903 (beaten by Bury).

In 1904–05 he was outstanding and capped off his season by collecting an FA Cup-winners' medal after Villa had beaten Newcastle United 2-0 in front of almost 102,000 fans in the Final at Crystal Palace.

He continued to perform with great authority in 1905–06 but injuries started to affect his game the following season, and after Chris Buckley and Roly Codling, plus Sam Greenhalgh, became the chosen half-backs Alex joined Burnley in December 1907, having played 141 first-class matches for Villa.

He eventually quit competitive League and Cup football at the end of the 1909–10 season with 464 senior appearances under his belt. He immediately returned to the Midlands where he joined Wednesbury Old Athletic as a player, retiring in May 1912.

Two months later Alex was appointed first-team trainer-coach at Crystal Palace and due to illness and injuries, he was actually placed on standby by England for games against Wales and Scotland at the age of 41.

After leaving Palace he served as trainer-coach at Merthyr Town for 13 years (from October 1919), before spending a season as head trainer with Walsall (September 1932 to May 1933).

Alex later coached at several schools and colleges around Britain for six years.

Besides his footballing exploits, Alex was an excellent swimmer who would dive to the bottom of the brine baths at Droitwich to retrieve a coin. He was also a fine track athletic, specialising in the 400 yards and hurdles events. Also a keen gardener and a blacksmith by trade, he was cousin of England international Jimmy Windridge who played for Chelsea, Middlesbrough and Birmingham between 1905 and 1916.

Brian Little

Date of birth: 25 November 1953, Horden, County Durham

Aston Villa record:
Appearances: League 242+5, FA Cup 15+1, League Cup 29+1, Europe 9
Goals: League 60, FA Cup 4, League Cup 15, Europe 3
Debut: League, 30 October 1971, substitute v Blackburn Rovers (h) won 4–1

Also played for: Trials for Burnley, Leeds United, Manchester City, Newcastle United, Stoke City, Sunderland, West Bromwich Albion, England (1 full cap)
Managed: Darlington, Wolverhampton Wanderers, Leicester City, Stoke City, West Bromwich Albion, Hull City, Tranmere Rovers

Having had trials with several top clubs, Brian Little signed apprentice forms for Aston Villa in 1969. Within a year, they found themselves in the Third Division for the first time in their history, but, unperturbed, Brian turned professional in June 1971 and 11 months later gained an FA Youth Cup-winners' medal.

Brian developed fast as a footballer, and with two senior games behind him (scoring in his second versus Torquay in April 1972) he established himself in the first team halfway through 1972–73.

Partnering Keith Leonard in attack, his enterprising, pacy runs, clever footwork and shooting ability were appreciated by the fans. He missed five League matches in 1973–74 and scored 24 goals in 1974–75, helping Villa win promotion and the League Cup.

Unfortunately, injuries sidelined Brian for half of Villa's games in 1975–76, but he was back to full fitness in 1976–77 when he collected his second League Cup-winners' medal, scoring a dramatic extra-time winner in the second replay of the Final against Everton, one of 26 goals that season.

Striking 19 goals in 117 appearances during the next three seasons, Brian's last efforts came in 1979–80, although over the next year he tried in vain to shake off a knee injury.

Brian may well have seen out his career with Birmingham City, but a proposed £610,000 transfer fell through after he had failed a medical examination on his damaged knee.

Besides his Villa exploits, Brian received one England cap as a late substitute for Mick Channon against Wales at Wembley in May 1975.

He remained on Villa's payroll and became youth-team coach, but his contract was terminated, along with that of manager Tony Barton's, in May 1984.

Appointed coach by crisis club Wolverhampton Wanderers early in 1986, he replaced manager John Barnwell when he resigned seven months later but quit himself in October 1986 to be replaced by Graham Turner, who had been sacked by Villa earlier that month.

After leaving Molineux, Brian coached at Middlesbrough under ex-Villa player Bruce Rioch. He left Ayresome Park in February 1989 to take charge of Darlington. Unable to prevent the Quakers from slipping into the Conference, he guided them to promotion at the first attempt and in 1991 won the Fourth Division title.

Bigger clubs were now chasing Brian, and in June 1991 Leicester City appointed him as manager in place of former Villa defender Gordon Lee. The Foxes reached the Division One Play-off Final three years running, losing the first two before winning the third against Derby County. However, after a difficult start to the 1993–94 Premiership season, Brian was tempted back to Villa Park as manager (November 1994), replacing Ron Atkinson.

He kept Villa from relegation, just, and built a new team. Things gelled together nicely and in 1996 Villa reached the FA Cup semi-finals and won the League Cup, beating Leeds in the Final to qualify for the UEFA Cup.

Brian, however, resigned in February 1998, replaced by ex-Villa midfielder John Gregory. He became manager of Stoke City but poor results led to him leaving to manage West Bromwich Albion. He did good business for the Baggies, signing Italian Enzo Maresca for nothing and selling him to Juventus for £4 million. But he failed to turn things round on the pitch and with relegation looming, he was sacked in March 2000 and replaced by Gary Megson.

A month later Brian took charge of Hull City, a club with huge debts. Things were sorted out and the Tigers reached the Division Three Play-offs. But in February 2002 Brian dropped a bombshell by resigning. Out of football for 18 months, he returned as Tranmere Rovers boss in October 2003 and guided them to the quarter-finals of the FA Cup in his first season and into the Play-offs in his second, before resigning in May 2005 after relegation had been avoided on the final day of the season.

Since then Brian has taken it easy, although he did put his name forward for the manager's job at Villa Park, which eventually went to Martin O'Neill.

Andy Lochhead

Date of birth: 9 March 1941, Lenzie near Milngarvie, Scotland

Aston Villa record:
Appearances: League 127+4, FA Cup 2, League Cup 20, FA Charity Shield 1
Goals: League 34, League Cup 10
Debut: League, 21 February 1970 v Bristol City (h) lost 2-0

Also played for: Renfrew Juniors, Burnley, Leicester City, Oldham Athletic, Denver Dynamo (NASL), Scotland (1 Under-23 cap)
Managed: Padiham (non-League)

Although centre-forward Andy Lochhead was associated with Aston Villa for only three and a half years, he was adored by the fans and his exploits as a goalscorer boosted the team no end, helping Villa reach the League Cup Final and win the Third Division Championship in successive seasons: 1970-71 and 1971-72.

In his heyday he was described as being a six-foot, bullet-domed central striker, who feared no-one, and there's no doubt that opposing defenders, some of them pretty useful and experienced, certainly knew they had been involved in a game when Andy was around.

Strong in the air, decisive and extremely competent on the ground, he loved to go in where it hurt and he received his fair share of head wounds during his professional career, which started in earnest at Burnley in December 1958 following his move from the Paisley junior side Renfrew Juniors.

Deputising initially for England international Ray Pointer, Andy gained a regular place in the Burnley side during the 1962-63 campaign – having represented Scotland in an Under-23 game versus Wales the previous year. Despite his noble efforts he failed to win a full cap, although he was named as a reserve on two occasions.

He did superbly well at Turf Moor, scoring 128 goals in 266 first-class matches before transferring to Leicester City for £80,000 in October 1968. In fact, he became the sixth and, indeed, last Burnley player to register a century of League goals, reaching that milestone on the final day of the 1967-68 season against Leeds United.

He is also one of only four Clarets players to net five goals in a competitive game, doing so on two separate occasions – against Chelsea in a home League fixture in April 1965 and versus Bournemouth in a third round FA Cup replay in January 1966.

In his first season at Filbert Street, Andy, partnering Allan Clarke in attack, helped the Foxes reach the FA Cup Final, but in the end he had to settle for a runners'-up medal after Manchester City's 1-0 win.

The club then slipped disappointingly into the Second Division at the end of his first season at Villa Park and once again he left Wembley Stadium a rather disappointed man when Spurs won the 1971 League Cup Final.

However, all was forgotten in 1971-72 as Andy, playing up front with Geoff Vowden and thriving on the wing play of Ray Graydon and Willie Anderson, top scored with 19 League goals (25 in all games) when Villa clinched promotion as Third Division champions. And to crown a great season Andy was also voted Midland Footballer of the Year, as well as being the recipient of the Terrace Trophy, awarded by the Villa supporters.

His goals dried up in 1972-73 but his effort and commitment never waned, as Villa just missed out on regaining their top-flight status by finishing third behind his former club Burnley (champions) and Queen's Park Rangers.

At that juncture manager Vic Crowe transferred Andy to Oldham Athletic (August 1973), and he won the Third Division title with the Latics in his first season at Boundary Park.

After a spell in the US with Denver Dynamo, Andy retired in the summer of 1974 to become a coach with Oldham, later taking over as manager of local non-League club Padiham (1975-76). He remained in the area and worked as a steward in the popular Ightenmount bowling club while scouting for a handful of Lancashire clubs, including two of his previous employers, Burnley and Oldham. He also attended various matches at Turf Moor as often as possible, choosing to watch the reserves more than the first team.

Unfortunately Andy suffered a heart attack in June 2004, but thankfully he regained his health and is now employed as host to the match sponsors at each of Burnley's home games. He also writes a weekly football column in the *Lancashire Telegraph*.

Stan Lynn

Date of birth: 18 June 1928, Bolton
Died: 28 April 2002, Birmingham

Aston Villa record:
Appearances: League 281, FA Cup 36, League Cup 6, FA Charity Shield 1
Goals: League 36, FA Cup 1, League Cup 1
Debut: League, 14 October 1950 v Huddersfield Town (a) lost 4-3

Also played for: Whitworth's FC, Accrington Stanley, Birmingham City, Stourbridge, Kingsbury United, Aston Villa Old Stars

The first full-back to score a hat-trick in a League Division One game was Stan Lynn for Aston Villa, against Sunderland, in January 1958, two of his bullet-like efforts hitting the net from the penalty spot in a 5-2 win.

Extremely well built, strong and solid, quick over the ground and possessing a crunching tackle, Stan could kick like a mule, especially from dead-ball situations.

During a wonderfully-consistent career in first-class football, he struck home 70 goals in 508 League and Cup appearances, making him one of the highest-scoring full-backs in the history of the game.

Stan initially had a trial as a stocky right-winger for Bolton schoolboys and worked in a mineral water factory before joining his first major club, Accrington Stanley, as an amateur full-back in August 1945. He turned professional in July 1947, two months after making his League debut in a memorable 8-4 home win over Lincoln City.

He remained at Peel Park until March 1950 and made 35 senior appearances for Stanley, before transferring to Aston Villa for what was to be a bargain fee of just £10,000 – manager Alex Massie pipping Newcastle United for his signature.

He netted three goals in 10 games during his first season at Villa Park, being used as an emergency centre-forward on three occasions, once against Derby County when he scored to salvage a point.

He eventually took over the right-back berth when Harry Parkes was switched to the opposite flank halfway through the 1951-52 campaign and he never looked back after that, going on to form a fine partnership and understanding (from 1954 onwards) with Peter Aldis, who had subsequently replaced Parkes on a regular basis in 1953.

Injuries apart, Stan held onto the number-two position until 1960, when first Gordon Lee and then John Neal pushed forward their claims for selection.

In 1956-57 he played his part, and did so exceedingly well, as Villa lifted the FA Cup by beating the favourites and double-chasing Manchester United 2-1 in the Final. And then, as an ever present, he played splendidly again in 1959-60 when Villa won the Second Division Championship at the first time of asking (following relegation). The following season scored a vital penalty in the League Cup semi-final replay victory over Burnley to set up a Final showdown with Rotherham United. Stan missed the first leg but played in the second and gleefully accepted his winners' prize after Villa came back from 2-0 down to clinch the trophy 3-2 on aggregate.

Stan eventually left Villa Park for neighbours Birmingham City in October 1961 for £15,000. Although 33 years of age at the time, and having lost some of his speed, some thought him to be over the hill when he switched to St Andrew's, but he remained fit and focussed and, performing with confidence and a lot of determination, went on to give Blues grand service for a period of four years.

In 1963 he helped Blues beat his former employers Aston Villa 3-1 on aggregate in the League Cup Final and two seasons later, in 1964-65, he surprisingly finished up as Blues' joint top scorer, his tally of 10 goals including a penalty in each of the first three League games. He netted only once from normal outfield play.

He moved into non-League football with Stourbridge in August 1966 and announced his retirement four years later, in May 1970, after a short spell with Kingsbury United.

A keen and enthusiastic golfer, Stan worked as a salesman for a plumbing company before taking employment as a warehouseman with the Lucas Industries Group while residing in Shirley. A football follower to the last he was almost 74 when he died in 2002.

Tommy Lyons

Date of birth: 5 July 1888, Littleworth, Hednesford, Staffordshire
Died: 4 October 1938, Hednesford

Aston Villa record:
Appearances: League 217, FA Cup 20, FA Charity Shield 1, Wartime 1
Debut: League, 7 December 1907 v Liverpool (a) lost 5-0

Also played for: Heath Hayes Boys, Hednesford Town, Hednesford Victoria, Bridgetown Amateurs, (wartime guest for Port Vale), Walsall (player-coach)

Rugged full-back Tommy Lyons, strong and resilient with good positional sense and a powerful kick, was a fearless tackler, but he was also a defender with an astute footballing brain who invariably played with his head bowed forward.

He was a registered player at Villa Park for over 12 years, signing professional forms in April 1907 after a month's trial and remaining there until after World War One.

In his younger days he occupied the centre-half position, also playing occasionally as a wing-half before being successfully groomed into an exceptionally-fine right-back. He went on to appear in 238 League and FA Cup games for Villa, mainly as partner to the reliable Freddie Miles.

Lyons made his senior debut in front of 30,000 spectators at Anfield in December 1907, after Villa had already used four different players in the right-back position during the opening 16 games of that season. But it was not a happy baptism, as Liverpool handed Villa a 5–0 beating and Lyons was having a hard time against the Reds winger Jack Cox, whose pace and crosses from the left helped create three of the goals.

But it was a completely different story a week later when Lyons lined up against Middlesbrough at Villa Park. He performed exceptionally well, never gave his opponent (Ernie Verrill) any time or space, and helped his side to a resounding 6–0 win – Lyons himself assisting in two of the goals.

Having impressed all and sundry in that game, he confidently held his place in the side, injuries and illness apart, until the end of the 1914–15 season when League football was abandoned due to the outbreak of World War One. In fact, in 1912 he came very close to representing England, being named as reserve to Bob Crompton in two internationals.

In 1909–10 Lyons was outstanding and missed only three games as Villa won their sixth League Championship. The following season he was disappointed, along with his colleagues, when the runners'-up prize was gained in the First Division, but it was joy again for the Hednesford-born defender in 1913 when Villa won the FA Cup, beating Sunderland 1–0 in the Final at Crystal Palace. Villa also finished second in the League to Sunderland, beaten by four points (54–50).

During the last two pre-World War One campaigns, Lyons's full-back partner was predominantly Tommy Weston in 1913–14 and Bill Littlewood in 1914–15, and, although Villa didn't play competitive football during the hostilities, he was a member of the first-team squad again when the Midland Victory League was introduced in March 1919, although he played in only one game.

This competition was arranged so that players could re-establish themselves as a unit in readiness for the recommencement of the Football League programme later that year. But, unfortunately, Lyons never got the chance to add to his senior appearance tally with Villa, leaving the club in August 1919 to sign for Port Vale, whom he had appeared for as a guest during the hostilities. He was handed 63 League and three FA Cup outings by the Valiants in three seasons, helping them win the Staffordshire Cup and share the Staffordshire Infirmary Cup in 1920.

He left the Potteries club in July 1922 to take over as senior player-coach of Walsall, a position he held until May 1923. He made just one League appearance for the Saddlers (versus Wrexham at Fellows Park in February 1923), but he was always willing to pass on his knowledge of the game to the up-and-coming youngsters at the club and to the two established full-backs in the side, Ben Timmins and Wally Webster.

After leaving Walsall, Lyons moved back to his native Hednesford and attended home games at Villa Park whenever he could, making his last appearance at the ground in 1936.

His brother, Bert Lyons, played for Clapton Orient and Tottenham Hotspur in the 1930s.

Paul McGrath

Date of birth: 4 December 1959, Ealing, London

Aston Villa record:
Appearances: League 248+5, FA Cup 23+1, League Cup 29+1, Europe 15+1
Goals: League 9, League Cup 1
Debut: League, 19 August 1989 v Nottingham Forest (a) drew 1–1

Also played for: Dalkey United, St Patrick's Athletic, Manchester United, Derby County, Sheffield United, Republic of Ireland (83 full caps)

Paul McGrath was the first black player to captain the Republic of Ireland and right now, for scores of supporters on the Emerald Isle, the former Aston Villa defender is a living legend.

No player in Ireland's history – and that includes some brilliant stars – has had more column inches written in his honour than Paul, yet the defender has always remained modest about his ability.

Born in Ealing, London, Paul spent the first 16 years of his life in an orphanage and started his football career with the Irish club Dalkey United in 1975 before joining St Patrick's Athletic, initially as a semi-professional.

Shortly after winning his country's Young Player of the Year award, Paul joined Manchester United for a bargain fee of £30,000 in April 1982, signed by manager Ron Atkinson.

Paul settled in easily at Old Trafford and produced several impressive displays in the second team, before having a run in the senior side in place of fellow countryman Kevin Moran.

Paul made 14 League appearances in 1982–83 and scored three goals, the first two in a 3-0 home win over Luton Town ahead of the FA Cup Final with Brighton & Hove Albion, when he was named as a reserve.

Three years later, after taking over at the heart of the defence, Paul helped the Reds to win the FA Cup. In the same year of that Wembley triumph (1985), he won the first of his 83 caps, though it wasn't until Jack Charlton took over as manager that he became a regular and, indeed, key member of the national side.

Chosen to play in midfield by Charlton, Paul helped the Republic of Ireland qualify for the European Championships in 1988 and the World Cup Finals two years later. Four years on, in 1994, he formed part of the Ireland side that qualified for their second World Cup.

However, the story was not as straightforward as it may sound. Paul twice missed Ireland matches, while at club level Manchester United decided to cut their losses and let him leave for Aston Villa. He had also become injury-prone, and during the course of his career the unfortunate Paul had eight knee operations, which meant that towards the end of his career he was not training in the accepted sense.

Signed for £450,000 in August 1989 by manager Graham Taylor, Paul became the idol of the Villa Park fans. He spent over seven years with the club, made 323 senior appearances and gained two League Cup-winners' medals, the first in 1994 when Villa beat his former club Manchester United 3-1 in the Final and the second in 1996 in a 3-0 win over Leeds United.

Well-built, tall, strong and commanding, steady and controlled under pressure, and with a useful turn of pace over short distances, Paul enjoyed superb partnerships at the heart of the defence with Dave Mountfield, Shaun Teale, Ugo Ehiogu and Gareth Southgate, in that order.

He moved to Derby County for £100,000 in October 1996 and then assisted Sheffield United from August 1997 before announcing his retirement in May 1998, with 648 club and international appearances under his belt.

It is a testament to Paul's natural fitness that despite all his injury worries and other annoying things in his life, he played his football at the highest level for 16 years. And to this day, he remains one of the greatest players, certainly central-defenders, ever to don the green jersey of the Republic of Ireland and the claret-and-blue of Aston Villa.

Paul's testimonial match – Aston Villa versus Birmingham City in May 1995 – attracted a crowd of 12,000 with receipts totalling almost £99,000.

William McGregor

Date of birth: 13 April 1846, Braco, Perthshire
Died: 22 December 1911, Birmingham

Aston Villa record:
Club organiser and administrator (July 1876), president (September 1880), director (August 1881), vice-chairman (August 1895), chairman (May 1897–June 1898)

Also: Founder of the Football League (1888), Football League chairman (1888–92), Football Association chairman (1888–94), Football League president (1892–94), life member of the Football League (1895–1911)

William McGregor first became interested in football as a young man in Scotland while serving his apprenticeship as a draper. At the age of 24 he followed his brother, Peter, down to Birmingham with a view to setting up his own drapery business in the city. He eventually rented premises on the corner of Brearley Street and Summer Lane, Aston – a rough area run by the notorious 'Harding Street Gang'. In fact, the infamous Aston Riots were instigated by this gang after a Tory Party meeting at the Lower Grounds (later to become Villa's occasional home ground) got out of hand in a big way.

William, an evangelist and dedicated Methodist, who was renowned for his sense of mirth, initially became involved with another local football club, Calthorpe, but after learning there was a strong Scottish contingent in the Aston Villa side he became a member of the club in 1876.

William bedded into his new surroundings and quickly helped mould Villa into one of the most powerful sides in Midland football. The club won its first trophy, the Birmingham Senior Cup, in 1880, at which point William became president.

Seven years later, in 1887, Villa won the FA Cup for the first time, beating arch-rivals West Bromwich Albion 2–0 in the Final to become the first Midland-based club to lift the silver prize.

Due to Aston Villa's success and the large crowds they were attracting, plus the fact that the game was also doing well in the north, he realised the general public were hungry for more competitive football. So, early in 1888, three years after football had become a professional sport in England, he wrote this letter to a number of clubs in England:

'Every year it is becoming more and more difficult for football clubs of any standing to meet their friendly engagements and even arrange friendly matches. The consequence is that at the last moment, through Cup-tie interference, clubs are compelled to take on teams who will not attract the public.

'I beg to tender the following suggestion as a means of getting over the difficulty: that 10 or 12 of the most prominent clubs in England combine to arrange home-and-away fixtures each season, the said fixtures to be arranged at a friendly conference about the same time as the International Conference.

'This combination might be known as the Association Football Union, and could be managed by a representative from each club. Of course, this is in no way to interfere with the National Association; even the suggested matches might be played under Cup-tie rules. However, this is a detail.

'My object in writing to you at present is merely to draw your attention to the subject, and to suggest a friendly conference to discuss the matter more fully. I would take it as a favour if you would kindly think the matter over, and make whatever suggestions you deem necessary.

'I am only writing to the following – Blackburn Rovers, Bolton Wanderers, Preston North End, West Bromwich Albion and Aston Villa, and would like to hear what other clubs you would suggest.

'I am yours, very truly, William McGregor (Aston Villa F.C.)

'P.S. How would Friday, 23 March, 1888, suit for the friendly conference at Anderton's Hotel, London?'

William laid out his proposal at that meeting at Anderton's Hotel, which actually took place on 22 March. After a second meeting, held at the Royal Hotel, Manchester, on 17 April, the following 12 clubs paid an annual subscription of £2.2s (£2.10) and formed the world's first Football League: Accrington, Aston Villa, Blackburn Rovers, Bolton Wanderers, Burnley, Derby County, Everton, Notts County, Preston North End, Stoke, West Bromwich Albion and Wolverhampton Wanderers.

The first games were played on 8 September 1888, with William's club, Aston Villa, drawing 1–1 away to Wolves. The League proved an instant success and William's dream had become a reality.

During his 18-year association with Aston Villa, William had seen the team win both the League title and the FA Cup on three occasions, with the double being completed in 1897, a fact that famously led him to say:

'For brilliance and, at the same time, for consistency of achievement, for activity in philanthropic enterprise, for astuteness of management and for general alertness, the superiors of Aston Villa cannot be found.'

William, who was involved in football at a serious level for 34 years, was taken ill in May 1910 and died at Miss Storer's nursing home in Newall Street, Birmingham, just before Christmas 1911. Soon afterwards, Aston Villa endowed a bed in his name in the children's ward of Birmingham's General Hospital, and two years later a drinking fountain, set in the wall of the Midland Bank on Lozells Road (the remains of which are preserved to this day at Villa Park), was unveiled by the Birmingham County FA in memory of William McGregor, who is buried in the grounds of St Mary's Church, Handsworth, Birmingham.

Ken McNaught

Date of birth: 17 January 1955, Kirkcaldy, Fife, Scotland

Aston Villa record:
Appearances: League 207, FA Cup 13, League Cup 17, European 22, FA Charity Shield 1
Goals: League 8, European 5
Debut: League, 20 August 1977 v Queen's Park Rangers (a) won 2-1

Also played for: Everton, West Bromwich Albion, Manchester City (loan), Sheffield United
Managed: Vale of Earn

In his early days, centre-half Ken McNaught represented Scotland at both Youth and Amateur international levels. He signed apprentice forms for Everton in July 1971 and was rewarded with a professional contract at Goodison Park in May 1972 by manager Harry Catterick.

After a series of fine performances in the second team, he developed into an excellent centre-half and made 86 first-team appearances for the Merseysiders before moving to Villa Park for £200,000 in July 1977, signed around the same time as his fellow countryman Allan Evans.

He and Evans subsequently formed an excellent partnership in the centre of Ron Saunders's defence, and McNaught was certainly in fine form during the League Championship and European Cup-winning campaigns of 1980–81 and 1981–82.

One of seven ever presents when the League title was claimed, unfortunately McNaught was forced to miss half of Villa's competitive games due to injury the following term, although when playing he was immense as Villa battled through some tough rounds in the European Cup.

Commanding in the air, positive and sure on the ground, wonderfully balanced with excellent positional sense, McNaught was also pretty quick over the ground and he was never really run ragged – even when given a tough time by an opposing striker. He certainly did a sound job in that European Cup Final victory over Bayern Munich, who had two of the best marksmen in the game in Hoeness and Rummenigge.

McNaught was absent from only two League games in his first season at Villa Park (1977–78), scoring two goals, his first earning a point at West Ham (2–2) and his second helping beat Coventry City 3–2 at Highfield Road. He missed 10 matches through injury in 1978–79 (netting one more goal in a 4–0 win at Wolves) and was absent from 12 the following season when he struck in a 2–1 win over his former club, West Bromwich Albion, before playing a major part in those three trophy wins in some two years, culminating with a European Super Cup victory over Barcelona in 1982, before injury (triggered off in the home League game against Stoke) curtailed his senior appearances once more

McNaught spent only one more full season at Villa Park, playing under Saunders's successor Tony Barton, who then chose to transfer him to nearby West Bromwich Albion for £125,000 in August 1983, signed by former Villa player Ron Wylie to replace John Wile.

At this juncture Villa's central-defensive pairing comprised Evans and Brendan Ormsby, and there were also a handful of other useful players at the club who could be utilised in McNaught's position, hence his departure to The Hawthorns.

Ironically, McNaught made his debut for the Baggies in a 4–3 League defeat in the local derby at Villa Park on the opening day of the 1983–84 season, and he was an ever present at the heart of Albion's defence that season before Martyn Bennett and Ally Robertson became the club's chosen defensive duo.

He remained at The Hawthorns until July 1985, making 50 senior appearances and scoring one goal, before switching his allegiance to Sheffield United, having had a loan spell with Manchester City halfway through the 1984–85 campaign.

Announcing his retirement in May 1986, basically through injury, McNaught returned home to Scotland to become first-team coach at Dunfermline Athletic, a position he held for just one season. After a brief association with Swansea City, where he assisted ex-Villa goalkeeper Jimmy Rimmer on the coaching staff, he went back to Scotland to take charge of non-League club Vale of Earn.

McNaught quit football in 1990 (after almost 20 years in the game) to take over as manager of the pro's golf shop at the famous Gleneagles golf course in Scotland. McNaught's father, Willie, was a full Scottish international who played for Raith Rovers and Brechin City.

THE LEGENDS OF ASTON VILLA

Peter McParland, MBE

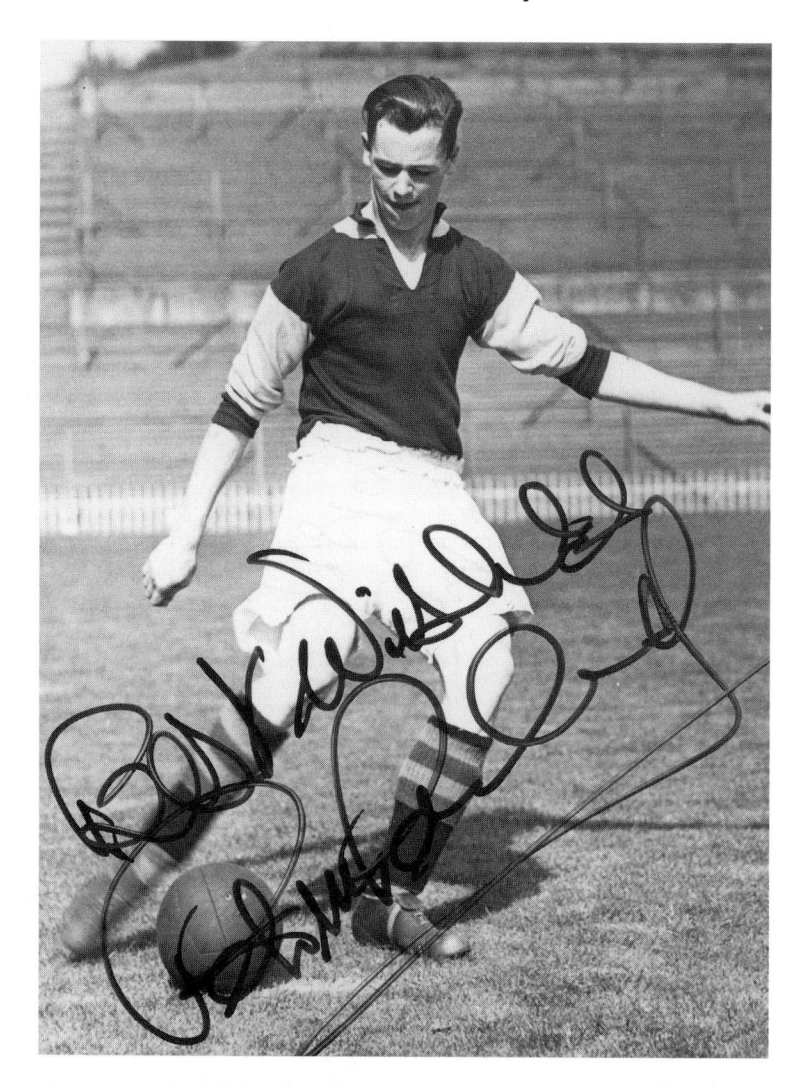

Date of birth: 25 April 1934, Newry, County Down, Northern Ireland

Aston Villa record:
Appearances: League 293, FA Cup 36, League Cup 11, Charity Shield 1
Goals: League 97, FA Cup 19, League Cup 4
Debut: League, 15 September 1952 v Wolves (h) lost 1-0

Also played for: Dundalk Juniors, Dundalk United, Wolverhampton Wanderers, Plymouth Argyle, Worcester City, Peterborough United, Atlanta Chiefs (NASL), Glentoran (player-manager), Northern Ireland (34 full caps)
Managed: No. 1 Club Kuwait (as coach-manager)

Peter McParland was a fast, direct, goalscoring left-winger, who could also play equally as well in the centre-forward position.

Many believe, certainly the older Villa supporters, that Peter – who was nicknamed 'Packy' – would have embraced the modern-day game, in which such players are few and far between.

Blessed with a powerful shot, mainly with his right foot, he was instrumental in helping Villa to much long-awaited success, and he also helped Northern Ireland reach the last eight of the 1958 World Cup Finals in Sweden.

Born in Newry, County Down – the town that also produced goalkeeping legend Pat Jennings – he was spotted playing for Dundalk United by Aston Villa manager George Martin and was signed as a full-time professional for £3,880 in August 1952.

He acted as reserve to Billy Goffin, Norman Lockhart and even Colin Gibson during his first season at Villa Park, before making the number-11 shirt his own halfway through the 1953–54 season.

He was a first-team regular for the next nine years and made over 340 senior appearances, scoring 120 goals, two of them in the 1957 FA Cup Final when Villa beat the favourites and double-chasing Manchester United 2–1.

Peter's goals were also influential in his team making it to Wembley that season. He scored in the third round against Luton Town, in two sixth-round encounters against Burnley and netted two more in the 2–2 semi-final draw with West Bromwich Albion at Molineux.

His double strike against the Busby Babes in the Final came after United's goalkeeper Ray Wood had left the field injured, following an aerial challenge by Peter, Wood fracturing his jaw.

As well as that Wembley triumph, Peter also gained a Second Division Championship medal in 1960 and was then a member of the Villa team that won the first League Cup competition in 1961, when Rotherham United were defeated 3–2 on aggregate in the two-leg Final. In fact, Peter grabbed the dramatic winner in the second game at Villa Park to become the first player ever to score in both an FA Cup and League Cup Final.

Peter's impact on the 1958 World Cup Finals in Sweden was nothing short of remarkable. An unheralded team, guided shrewdly by the Tottenham Hotspur captain and former Villa player Danny Blanchflower, opened with a 1–0 win over Czechoslovakia.

Peter then scored in the 3–1 defeat by Argentina and followed up with two important goals to earn a 2–2 draw with the defending champions West Germany. He then struck twice more as the Czechs were beaten 2–1 in a Play-off match.

Although France proved far too strong for the Irish lads in the quarter-finals, winning 4–0, Peter had proven himself to be one of the best forwards in the tournament. In all, he won 34 caps for his country and scored 10 goals. He also represented the Football League against the Italian League in 1960.

After 10 excellent years at Villa Park, Peter was transferred to neighbouring Wolves for £35,000 in January 1962. He never really settled at Molineux, making only 21 appearances and netting 10 goals. In January 1963 he moved to Devon and signed for Plymouth Argyle for £30,000, then had spells with Worcester City and Peterborough United, and he went to play for Atlanta Chiefs in the NASL in America.

Returning to the UK in December 1968, he took over as player-manager of Glentoran, steering the club to the Irish League title ahead of a Linfield side managed by his former international teammate Billy Bingham.

After a successful scouting mission for Chelsea early in 1972, Peter accepted a coaching position in Kuwait with the Quadsiai club. He later held similar positions in Cyprus, Libya and Hong Kong (the latter for five months) before returning to Kuwait to coach and manage the country's No. 1 Club in 1979–80.

After returning from his activities in the Far East, Peter settled in Bournemouth where he ran a property business for many years before retiring.

Con Martin

Date of birth: 20 March 1923, Rush, Dublin

Aston Villa record:
Appearances: League 194, FA Cup 19
Goals: League 1
Debut: League, 2 October 1948 v Sheffield United (h) won 4–2

Also played for: Drumcondra, Glentoran, Leeds United, Waterford (player-manager), Cork Hibernians, Northern Ireland (6 full caps), Republic of Ireland (30 full caps)
Managed: Shelbourne

The first player to represent the Republic of Ireland and Northern Ireland in the same year, 1949, was Aston Villa's Con Martin.

Three years earlier, while playing for his first major club, Glentoran, he won the first of six full international caps for what was then known as the Irish Free State (later Northern Ireland). In his first two outings he played a starring role in goal, keeping a clean sheet in both games and acquiring the remarkable record of being the only Irish international goalkeeper in history who never had a goal scored against him.

In time, however, Con became a legendary defender and added 30 more caps to his collection with the Republic of Ireland (dual representation was permitted up to 1950).

It was while playing for Aston Villa that he was selected for the historic game against England at Goodison Park in September 1949 – and he played his part as the Irish inflicted upon the English their first-ever defeat on home soil by a foreign team.

'England were the best team in Europe at the time' said Con, on an Irish radio programme in February 2006. 'Our team really hadn't got a chance, but we had a great game, our defence played very well and lucky enough we came out winners, 2–0.

'One particular columnist said at the time that he'd eat his hat if Ireland beat England. I don't know whether he ever did eat his hat or not, but that was a historic victory and the result was great for us. It was a great occasion.'

Con was signed by Aston Villa from Leeds United for a bargain fee of £3,000 in September 1948. He became a central figure in the club's League and Cup campaigns, producing some tremendous performances at the heart of the defence and, indeed, in goal.

He recalled 'Villa had a pretty strong team at the time. We finished 10th in 1948–49 and sixth in 1951–52 – and on many occasions we had some splendid battles with Manchester United, who I always enjoyed playing against.

'I can remember the two League games against them in the 1948–49 season. They were the FA Cup holders at the time, and we lost 3–1 at Old Trafford but were lucky enough to beat them 2–1 at Villa Park when over 68,000 fans were present. This was a wonderful game of football, and I recall clearing two shots off the line and hitting the United woodwork with a header late in the game.

'I also recall some terrific tussles with Wolves, who were a force to be reckoned with in the late 1940s and early 50s. On Christmas Day 1948 we lost 4–0 at Molineux, but 24 hours later we turned things round by winning 5–1 at Villa Park, Trevor Ford scoring four times. These sort of games seem to stick out.

'Twelve months later we met again over the same period and this time we won at Molineux and Wolves did likewise at Villa Park. Funny old game, football.'

During the 1951–52 season Con was Villa's first-choice goalkeeper – and he did very well, playing in 28 games. But it was as a centre-half that he performed best, and he continued to play for the Republic of Ireland up to 1956, earning his final cap in a 4–1 victory in Holland. In July of that same year he also quit playing for Aston Villa, moving back to Ireland to become player-manager of Waterford, where he remained until May 1964. He assisted Cork Hibernians briefly after that and his distinguished football career came to a close in 1965 at the age of 42.

Con remembered 'I had a wonderful career. I have very fond memories of all those players I played against and with, players like Stan Mortensen and Stanley Matthews and Tom Finney. I won a lot of trophies and a lot of medals. I look back on it with fond memories.'

He worked as an insurance agent in Dublin until retiring in 1988. His son, Mick, played in midfield for the Republic of Ireland as well as for the Bohemians, Manchester United, West Bromwich Albion, Newcastle United and Preston North End among others during the 1970s and 80s. His grandson, Owen Gorvan plays for Ipswich Town (2007).

Alex Massie

Date of birth: 13 March 1906, Possilpark, Glasgow
Died: 20 September 1977, Welwyn Garden City, Herts

Aston Villa record:
Appearances: League 141, FA Cup 11, Wartime 131
Goals: League 5, Wartime 8
Debut: League, 17 December 1935 v Manchester City (a) lost 5-0

Also played for: Shawfield Juniors, Partick Thistle, Petershill (Glasgow), Glasgow Juniors, Glasgow Benburb, Glasgow Ashfield, Ayr United, Bury, Bethlehem Steel Corporation (US), Dublin Dolphins, Heart of Midlothian (2 spells), (wartime guest for Birmingham, Nottingham Forest, Notts County, Portsmouth, Solihull Town), Scotland (18 caps)
Managed: Torquay United, Hereford United

Scottish international Alex Massie played mainly in the right-half position. He began his professional career with Partick Thistle, whom he joined from Shawfield Juniors in 1924. He moved to Petershill in 1925, then assisted Glasgow Benburb, had a spell with Glasgow Ashfield and also with Ayr United, before entering the Football League with Bury in January 1927, signed for a fee of £1,000.

He was at Gigg Lane for 18 months, up to August 1928 when he switched to the United States to play for Bethlehem Steel Corporation in the American Soccer League. After just seven games, however, the Steel were suspended and subsequently joined the Eastern Soccer League, Alex spending the 1929-30 season playing on the Atlantic coast before returning to Europe with the Irish side Dublin Dolphins in August 1930. Two months later he returned to his native Scotland to join Heart of Midlothian for £900.

His performances at wing-half, and occasionally at inside-forward, soon won him international recognition, his first full Scotland international cap coming in September 1931 against Ireland at Ibrox Park when he starred in a 3-1 win.

He was appointed captain of his country during the 1934-35 season and took his total number of senior caps to 11, as well as representing the Scottish League on six occasions before moving to Villa Park in December 1935, signed for a fee of £6,000.

Unfortunately, despite many excellent performances, Alex – who always wore odd-sized boots incidentally – was unable to prevent Villa from slipping into the Second Division for the first time in the club's history.

He battled on at a lower level for two years, produced several more impressive displays and captained Villa to the Second Division Championship in 1938.

He also played in 131 regional games for Villa during World War Two, scoring five goals in a 14-1 Birmingham League Cup win over RAF Hednesford in January 1942. He also gained a Wartime Football League (North) Cup-winners' medal when Villa beat Blackpool over two legs in the Final in 1944.

Alex ended his international career with 18 senior caps under his belt, winning his last against Wales at Cardiff in October 1937, scoring in a 2-1 defeat.

During the hostilities Alex guested for a number of top sides, including Birmingham, Nottingham Forest, Notts County and Portsmouth, and he also played a few games for local side Solihull Town and turned out for an international XI against a District XI in 1940.

He retired from playing in September 1945 and was immediately appointed manager of Aston Villa. He made some important signings and guided the team to the runners'-up spot in the Football League South behind Birmingham City in his first season in charge, followed by top-10 finishes in the first three post-war League seasons of 1946-47, 1947-48 and 1948-49, despite not having complete control of the playing side of things at Villa Park.

In 1949-50 Villa struggled at times and eventually had to settle for 12th spot. Having been barracked by a small minority of fans, Alex eventually left the club in August 1950.

He was out of the game for just three months, returning in the November as manager of lowly Torquay United, where he succeeded the former Arsenal player Bob John. The Gulls struggled, eventually finishing in 20th place at the end of the season, and two months into the start of the next campaign (September 1951) Alex resigned. Again taking time out to reflect on matters, he once again took a managerial position in January 1952 with Hereford United, where he remained in charge for almost a year.

He later coached local sides in and around the area of Welwyn Garden City where he died in September 1977, at the age of 71.

Freddie Miles

Date of birth: 12 January 1884, Aston, Birmingham
Died: 8 February 1926, Wylde Green, Sutton Coldfield

Aston Villa record:
Appearances: League 249, FA Cup 20, FA Charity Shield 1
Debut: League, 19 December 1903 v Nottingham Forest (a) won 7–3

Also played for: Heath Villa (Birmingham), Aston St Mary's

Tommy Lyons's full-back partner at Villa Park for almost five years, from December 1907 to September 1912, Freddie Miles was the idol of the crowd, a wonderful captain and a sportsman to the last.

Following rudimentary experience with local sides Heath Villa and Aston St Mary's, for whom he once scored two penalties in a game, he signed as a full-time professional in July 1902 and remained at the club until May 1914 when he announced his retirement from competitive football, although he did participate in various charity matches over the next two years or so before being engaged in wartime activities, serving in the British Army in France where he was badly wounded and admitted to hospital, remaining there for 15 months.

Returning to England in December 1918, he was then appointed first-team trainer at Villa Park in January 1919, a position he retained until August 1925. He was working at Kynochs (Birmingham) at the time of his death.

A very spirited defender, good on the ball with a strong left-footed kick, Miles was the embodiment of pluck and determination. He possessed a never-say-die attitude, but unfortunately he was not too strong constitutionally, often missing training through illness as well as a handful of first-class matches, calling off at the last minute after feeling unwell.

He had represented the Birmingham Juniors against the Scottish Juniors in April 1902, before making his senior debut for Villa in a resounding 7-3 League win at Nottingham Forest a week before Christmas 1903, when he took over from Albert Evans. In fact, Miles made one of Joe Bache's three goals in that game with an almighty clearance downfield, which fell nicely for his colleague to net from 12 yards.

Miles played in 17 games that season, including his first FA Cup-tie against Tottenham Hotspur at White Hart Lane, and the following term he was quite outstanding alongside Howard Spender, helping Villa finish fourth in the First Division and win the FA Cup, beating Newcastle United 2-0 at Crystal Palace before a crowd of 101,117. When he collected his winners' medal, Miles had only 52 senior games under his belt.

Injured for most of the 1905-06 campaign, he was back to his best in 1906-07 when he switched to right-back to accommodate James Logan and again the pairing was spot on, Villa finishing fifth in the League as Miles made some outstanding performances.

Lyons then arrived on the scene, and he teamed up with Miles for the first time against Liverpool at Anfield in December 1907, Villa losing 5-0. After that debacle, the duo performed superbly well together, and in 1909-10 they helped Villa clinch the League Championship for the sixth time, Lyons missing three games and Miles 11, the latter mainly through injury (a troublesome ankle).

Still producing excellent form, Miles made 32 appearances in 1910-11, 28 the following season and 11 in 1912-13, missing out on a second Cup-winners' medal, having been replaced at left-back by Tommy Weston.

With Lyons and Weston the preferred full-back partnership, Miles happily played in the reserves for a season, getting an occasional call-up when the latter was unavailable.

After his exploits during the war, Miles then gave Villa great service as head spongeman, sitting on the bench at the 1920 and 1924 FA Cup Finals, seeing Villa beat Huddersfield Town in the first (thus earning him a second winners' medal) and losing to Newcastle United in the second (the first all-ticket Final at Wembley).

Dr Vic Milne

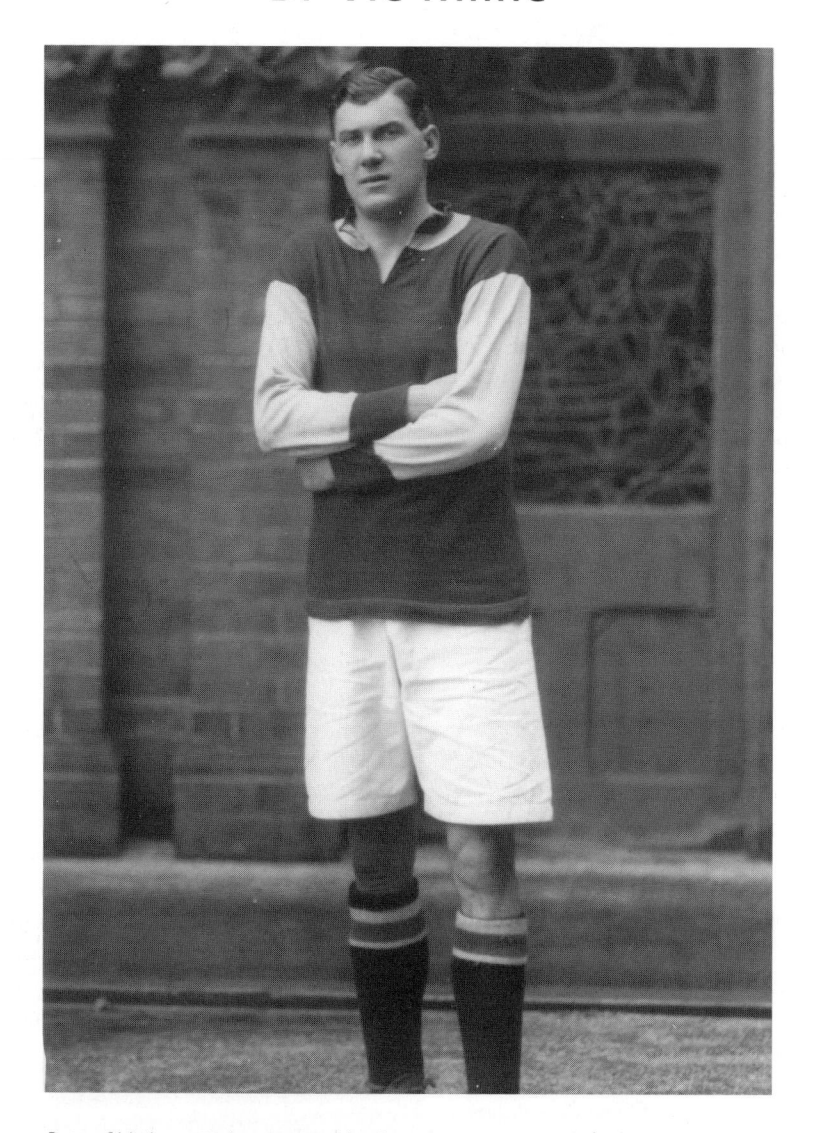

Date of birth: 22 June 1897, Aberdeen
Died: 6 September 1971, Little Aston, Sutton Coldfield

Aston Villa record:
Appearances: League 157, FA Cup 18
Goals: League 1
Debut: League, 15 September 1923 v Chelsea (h) drew 0-0
Also played for: Aberdeen Boys' Brigade football, Aberdeen City Boys, Robert Gordon's College (Aberdeen), Aberdeen University, Royal Engineers, Aberdeen

Dr Vic Milne was registered with Aston Villa from August 1923 until May 1929, and shortly after retiring (through injury) he served as Villa's official club doctor for three years from July 1930 to June 1933.

Signed initially as experienced cover for the young Tommy Ball, who had taken over from Frank Barson (sold to Manchester United) at the heart of Villa's defence, Vic subsequently claimed the centre-half spot for himself when Ball was tragically killed – murdered by his neighbour, policeman George Stagg.

Described as being an 'Apollo-sized' defender, Vic played in the 1924 FA Cup Final defeat by Newcastle United at Wembley but was in and out of the side during the 1924–25 and 1925–26 seasons, when he shared the central-defensive duties with first Percy Varco and then Alex Talbot – the player who eventually took over from Vic on a permanent basis in 1929.

Vic, tall and lanky, strong and commanding, powerful in the air and robust in the tackle, had an excellent 1926–27 campaign, missing only seven games, and in 1927–28 he was absent from just five matches when he played some of the best football of his career, twice containing the threat of Everton and England's prolific goalscorer Dixie Dean, helping Villa win both League games, 2–0 at home and 1–0 away.

In his last season at Villa Park, Vic struggled with a niggling knee injury, and he also suffered from back trouble. He appeared in only 16 games before Talbot took over as first-choice pivot.

Vic was forced to retire as a player in the summer of 1929, having made 175 senior appearances for the club and scoring just one goal, in a 2–1 home League win over Notts County in September 1925.

Born in Scotland's Granite City, Vic began his medical studies in earnest at Aberdeen University in 1915, but World War One interrupted his work. He was called up, as a student with some knowledge of chemistry, to serve in the Royal Engineers, being transferred 500 miles south to Plymouth in 1916. He played football for his depot team and was then despatched to France to serve his country.

Returning to Aberdeen University unscathed in late 1918, he gained blues at both football and cricket, and earned a half blue on the athletics track – competing in the 400 and 800-yard events – before signing amateur forms for Aberdeen in August 1919.

Continuing his medical studies, he did exceedingly well at Pittodrie Park, captaining the side on several occasions in the absence of Bert MacLachlan. He made his Scottish League debut in March 1920 against Raith Rovers and, after upgrading his status to semi-professional level, he went on to score seven goals in 122 competitive games for the Dons, helping them reach the semi-final of the Scottish Cup in 1922 when they were beaten 3–1 by Morton, Vic netting his side's consolation goal.

Vic was in superb form in 1922–23 when he missed only two League games and was mighty close to winning a full cap for Scotland, being named as standby reserve for Celtic skipper Billy Cringan for the Home Internationals against Wales and England.

He qualified as a doctor in April 1921 and gained a diploma in Public Health in 1923, shortly before joining Aston Villa.

After giving Villa six years' excellent service, Vic concentrated on his duties as a doctor, returning to Villa Park to replace Dr Jessop as the club's official practitioner in 1930 when he was working in his surgery in nearby Aldridge. He attended several matches at Villa Park up to his retirement as a doctor in 1968.

Vic's father was chairman of Aberdeen FC.

Tony Morley

Date of birth: 26 August 1954, Ormskirk

Aston Villa record:
Appearances: League 128+9, FA Cup 8, League Cup 14, Europe 19+1, FA Charity Shield 1
Goals: League 25, FA Cup 1, League Cup 3, Europe 5
Debut: League, 18 August 1979 v Bolton Wanderers (a) drew 1–1

Also played for: Ormskirk and District Schools, Preston North End, Burnley (2 spells), West Bromwich Albion (2 spells), Birmingham City, FC Seiko (Japan), Den Haag (Holland), Walsall (trial), Notts County (trial), Tampa Bay Rowdies (NASL), Hamrun Spartans (Malta), Sutton Coldfield Town, Bromsgrove Rovers (player-coach), Stratford Town, Aston Villa Old Stars, England (1 B, 1 Under-21 and 6 full caps)

Signed from Burnley for £200,000 in June 1979, Tony Morley was a highly-skilful left-winger who could use both feet. He was fast and direct, possessed great skill and flair, and, without doubt, enjoyed the best days of his career at Villa Park.

He was seen as a wayward genius at times, but was gently moulded by his manager Ron Saunders into one of the most dangerous wide players in the game.

Famed for scoring spectacular goals, the one he cracked home in a 3-1 win over Everton at Goodison Park in February 1981 won him the Goal of the Season award and at the same time helped Villa on the way to their first League Championship triumph for 71 years.

He was a vital cog in the Villa side during that terrific season, playing down the left flank in front of full-back Colin Gibson and being fed with sublime passes most of the time by hard-working midfielders Gordon Cowans, Dennis Mortimer and Des Bremner. An ever present, he struck home 10 First Division goals, including two in a 3-0 win over Spurs, another that earned a point against Arsenal (1-1) and crucial efforts in 2-1 away wins over Coventry City, Leeds United and Southampton.

He also shone the following term, too, helping Villa win the coveted European Cup in Rotterdam. He had tricked his way down the left wing for well over an hour that May evening in 1982, before eventually finding enough space to whip over a cross that found striker Peter Withe, who shinned the ball past the Bayern Munich 'keeper Muller for the deciding goal.

Tony also helped Villa win the European Super Cup as well as making 180 senior appearances and scoring 34 goals (while creating many more) during his time with the club.

Tony also played in one B, one Under-21 and six full internationals for England.

His senior debut couldn't have been more high profile. England hadn't played in the World Cup Finals since 1970 and needed at least a point in their final qualifying game for Spain '82 against Hungary.

There was a lot of pressure on the team, and in front of a full house of 92,000 at Wembley they won the match 1-0. Unfortunately, Tony was not named in Ron Greenwood's squad for the Finals and this proved a huge disappointment.

At the time Greenwood loved to play attacking football, but he elected to do away with fast-raiding wingers in Spain, his only wide man being Steve Coppell, although he did select two other pacy forwards in Kevin Keegan and Trevor Francis.

After four successful years at Villa Park, Tony was transferred to local rivals West Bromwich Albion in December 1983 for £75,000.

He later assisted Villa's arch-rivals and second city neighbours Birmingham City, played in Japan, did well in Holland (where he won the Dutch Cup and gained promotion with Den Haag in 1987), starred in the NASL and also played in Malta. During his lengthy and, indeed, varied career, he amassed well over 450 appearances (at competitive level) and scored 65 goals.

Tony also coached in Australia and Hong Kong, and, when time (and fitness) allowed, he played for the Villa Old Stars team in various charity matches and occasionally provided commentary for radio broadcasts on the official Aston Villa FC website.

His job today is coaching kids from the ages of seven to 16 in and around the Midlands area.

Tommy Mort

Date of birth: 1 December 1897, Kearsley near Bolton
Died: 6 June 1967, Wigan, Lancashire

Aston Villa record:
Appearances: League 337, FA Cup 31
Goals: League 2
Debut: League, 15 April 1922 v Bolton Wanderers (h) won 2-1

Also played for: Kearsley St Stephen's, Newton Lads' Club, Lancashire Fusiliers, Altrincham, Rochdale, England (2 full caps)

Lancastrian Tommy Mort was a fine full-back, skilful in judgement, intercepting passes and anticipation, and renowned for his excellent sliding tackle.

He became a magnificent partner to Tommy Smart, the pair being affectionately known as 'Death and Glory' by the Villa supporters as they defended with grim determination and no mean skill over a period of at least 10 years, disrupted only by injury, sickness and international calls.

After serving in the armed forces with the Lancashire Fusiliers and doing well for almost two-and-half seasons with non-League side Altrincham, Mort was 23 years of age when he was signed as a full-time professional by Third Division North side Rochdale in June 1921. After a season at the Willbutts Ground (now Spotland) he was transferred to Aston Villa for £1,000 in April 1922 and made his First Division debut just 48 hours later, taking the place of the injured Tommy Smart against the club he supported as a lad, Bolton Wanderers, starring in a 2-1 win.

Over the next two seasons he missed only 14 League games, played in the 1924 FA Cup Final defeat by Newcastle United when he made two goal-line clearances and gained two full England caps, lining up in a 2-1 defeat by Wales at Ewood Park, Blackburn, shortly before the Cup Final when Smart played alongside him and in a 3-1 win over France in Paris, in May of that same year. He went on to win a third cap, in a 2-0 reverse by Scotland at Old Trafford in April 1926, and he also took part in three international trials between 1924 and 1926 when England were searching for two settled full-backs, having fielded 16 different partnerships during the previous five seasons.

Not the tallest or, indeed, heftiest of defenders, standing just 5ft 8in tall and weighing around 12st, Mort was nevertheless a solid competitor, never short on confidence and always ready for a battle. He was hardly ever given the runaround by an opposing winger, and although at times he was beaten for pace his positional sense and manoeuvrability was second to none. Several times he was Villa's most accomplished defender and would often appear in the centre of defence, clearing danger with one almighty downfield kick.

He only scored two competitive goals in his 368 League and Cup appearances for Aston Villa. The first was crucial, salvaging a point from a 1-1 home draw with Bury in March 1926, while his second found the back of the Middlesbrough net in a resounding 7-1 win at Villa Park on Christmas Day 1931. He came close to adding to that tally when efforts against Arsenal (in April 1932), Manchester City (in April 1933) and Tottenham Hotspur (in January 1934) all crashed against the woodwork. He also had shots booted off the line in the local derby with Birmingham in April 1932 and December 1933, the latter when he starred at right-back.

Mort had a lean spell in the side during the late 1920s when he was pushed all the way by Teddy Bowen, but he bounced back, played some excellent football and was immovable between 1929 and 1933, producing some exquisite performances.

In season 1933-34, Villa chose Danny Blair and Joe Nibloe as their two main full-backs, with Mort acting mainly as a reserve, doing likewise the following term when George Beeston entered the fray. In fact, during those two campaigns Mort appeared in only 18 League games and three FA Cup matches. He eventually announced his retirement in the summer of 1935 after spending a season in the reserves.

Mort subsequently returned 'home' to Lancashire where he started his own business in Wigan, only occasionally visiting Villa Park, although he did watch his former club in action when playing away at Bolton, Burnley and Preston.

Dennis Mortimer

Date of birth: 5 April 1952, Liverpool

Aston Villa record:

Appearances: League 316+1, FA Cup 21, League Cup 38, European 27, others 2

Goals: League 31, FA Cup 1, League Cup 2, European 2

Debut: League, 21 August 1976 v West Ham United (h) won 4–0

Also played for: Kirby Boys, Coventry City, Sheffield United, Brighton & Hove Albion, Birmingham City, Kettering Town, Redditch United (player-manager), West Bromwich Albion (reserve player-coach), Aston Villa Old Stars, England (6 youth, 6 Under-21 and 3 B caps)

Midfielder Dennis Mortimer became the first Aston Villa captain to lift a major European trophy, doing so after the German champions Bayern Munich had been beaten 1–0 in the 1982 European Cup Final in the De Kuip Stadium, Rotterdam, Peter Withe's tap-in goal deciding the contest in the second half.

Dennis, after schooling in Kirby with a future playing colleague Kenny Swain, began his career with Coventry City, signed initially as an apprentice in July 1967 and taking professional status in September 1969.

He came through the ranks at Highfield Road and made 215 senior appearances, netting 10 goals for the Sky Blues as he developed into a player of considerable talent. Indeed, it was his accomplished displays for Coventry that attracted the attention of several top clubs. In the end, Dennis, persuaded by manager Ron Saunders, chose to join Aston Villa for £175,000 in December 1975 – and, in truth, he never regretted the move.

Success followed quickly, and he went on to become one of the club's all-time greats, his triumphs exceeding all expectations. Full of power and determination, passion and skill, he had the will to win.

He was, without doubt, the driving force in Villa's engine room and was one of a band of players who, for reasons best known to successive England managers, was denied full international honours. Six Youth, six Under-23 and three B caps, plus a trip with the FA touring party to Australia in 1971, were scarcely a fitting reward for someone who can only be considered a legendary player.

During the decade up to 1985, Dennis made over 400 senior appearances for Villa, scoring 36 goals.

With Des Bremner and Gordon Cowans either side of him in midfield, he was the vital cog in the Villa team that won the League Cup in 1977, the Football League Championship in 1981, and both the European Cup (mentioned above) and the European Super Cup in 1982. He skippered the side in each of the last three triumphs and, in fact, proved to be one of the club's finest leaders in post World War Two football.

A regular in the Villa side for eight years, from August 1976 to September 1984, Dennis was an ever present in 1977–78 and 1980–81. He made his 100th senior appearance for the club versus arch-rivals and future club Birmingham City in February 1978, played in his 200th game against Derby County in March 1980, reached the milestone of 300 games versus Southampton at The Dell in September 1982, and made his 400th first-class appearance against his first employers, Coventry City, at Villa Park on the opening day of the 1984–85 season (August).

Dennis had a loan spell with Sheffield United in December 1984, and eight months later he moved to Brighton & Hove Albion. He was with the seaside club for only a year, returning to the Midlands to sign for Birmingham City in August 1986, thereby breaking the second-city taboo by playing for the two rival clubs.

After a brief spell with Kettering Town (July–November 1987), Dennis became player-manager of Redditch Town, a position he held until October 1988. He was then appointed Football in the Community Officer by West Bromwich Albion (August 1989) and was later placed in charge of the Baggies second team, having a handful of outings for the reserves. He later returned to Villa Park as a coach.

Dennis regularly attends Aston Villa games to this day and sometimes provides commentary on the home matches with the club's radio station, The Villan.

He is regarded by many as one of Aston Villa's true legends.

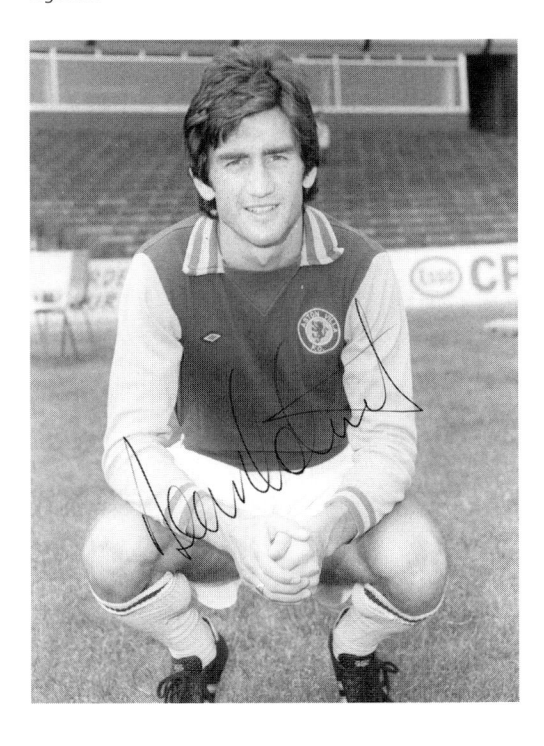

Harry Morton

Date of birth: 7 January 1909, Chadderton, Lancashire
Died: c.1975, Burnley, Lancashire

Aston Villa record:
Appearances: League 192, FA Cup 15
Debut: League, 28 November 1931 v Manchester City (a) drew 3-3

Also played for: Chadderton Sunday School, Oldham Boys, Platt Brothers Ironworks, Middleton Road Primitives, Bury (trial), Bolton Wanderers (trial), Southampton (trial), Everton, Burnley

Goalkeeper Harry Morton, a former fireman and Rugby League full-back, made his Football League debut in unusual circumstances. As a reserve in Aston Villa's first-team squad that travelled to Manchester for a First Division encounter against City at Maine Road, Morton was sitting in the main stand waiting for the kick-off when, just before the teams were due out onto the field of play, he received a call asking him to come down to the dressing room quickly.

Regular custodian Fred Biddlestone had unfortunately (or fortunately in Morton's case) injured his knee during the pre-match kick about and was forced to pull out, Morton taking over between the posts. He conceded three goals that afternoon but did reasonably well, producing several fine saves and helping Villa earn a point from a 3–3 draw.

One of the smallest 'keepers of his day, standing a fraction over 5ft 9in tall and weighing around 11st, Morton retained the number-one position for the remainder of that season as Villa finished a creditable fifth in the table.

He missed only one game in 1932–33 (against the FA Cup holders Newcastle United at home), and he was quite outstanding as an ever present during the next two campaigns, producing several brilliant displays and helping Villa reach the semi-final of the FA Cup in March 1934 when they were beaten by Manchester City at Huddersfield.

During the 1935–36 campaign, when a poor Villa defence leaked goals left, right and centre, the luckless Morton played in half of the 42 League games and was on the receiving end of some heavy defeats. He couldn't cope with Ted Drake's lethal finishing when the Arsenal striker bagged all his side's goals in a 7–1 win at Villa Park, and he also let in seven against Middlesbrough, six against Grimsby Town and five at both Blackburn and Manchester City, but still came up smiling.

Although he took over owing to an injury to his predecessor, Morton was nevertheless pressed all the way by the fit-again Biddlestone. He maintained a high level of consistency, was both brave and daring, commanded his area well and could kick long and straight when clearing his lines, once sending the ball to bounce into the opposing penalty area.

He was also a safe handler of the ball, but was, it must be said, rather vulnerable at times when going for high crosses, especially when he was challenged by a robust centre-forward, such as the aforementioned Drake. He was also an England international trialist in 1934 and was a reserve for the game against Wales that same year.

After occupying a variety of positions when assisting several local teams, and having unsuccessful trials as a goalkeeper with Bury, Bolton Wanderers (the team he supported as a lad) and Southampton, Morton joined the army and served with the Welch Fusiliers.

Playing regularly for his unit, he lined up in goal against Aston Villa in a friendly in October 1930, and despite conceding seven goals he impressed the Villa directors and committee members, who offered him a trial. This proved to be successful and a month later Morton became a full-time professional at the age of 21, signing as reserve to Fred Biddlestone.

After his initial outing, injuries and illness apart, and for a period in 1931 when he was rested, Morton remained first choice between the posts at Villa Park until February 1937, when Biddlestone returned to the side. A month later he was transferred to Everton for a small fee, as cover for England international Ted Sagar. He made his debut for the Merseysiders against West Bromwich Albion soon after joining, and his 29th and last senior outing was against Wolverhampton Wanderers at Molineux in February 1939 when the Blues lost 7–0. This was, in fact, his only game that season as Everton went on to win the League title.

Morton signed for Burnley just prior to the outbreak of World War Two, and after playing in a handful of regional games he announced his retirement in April 1940. He remained in the area until his death in the mid-1970s.

Frank Moss, senior

Date of birth: 17 April 1895, Aston, Birmingham
Died: 15 September 1965, St George's, Worcester

Aston Villa record:
Appearances: League 255, FA Cup 28
Goals: League 9
Debut: League, 5 April 1915 v Notts County (a) drew 1–1

Also played for: Aston manor, Walsall, Bellis & Morcom (guest), Aston Park Rangers, Smethwick Carriage Works FC, Bradford City, Cardiff City, Oldham Athletic, Bromsgrove Rovers (player-manager), Worcester City, England (5 full caps)

When left-half Jimmy Harrop was forced out of Aston Villa's 1920 FA Cup Final side through injury, his replacement was blond Frank Moss, a well-built, solid and workmanlike defender, who had just two League games under his belt. Moss played a 'blinder' at Stamford Bridge against Huddersfield Town, and along with his centre-back partner, Frank Barson, completely blocked out the threat of strikers Frank Mann and Sammy Taylor as Villa won the trophy 1–0 after extra-time.

There was nothing flashy about Moss's play. He was rugged, resolute, strong in the air and on the ground, and cleared his lines without fuss or bother, often belting the ball downfield as far as he could – well away from danger. His motto, in so many words, was 'when in doubt, kick it out', and he did just that for well over a decade for Aston Villa.

Nicknamed 'Snowy', he joined Villa as a full-time professional in February 1914, but had to bide his time as a footballer owing to the outbreak of World War One. Serving as a corporal in the 4th Lincolnshire Regiment, based at Bouchezvenes, France, he kept himself fit and active in the physical training centre and played as a guest for Walsall, the club where he was groomed as a young lad immediately prior to his switch to Villa Park.

However, in 1917 he suffered a severe wound to his left knee which threatened his career. Thankfully, after a lot of strict medical care and attention throughout a difficult period, the wound healed, and within two years he was fighting fit, eager to resume his association with Villa.

Moss went on to captain Aston Villa and England, having the pleasure of leading both club and country out at Wembley – Villa for the 1924 FA Cup Final encounter with Newcastle United, which they lost 2–0, and England against Scotland that same year, the first international staged at the Empire Stadium which ended in a 1–1 draw, Moss's clubmate Billy Walker netting for England.

That was the first of five full caps Moss gained during his playing days. He also represented the Football League in games against the Scottish League in successive seasons of 1922–23 and 1923–24, when he was regarded as one of the best defensive wing-halves in the country.

Moss was, without doubt, a star performer in the Villa side (injuries permitting) for eight years (1919–27). He had several defensive partners including Tommy Ball, Dr Vic Milne, Percy Varco and Jimmy Gibson, and he maintained a very high level of consistency.

Eventually losing his place in the middle-line during the 1928–29 season, when Joe Tate and Alec Talbot established themselves, Moss remained loyal to the club until January 1929 when he was transferred to Cardiff City for £2,500 – just after the Welsh club had been hammered 6–1 by Villa in an FA Cup tie! Six months later he moved north to Oldham Athletic and, after a spell as player-manager of non-League side Bromsgrove Rovers and a brief association with Worcester City (as a player), he retired in May 1934 to become licensee of the Grosvenor Arms public house in Worcester, remaining in the city until his death in 1965 at the age of 70.

Both Moss's sons, Amos and Frank junior, went on to play, and play well, for Aston Villa. And between them all three Mosses accumulated 706 senior appearances in the claret-and-blue strip.

Frank Moss, junior

Date of birth: 16 September 1917, Aston, Birmingham
Died: 5 May 1997, Looe, Cornwall

Aston Villa record:
Appearances: League 297, FA Cup 17, Wartime 11
Goals: League 3, FA Cup 0, Wartime 0
Debut: League, 5 September 1938 v Everton (h) lost 3-0

Also played for: Worcester Nondescripts, Worcester City (2 spells), Wolverhampton Wanderers, Sheffield Wednesday, (wartime guest for Birmingham, Northampton Town, Wrexham, Stourbridge, Southampton, Watford)

Blond-haired defender Frank Moss, resourceful and totally committed, was a fighter for both his clubs (football) and country (war).

As a youngster, Moss played in the North versus South Schoolboy international trial in 1932 and was selected for the Final of the English Schools Trophy that same season. After a spell with Worcester City (from August 1933) and a trial with Wolverhampton Wanderers (1934), Moss signed as an amateur for Sheffield Wednesday in November 1935, taking professional status at Hillsborough in May 1936 and making his League debut in a 2-2 draw at Liverpool six months later – the first of 23 appearances for the Owls.

However, with several players of similar style and, indeed, able to occupy the same position, Moss was transferred to Aston Villa in May 1938 for £2,000, and he remained at the club until June 1955, appearing in 325 first-team matches, the first as an emergency centre-forward against League champions-elect Everton at Villa Park in September 1938 when injuries ruled out several other forwards.

He played in one other game that season – at centre-half in the home clash with Arsenal when a crowd of 57,453 saw him struggle to cope with the threat of John Lewis, who scored twice for the Gunners in their 3-1 win.

Moss played the remainder of his League games for Villa at the heart of the defence, making his last appearance in a 6-1 League defeat at Charlton in February 1955, when he was deputising for Irish international Con Martin, the player who had taken over his centre-half position at the start of that season.

In fact, Moss's first senior outing for Villa was in the right-half position, alongside Harry Parkes and Eddie Lowe, against Derby County in an FA Cup quarter-final first leg home encounter when a record crowd of 76,588 saw the Rams win 4-3.

Operating gunboats and destroyers during World War Two in the Middle East, Moss played football on a regular basis, guesting for several clubs during the hostilities, four of them major ones including Villa's arch-rivals Birmingham, and when he returned to England he had 12 outings in Villa's first team during the transitional season of 1945-46 before establishing himself in the League side the following campaign.

A strong, reliable defender, good in the air and on the ground, fair and resolute, Moss held his position in the middle of the back line for eight years, being an ever present in 1949-50 and missing only three games in both 1951-52 and 1953-54.

He scored just three League goals for the first XI – in the 2-2 home draw with Burnley in November 1947, the winner against Manchester City at Villa Park in December 1949 (1-0) and a second-half equaliser at home to Liverpool (1-1) in September 1950.

During his time with Villa, Moss had several defensive partners, among them Parkes, Lowe and Martin (already mentioned), plus Dicky Dorsett and his bother Amos Moss, who was on Villa's books during the same period of time from 1945 to 1956.

After hanging up his boots when approaching his 38th birthday, Moss spent one season as a coach at Villa Park (1955-56) before leaving to concentrate on his business in Kingstanding, Birmingham, which he started initially in 1940.

In 1969 he decided to move to the Cornish seaside resort of Looe, where he remained for the rest of his life, hardly ever venturing north to watch the Villa in action.

His father, Frank senior, also played for Aston Villa and England (see previous entry).

Chris Nicholl

Date of birth: 12 October 1946, Wilmslow, Cheshire

Aston Villa record:

Appearances: League 209, FA Cup 12, League Cup 27, European 2, FA Charity Shield 1
Goals: League 11, FA Cup 4, League Cup 5
Debut: League, 11 March 1972 v Rotherham United (a) won 2–0
Also played for: Macclesfield Schools, Witton Albion, Burnley, Halifax Town, Luton Town, Southampton, Grimsby Town, Northern Ireland (51 full caps)
Managed: Southampton, Grimsby Town, Walsall

Rugged centre-half Chris Nicholl played for Witton Albion, Burnley (reserve-team football for three years), Halifax Town (season 1968–1969 when they finished runners-up in Division Four) and Luton Town, for whom he made over 100 senior appearances before establishing himself at the heart of Aston Villa's defence in the 1970s.

He was signed by manager Vic Crowe for £90,000 in March 1972 to take over from veteran George Curtis and played a crucial role at the end of that season, helping Villa secure the Third Division title.

He went on to give the club great service, playing in almost 250 first-class matches over a period of five years and gaining two League Cup-winners' medals in three years, the first in 1975 versus Norwich City, the second versus Everton in 1977.

Chris captained Villa to victory (after two replays) in the latter Final and, in fact, the third game at Old Trafford is fondly remembered for one of the greatest goals in any Aston Villa match – Chris netting with a brilliant 40-yard left footer which helped take the match to extra-time.

During his time with Villa, he also won the first 12 of what was to be an overall of 51 full caps for Northern Ireland, frequently appearing alongside his cousin Jimmy Nicholl, who served with Manchester United and West Bromwich Albion, among others.

A strong, honest tackler, powerful in the air with expert positional sense, Chris never gave his opponent too much space in which to manoeuvre and was capable of producing some nifty footwork in tight positions. He was also dangerous at set pieces – at both ends. During a League game against Leicester City in March 1976 he had the misfortune of conceding two own-goals while also scoring twice at the other end of the field for Villa in a 2-2 draw. He is the only player (so far) to achieve this unlikely feat.

Chris left Villa Park for Southampton in June 1977 and became the backbone of a successful Saints side, scoring eight goals in 228 League appearances and playing in the 1979 League Cup Final defeat by Nottingham Forest. He switched to Grimsby Town in August 1983, as player-assistant manager, and after adding a further 70 League outings to his career tally in three years at Blundell Park, Chris retired from the playing side in July 1985.

He returned to Southampton a month later as manager, taking over from Lawrie McMenemy who had signed him initially for the club eight years earlier.

Chris kept the Saints in the First Division but was sacked in May 1991 after failing to keep them out of the bottom half of the top flight.

After a brief scouting mission with Wigan Athletic, Chris decided to take a break from football, returning to the game early in the 1994–95 season when he replaced Kenny Hibbitt as manager of Walsall.

In his first season with the Saddlers, they gained promotion from the Third Division as runners-up. He then saw his charges finish in the top half of the Second Division during the next two seasons, before quitting his position at The Bescot Stadium in May 1997 after failing to get Walsall into Division One, citing his family as his reason for leaving.

Chris then spent the next two years acting as assistant manager of the Northern Ireland national team, working alongside his former boss, Lawrie McMenemy.

He made a brief return to Walsall as assistant manager to the then-manager and a former Villa teammate Ray Graydon in November 2001, but left in January 2002 through loyalty to Graydon, who had been sacked.

Out of the game for quite a while, and following the sacking of former Walsall player-manager Paul Merson in February 2006, Chris offered his services to the club within hours of Merson's departure, but he was not successful with his venture, Saddlers handing the former Birmingham City player, Kevan Broadhurst, the job instead.

Nevertheless, Chris is still a regular at the Bescot Stadium, both as a supporter and as a commentator for local radio. He remains very popular among Walsall fans, and he is, of course, fondly remembered for his efforts at the heart of Aston Villa's defence.

Chris's brother Terry played for Crewe Alexandra, Southend and Gillingham.

Harry Parkes

Date of birth: 4 January 1920, Erdington, Birmingham

Aston Villa record:
Appearances: League 320, FA Cup 25, Wartime 134
Goals: League 3, FA Cup 1, Wartime 41
Debut: FA Cup, 28 January 1946 v Millwall (h) won 9-1

Also played for: GEC Works team (Witton), Boldmere St Michael's, Northampton Town (guest), West Bromwich Albion (guest)

'Happy Harry' Parkes was described as the resident comedian at Villa Park, a real joker in the pack who kept the dressing room alive and buzzing, even in the darkest times.

He certainly proved himself a lucky pick up from the junior field as he went on to serve the club for over 16 years, accumulating more than 480 first-team appearances.

Originally a stocky outside-left, he joined Villa as an amateur inside-forward from Boldmere St Michael's in April 1939 (having had an unsuccessful trial with the club four years earlier at the age of 15) and over the next nine seasons or so appeared in 10 different positions at senior level before finally settling down at full-back from December 1948 onwards.

A permanent fixture in the Villa side from 1946 until 1954, he started the first post-war League campaign in the right-half position and, as the season progressed, also turned out in both inside-forward berths, led the attack, played on the right-wing, deputised for Frank Moss at centre-half, as well as lining up at left-half when Eddie Lowe was sidelined. 'Mr Versatility' certainly, but Parkes would play anywhere just to get a game of football, even taking over in goal during practice sessions.

A scorer on his debut in wartime football at Hednesford, Parkes struck his first senior goal in a 9-1 FA Cup win over Millwall in January 1946, netting his first goal in League football 11 months later in a 2-2 home draw with Huddersfield Town.

During Wartime football, Parkes had done exceptionally well as a marksman, netting 41 times for Villa, mainly from the inside-left channel, including four in a 19-2 home win over RAF (Lichfield) in the Birmingham League in March 1942. He bagged two fine efforts in an 8-2 home win over West Bromwich Albion in a League North game seven months later and two more in a 4-0 victory over Stoke City at Villa Park in August 1944, one of his shots almost ripping through the back of the net.

At the end of the 1943-44 wartime season, Harry won his only senior medal with Villa, helping them beat Blackpool 5-4 on aggregate in a thrilling Football League North Cup Final. He played at centre-forward in both legs, having a hand in Bob Iverson's goal in the second leg at Villa Park which Villa won 4-2 in front of a near-55,000 crowd.

Two years later Parkes played for Villa against Derby County in an FA Cup quarter-final encounter, when a crowd of 76,588 (a record to this day) packed into Villa Park to see the Rams win 4-3.

After the war, and once he had firmly established himself as a full-back, he starred alongside several fine players including Dicky Dorsett, Peter Aldis and Stan Lynn. A model of consistency, he missed only 14 games out of a possible 330 between April 1947 and October 1954, being an ever present in 1951-52 and making 41 League appearances in 1950-51 and 40 in three other seasons.

He retired as a player in June 1955 to concentrate wholly on running his sports shop on Corporation Street, Birmingham, which he bought in the early 1950s. This flourished for over 40 years, attracting many 'football-minded' customers who just popped in to have a chat with the former Villa player!

In later life Parkes became a director at Villa Park and he also served on the board of rivals Birmingham City, albeit briefly.

A hard-boiled 'Brummie,' strong in all aspects of defensive play, he was quick over the ground, a positive kicker and was one of the few players to contain the likes of Stanley Matthews and Tom Finney. Indeed, Matthews once said that he 'Hated playing against Parkes...He never gives you a yard in which to work.'

David Platt

Date of birth: 10 June 1966, Chadderton near Oldham, Lancashire

Aston Villa record:
Appearances: League 121, FA Cup 9, League Cup 14, Europe 4, others 7
Goals: League 50, FA Cup 2, League Cup 10, Europe 2, others 4
Debut: League, 20 February 1988 v Blackburn Rovers (a) lost 3–2

Also played for: Chadderton, Manchester United, Crewe Alexandra, Bari (Italy), Juventus (Italy), Sampdoria (Italy), England (62 full caps)
Managed: Nottingham Forest, England Under-21 team

Having trained with Steve Coppell, Bryan Robson, Frank Stapleton, Norman Whiteside and Ray Wilkins, David Platt was rejected by Manchester United and elected to join Crewe Alexandra in February 1985.

At Gresty Road he quickly gained a reputation as a strong-running, free-scoring midfielder, and, as a result, scouts and managers from several top clubs came to look at Dario Gradi's promising young star.

After three years with the 'Alex', David was snapped up by Aston Villa, signed for £200,000 in February 1988 by Graham Taylor.

Adapting quickly to Second Division football, David scored five goals in 11 games at the end of that season, helping Villa regain top-flight status at the first attempt. He added 14 goals to his tally in 1988–89 and, maintaining his form, won his first full England cap in a friendly against Italy in November 1989.

He added four more caps to his tally over the next seven months and also finished up as Villa's top scorer in 1989–90 with 21 goals. His efforts, plus his versatility and reliability, duly earned him a place in Bobby Robson's World Cup squad for the Finals in Italy.

On the bench for all of England's group games, he was sent on as an extra-time substitute in the second-round clash with Belgium and responded superbly by volleying home a memorable last-minute winner – his first goal for his country – to clinch a place in the quarter-finals.

With skipper Bryan Robson sidelined, David started against Cameroon and struck the opening goal in a 3–2 victory. He also appeared in the semi-final against West Germany which went to a penalty shoot-out. David scored his side's third spot-kick, but the next two were missed and sadly England were eliminated.

After an outstanding World Cup, he quietly settled back into his captain's role at Villa Park while also retaining his place in the England team, now managed by Graham Taylor, his former boss.

David was one of England's most consistent players during the early 1990s, scoring goals with frequency from midfield and proving an inspirational leader, sharing the captaincy with Arsenal's Tony Adams.

England crashed out of Euro '92 after failing to win any of their group games, David obliging with their only goal in a 2–1 defeat by Sweden.

Despite David's drive and enthusiasm, England failed to qualify for the 1994 World Cup and, as a result manager Taylor quit, replaced by Terry Venables, and it was David who scored the first England goal of the Venables era. However, by the time Euro '96 came round, David was on the bench with the two Pauls, Ince and Gascoigne, manning the midfield.

He appeared as a substitute in most of the Euro '96 games, starting the quarter-final clash with Spain. In the semi-final he again netted in a penalty shoot-out versus Germany, but, equally similarly, ended up on the losing side. David retired from international football soon afterwards with 62 caps to his credit (13 as captain) and an impressive 27 goals. He had also represented his country in three B and three Under-21 matches.

Meanwhile, in July 1991, he had left Villa Park for Italy, where he remained for four years, serving in turn with Bari, Juventus and Sampdoria – his moves costing £17.25 million in transfer fees.

Arsenal recruited him for £4.75 million in 1995 and he finally won domestic honours three years later when the Gunners completed the Premiership and FA Cup double.

He left Highbury in August 1998 to become player-coach of Sampdoria and his controversial stint ended prematurely when other clubs protested vehemently that he did not have the appropriate coaching qualifications for managing in Serie 'A'.

In 1999 he became player-coach of Nottingham Forest, but his reign at The City Ground was unsuccessful as he spent several million pounds on players who did not perform well, thus plunging the club into large sums of debt. He also had disagreements with several experienced, long-serving players, which led to them being isolated from the first-team picture and subsequently released by the club.

Manager of the England Under-21 side from 2001 to 2004, he tasted moderate success, qualifying for the European Championships in 2002. After failing to qualify for the 2004 tournament he was succeeded by Peter Taylor. David, who has owned a race horse and a Wolverhampton night club, is now a media pundit and writes a regular column for *Four Four Two* magazine.

George Ramsay

Date of birth: 3 March 1855, Cathcart, Glasgow, Scotland
Died: 7 October 1935, Llandrindod Wells, Wales

Aston Villa record:
Secretary-manager: 1884–1926.
Debut: Friendly, 15 October 1876 v Stafford Rangers (h) won 9–0

Also played for: Cathcart Schools, Oxford FC (Glasgow), Glasgow Rangers (trial)

George Burrell Ramsay is an important figure in the history of Aston Villa football club. He was secretary-manager during the most successful period of their history.

Had the rough and ready Scotsman not come across a group of inexperienced cricketer-footballers from a local church practicing their ball skills on a strip of wasteland in 1876, it is unlikely that Aston Villa would be a household name today.

In fact, the infant club – which had been going for some two years – would probably have gone out of existence if it hadn't been for George, such was the impact he had on the club's early years.

George was a gifted footballer himself, having come very close to joining Rangers before venturing south to look for work in Birmingham and, on seeing these 'young men' trying to play football, he later described their approach to the game as 'a dash at the man and a big kick at the ball'.

George was asked if he would like to join in the action. He had no hesitation and immediately these young footballers were amazed by his dribbling and control, so much so that he was persuaded to become a member of the team and was quickly made captain.

One of the first things George did was get Villa a ground, suitable to play competitive matches in front of paying spectators. He found one in nearby Perry Barr, which meant that Villa were able to charge admission for the first time. He also took charge of training sessions, which saw a dramatic improvement in general results.

Villa improved greatly under his guidance and the team won its first trophy in 1880, with George, who always wore a smart, tight-fitting polo hat and long, baggy shorts, leading the team to a 3–2 victory over Saltley College in the Birmingham Senior Cup Final.

Having been troubled by foot and knee injuries for over a year, George chose to retire from playing in the summer of 1882 but continued in the capacity as trainer and coach. He assumed the dual role of secretary-manager in August 1884 and retained that position for a total of 42 years, until August 1926.

In that time he was assisted superbly well by three excellent chairmen: Josuah Margoschis, who held office from 1885 to 1897, William McGregor, founder of the Football League, who was the 'chair' for the 1897–98 season and Fred Rinder, who presided over events from 1898 to 1925.

George was subsequently employed by the club as honorary advisor and, in later years, he served as vice-president.

During his time as secretary-manager, Villa won the Football League title on six occasions: 1894, 1896, 1897, 1899, 1900 and 1910, and they also lifted the FA Cup six times: 1887, 1895, 1897, 1905, 1913 and 1920, establishing themselves as the premier football club in England in 1897 when they equalled Preston North End's feat of completing the double.

The team also finished runners-up in the First Division six times: in 1889, 1903, 1908, 1911, 1913 and 1914, and were beaten in the FA Cup Finals of 1892 and 1924.

In all, George Ramsay – who received two long-service medals from the Football League (1909 and 1927) – served Aston Villa for a total of 59 years. Six months after his death the club was relegated to the Second Division, an unthinkable notion in the Ramsay era.

It is said that George was the first man to kick a ball at Villa's first ground (Perry Barr) and their last (Villa Park).

Jimmy Rimmer

Date of birth: 10 February 1948, Southport, Lancashire

Aston Villa record:
Appearances: League 229, FA Cup 12, League Cup 22, Europe 22
Debut: League, 20 August 1977 v Queen's Park Rangers (a) won 2–1

Also played for: Manchester United, Swansea City (2 spells), Arsenal, Hamrun Spartans (Malta), England (1 full cap)

After representing Southport and Merseyside Schools, goalkeeper Jimmy Rimmer joined Manchester United in May 1963 and turned professional two years later after gaining an FA Youth Cup-winners' medal.

Acting chiefly as understudy to England's Alex Stepney, he made just 46 first-class appearances in his 11 years at Old Trafford. He was a member of United's winning squad versus Benfica in the 1968 European Cup Final at Wembley, having made his League debut versus Fulham only a few weeks earlier, although his first taste of football with the Reds was on the club's Australian tour in the summer of 1967. He also played in the 1969 European Cup semi-final defeat to AC Milan.

Jimmy had loan spells with Swansea City from October 1973 to February 1974 and Arsenal during February 1974, before moving to Highbury on a permanent basis for £40,000 two months later.

With Stepney prevalent between the posts, Jimmy managed only 46 senior appearances for United and was thought to be the ideal replacement, in the long term, for Bob Wilson at Arsenal.

He made only one first-team appearance in 1973-74, keeping a clean sheet on his debut against Liverpool, but when Wilson announced his retirement at the end of that season Jimmy stepped up to become Arsenal's number one. He held that position for the next three years, being a near ever present for the Gunners in that time when he also won his one and only full England cap, although it was not an auspicious match – lining up against Italy in a friendly in New York in May 1976 when he conceded two goals in the first-half before being substituted at half-time by Joe Corrigan. Thankfully, England recovered and went on to win 3-2.

Once the Tottenham Hotspur manager Terry Neill had taken over the reins at Arsenal, he signed Pat Jennings from his former club and Jimmy, after 146 outings for the Gunners, was duly sold to Aston Villa for a fee of £65,000 in August 1977.

Jimmy replaced John Burridge at Villa Park and remained in charge of the goalkeeping position for the next six seasons, winning a First Division Championship medal in 1981, and both European Cup and European Super Cup-winners' medals the following year, although in the Final of the European Cup in Rotterdam he was injured very early on in the proceedings and had to be replaced by the young Nigel Spink.

And as a result of that victory over Bayern Munich, Jimmy became the first English-born player to win a European Cup-winners' medal with two different clubs, despite the fact that he only ever played for nine minutes in the two matches!

Agile and positive, a clean handler of the ball and brave in 50:50 situations, Jimmy played with great assurance and gave the defenders in front of him a lot of confidence, knowing that most times he would claim a high cross. He went on to appear in 287 senior games for Villa and, after being replaced by Nigel Spink, he returned to Swansea City in August 1983. He later assisted the Maltese club, Hamrun Spartans (from August 1986 to June 1987), and had a third spell at the Vetch Field as a coach during the 1987-88 season.

Thereafter he spent several years in China, working as a goalkeeping coach for the Chinese national team and he also assisted with coaching in Dalian Shide before taking a similar position in Canada. He returned to Wales in the mid-1990s to run a gold centre near Swansea.

Jimmy's career boasts a total of 550 senior appearances at club level (470 in the Football League).

Bruce Rioch

Date of birth: 6 September 1947, Aldershot

Aston Villa record:
Appearances: League 149+5, FA Cup 7, League Cup 14, FA Charity Shield 1
Goals: League 34, League Cup 3
Debut: League, 9 August 1969 v Norwich City (h) lost 1–0

Also played for: Dynamo Boys' Club, Luton Town, Derby County (2 spells), Everton, Birmingham City, Sheffield United, Seattle Sounders (NASL), Torquay United (player-manager), Scotland (24 full caps)
Managed: Seattle FC (NASL), Middlesbrough, Millwall, Bolton Wanderers, Arsenal, Norwich City, Wigan Athletic, Odense BK

Having represented Cambridge & District Schools, Bruce Rioch joined Luton Town as an apprentice in September 1962, turning professional two years later. Making his League debut in November 1964 against Southend United, he spent a couple of years establishing himself at Kenilworth Road and helped the Hatters win the Fourth Division title in 1968 (scoring 24 goals).

He moved to Villa Park in July 1969, signed by manager Tommy Docherty for a then record fee for a Second Division club of £100,000 (with his brother Neil). He gained a League Cup runners'-up medal in 1970 when Villa lost 2-0 to Tottenham and in 1972 was instrumental in helping Villa win the Third Division title.

The son of a Scottish sergeant major, Bruce was an all-action, hard-shooting midfielder who loved to drive forward with the ball and would let fly at goal from any distance, even trying his luck from 40 yards if allowed!

A huge favourite with the fans (especially the female variety), he remained at Villa Park until February 1974 when he moved to Derby County for £200,000. He helped the Rams win the League Championship in 1975 before switching to Everton in December 1976, returning to The Baseball Ground in September 1977.

However, after a dispute with his former manager (Docherty) and loan spells with Birmingham City (December 1978) and Sheffield United (March 1979), Bruce elected to join the NASL club Seattle Sounders.

On his return to England in October 1980 he was appointed Torquay United's player-coach, working under Mike Green and later Frank O'Farrell, but he left Plainmoor after a training ground incident with Colin Anderson in January 1984. Taking a rest from football for 13 months, he re-entered the game as manager of Seattle (NASL) but never settled and resigned in September 1985.

His next appointment was as manager of Middlesbrough (February 1986) and at the end of a season, which had started with 'Boro hovering on the brink of bankruptcy and being locked out of their Ayresome Park home by the official receiver, he guided the Teessiders to promotion from the Third Division.

A year later Boro claimed a second successive promotion, this time as winners of the Second Division Play-off Final. However, the team found it difficult to adjust to the pace of top-flight football and after a season fighting against relegation Bruce was sacked.

He made a quick return to the game as boss of Millwall, whom he guided to the Second Division Play-offs in 1991, but left in March 1992, taking over the reins at Bolton Wanderers two months later.

In his first season, the Trotters finished runners-up in Division Two and two years later lost to Liverpool in the League Cup Final while beating Reading 4-3 after extra-time in the Play-off Final to clinch a place in the Premiership.

That Play-off Final victory was Bruce's last game as Bolton manager. A few weeks later he accepted the Arsenal job. In his only season at Highbury, he guided the Gunners to a UEFA Cup place and also reached the League Cup semi-finals, but lost on the away-goal rule to Aston Villa.

Just before the start of the 1996-97 campaign Bruce was sacked after a dispute with the Arsenal board of directors over transfer funds. His enduring legacy at the club was the signing of Dennis Bergkamp from Internazionale; the Dutchman would go on to become one of the club's greatest players.

After leaving Arsenal, Bruce served as assistant manager at Queen's Park Rangers, managed Norwich City (June 1998-April 2000), was in charge of Wigan Athletic (July 2000-February 2001) and turned down an offer of managing his former club Derby. It was four years before he returned to the game, taking over as chief coach of Danish side Odense BK in June 2005.

During his playing career Bruce amassed over 600 senior appearances and represented Scotland on 24 occasions, being the first 'English-born' player (by virtue of his father's birthplace) to captain his adopted country.

Bruce's son Gregor also served with Luton as well as Barnet, Peterborough and Hull City.

Ian Ross

Date of birth: 26 November 1947, Glasgow

Aston Villa record:
Appearances: League 175, FA Cup 10, League Cup 17, Europe 2, FA Charity Shield 1
Goals: League 3
Debut: League, 26 February 1972 v Port Vale (h) won 2–0

Also played for: Liverpool, Notts County (loan), Northampton Town (loan), Peterborough United (loan and player-coach), Santa Barbara (NASL), Wolverhampton Wanderers (player-coach), Hereford United (player-coach)
Managed: Huddersfield Town, Berwick Rangers, FC Valur (Iceland), Keflavik (Iceland)

Signed by Liverpool from junior football in his native Glasgow in June 1963, having been a close friend of Kenny Dalglish, Ian Ross's aptitude for many roles rather than a specific position probably robbed him of many more appearances than the 68 he did make in Anfield colours following his debut in 1967.

He would be remembered specifically for two crucial missions given to him by manager Bill Shankly: the first in December 1969 when he was told to shackle the menacing talents of Alan Ball in the Goodison derby against the reigning League champions Everton, which Liverpool, without two key players (Roger Hunt and Tommy Smith, both injured), won in style by 3-0. And the second, the following season, when he was ordered to do a similar job on the great Franz Beckenbauer in a European Fairs Cup quarter-final second leg encounter with Bayern Munich in Germany. Again, Ian's efforts were bathed in success as Liverpool drew 1-1 for a 4-1 aggregate triumph. Beckenbauer hardly had a kick and Ian also had the pleasure of scoring his side's goal, one of only four in his Anfield career.

In February 1972 Ian joined Aston Villa for £70,000 and quickly became a firm favourite with the supporters, as Vic Crowe's side went on to complete a fine season by winning the Third Division Championship – Ian gaining a medal by playing in 17 matches and netting his first goal for the club against Chesterfield on the final day of the season to secure a 1-0 victory.

During the 1972-73 campaign he took over the captaincy (from Brian Tiler) and missed only five League games as Villa narrowly missed out on a second successive promotion, finishing third in the table. He was an ever present in 1973-74 and likewise in 1974-75, when his leadership went a long way in helping Villa win the League Cup by defeating Norwich City 1-0 in the Wembley Final and claim the runners'-up spot in the Second Division, therefore regaining their place in the top flight after an absence of eight years.

A fine professional and a trier to the last, Ian simply loved playing football. He wasn't one of the greatest, far from it. But he was as consistent as anyone in the game and he battled through every match with enormous enthusiasm and total commitment.

After loan spells with Notts County, Northampton Town and Peterborough United in the space of three months in the winter of 1976 – he actually played for four different clubs in four months during that same year – Ian left Villa Park for a stint in the NASL with Santa Barbara. He returned to England in August 1979 to take over as player-coach of Wolverhampton Wanderers, switching to Hereford United in the same capacity but on a non-contract basis in October 1982.

A second spell at Molineux followed early in 1983 before he went abroad again, this time to Oman as a senior coach, returning to serve briefly on Birmingham City's coaching staff prior to taking up a senior position as coach/manager of Valur in Iceland.

He remained in office for almost four years, from August 1984 until June 1988, when he chose to try his luck at coaching in South Africa and then in Australia, also serving as manager of another Icelandic club, IBK Keflavik, in between times.

In March 1992 Ian took over as team manager of Huddersfield Town, guiding the Terriers into the Play-offs in 1992. He retained his position with the Yorkshire club until May 1993 and after managing Berwick Rangers (1995-96) he retired from the game, becoming a licensee of the Gardener's Arms at Timperley near Altrincham.

Dean Saunders

Date of birth: 21 June 1964, Swansea

Aston Villa record:
Appearances: League 111+1, FA Cup 9, League 15, Europe 8
Goals: League 37, FA Cup 4, League Cup 7, Europe 1
Debut: League, 13 September 1992 v Leeds United (a) drew 1–1

Also played for: Swansea City, Cardiff City, Brighton & Hove Albion, Oxford United, Derby County, Liverpool, Galatasaray (Turkey), Nottingham Forest, Sheffield United, Benfica (Portugal), Bradford City, Wales (73 full caps)

The son of Roy Saunders (a former Liverpool player), Dean Saunders was one of the game's most prolific marksmen. After having both cartilages removed from his left knee as an 18-year-old, he scored his first League goal for Swansea City against Oldham Athletic in March 1984 and his last some 16 years later in the Premiership for Bradford City against Arsenal in February 2000.

A positive, all-action, unselfish striker, who simply knew where the net was, Dean retired with a superb record under his belt of 806 club and international appearances and 276 goals – and at one time, along with another Liverpool striker Ian Rush and midfielder Peter Nicholas, he was Wales's most capped outfield player with a total of 73, which was later surpassed by Gary Speed in 2004.

Surprisingly, in a wonderful and consistent career, during which he consulted his father on many occasions, especially in his early days at Swansea and Brighton, Dean received only two medals at club level. He helped Liverpool win the FA Cup in 1992 and Aston Villa lift the League Cup in 1994 when he scored twice (one a penalty) in a 3-1 win over Manchester United in the Final.

His best performances, on the whole, came with Derby County, for whom he struck 57 goals in 131 outings between October 1988 and July 1991, and also with Villa, for whom he struck 49 goals in 144 competitive games.

Dean was always popular with the fans, whoever he played for. He scored a dramatic goal just 16 seconds from the end of a League game against Luton Town in May 1987 to save Oxford United from relegation and during his only season at Anfield he certainly produced the goods, top scoring in 1991–92 with 23 goals, nine coming in the UEFA Cup competition – including a dynamic four goals in a 6-1 home win over Kuusysi Lahti and a smartly-taken hat-trick against Swarovski Tirol.

Dean effectively took over from the former West Bromwich Albion, Coventry City and England international striker Cyrille Regis as leader of Villa's attack and, partnering Damian Atkinson and occasionally Dwight Yorke, he top scored in each of his three seasons with the club.

He struck home 17 in 1992–93 when Villa finished runners-up to Manchester United in the Premiership; he notched 16 the following term including a hat-trick in a 5-0 home win over Swindon Town and bagged another 17 in 1994–95, scoring winners against his future club Nottingham Forest (2-1 at The City Ground) and Tottenham Hotspur (1-0 at Villa Park). His brace also earned a victory at one of his lucky grounds, Hillsborough, when Sheffield Wednesday were beaten 2-1.

In July 1995 Dean moved to a hotter climate, joining the Turkish club Galatasaray for £2.25 million. He remained there for 12 months before returning to England to assist Nottingham Forest (recruited by manager Stuart Pearce for £1.5 million), later plying his trade with Sheffield United, then the Portuguese giants Benfica (signed for £500,000 in December 1998) and finally Bradford City, eventually retiring as a player in July 2001 after more than 20 years in the game.

He then held the position of first-team coach under ex-Liverpool midfielder Graeme Souness at both Ewood Park and St James' Park, and in 2007 was appointed assistant manager of the Welsh National team.

In 1994 a case began at the High Court (London) involving defender Paul Elliott (Chelsea) and Dean Saunders (then of Aston Villa). It revolved around a tackle by Dean (who was playing for Liverpool at the time) on Elliott, which effectively ended the latter's playing career. Elliott lost the case and was faced with a legal bill of £500,000.

Ron Saunders

Date of birth: 6 November 1932, Birkenhead

Aston Villa record:
Manager: June 1974–February 1982

Played for: Everton, Tonbridge, Gillingham, Portsmouth, Watford, Charlton Athletic, Yeovil Town

Also managed: Yeovil Town, Norwich City, Manchester City, Birmingham City, West Bromwich Albion

As a player – a real tough, rugged, centre-forward – Ron Saunders scored well over 200 goals in the space of 13 years while serving with Everton, Tonbridge, Gillingham, Portsmouth, Watford and Charlton Athletic.

He commenced his career at Goodison Park in 1947 and turned professional in 1951 but found it hard going on Merseyside, making only three appearances before having a spell with Tonbridge. He returned to League action with Gillingham in May 1957 and switched to Portsmouth in September of the following year.

He was leading marksman for six consecutive seasons at Fratton Park and it was largely his goals that won Pompey the Third Division Championship in 1962. He remains their third highest scorer to this day with a total of 155 goals in League and Cup competitions.

In September 1964 Ron moved to Watford; he then assisted Charlton from August 1965 until his retirement in April 1967. At that point he took over as general manager of Yeovil Town and thereafter was in charge of Oxford United (February-July 1969), Norwich City (July 1969 to December 1973) and Manchester City (December 1973 to April 1974). He guided Norwich to the Second Division Championship in 1972 and to League Cup runners-up a year later, while Manchester City also reached the League Cup Final in 1974, beaten by Wolves.

He was recruited by Aston Villa in June 1974, taking over the hot seat from Vic Crowe. And there's no doubt he did a superb job during his eight years in charge.

Ron then became the first manager to lead three different teams to successive League Cup Finals when Villa won the trophy in his first season, beating his former club Norwich City in the 1975 Final and two years later the same trophy was won again, this time at Everton's expense, although it took Villa three attempts to see off another of Ron's old clubs.

He signed some brilliant footballers in his first three years, including striker Andy Gray, midfielder Dennis Mortimer, defenders Allan Evans and Ken McNaught, and goalkeeper Jimmy Rimmer. He later added some more splendid players, among them right-back Kenny Swain, midfield workhorse Des Bremner, winger Tony Morley and target man and goalscorer Peter Withe. And the majority of these served the club wonderfully well for several seasons.

There's no doubt that Ron assembled some very fine teams, despite his style and attitude not pleasing everyone.

His efforts and commitment paid dividends again in 1981 when he took the club to its first Championship success for 71 years. He used only 14 players in First Division action, seven of whom were ever presents. Villa beat Ipswich Town by four points to clinch the title by winning 26 of their 42 matches, their highest total ever in the top flight.

However, to the amazement of hundreds of diehard supporters, in February 1982 Ron resigned his position as team manager when Villa were on the verge of the club's greatest achievement, winning the European Cup. This was all down to an unconfirmed disagreement with the board of directors over his contract.

Surprisingly, he moved straight across the city to take over as manager of Villa's arch-rivals, Birmingham City. The Blues went down in 1984 but Ron got them back into the top flight at the first attempt before causing another major shock in Midlands football by walking out of St Andrew's in January 1986, at a time when Blues were again battling against relegation.

His next port of call was just five miles down the road to The Hawthorns, home of Blues's fellow strugglers, West Bromwich Albion.

He was unable to prevent the Baggies from sliding into the Second Division and a year later, after selling star-of-the-future Steve Bull and young Andy Thompson to Wolves, and with his team failing to win promotion, he was sacked in his 55th year.

Ron quit football at that point and chose to play golf instead. He now resides in Solihull and follows the football from his armchair rather than from a seat in the stand!

Jackie Sewell

Date of birth: 24 January 1927, Kells Village, Whitehaven, Cumberland

Aston Villa record:
Appearances: League 123, FA Cup 21, FA Charity Shield 1
Goals: League 36, FA Cup 4
Debut: League, 3 December 1956 v Sheffield United (a) drew 2–2

Also played for: Kells Miners' Welfare, Whitehaven Town, (wartime guest for Carlisle United, Workington), Notts County, Sheffield Wednesday, Hull City, Lusaka City (Zambia), Zambia (2 games as player-coach), England (6 full caps)

When I chatted with Jackie Sewell at an ex-player's reunion some years ago, he was rather disillusioned with the game of football, saying 'I don't go to watch matches as a fan anymore...I just make the odd trip as a scout to see a player at Derby or in non-League action. The unruly behaviour of certain supporters, those so-called morons, turns me off completely...and I'm sure several other people feel the same way. In my days as a player, I know for sure, that the majority of rival fans stood shoulder to shoulder on the terraces, enjoying some banter. After the game, irrespective of the result, they shook hands and went home. That doesn't happen now. Sorry, but to me the average supporter is not a lover of football and, another thing, the cost of a ticket for a match these days is obscene.'

Jackie played football for over 20 years. War broke out when he was at school and during the hostilities he became a Bevin Boy. Playing as a guest for Carlisle United and Workington, he signed amateur forms for Notts County in May 1942 and turned professional under manager Major Frank Buckley in October 1944.

He did very well with the Magpies and in a little over four years broke the club's individual scoring record, surpassing Tommy Keetley's tally of 94 goals.

A quick thinker with an excellent first touch and a strong right-foot shot, Jackie possessed plenty of craft and imagination and above all was a terrific opportunist.

There's no doubt his development at Meadow Lane was greatly assisted by England's Tommy Lawton. In the first season after the war (1946-47) Jackie hit 21 League goals and three years later, having helped County win the Third Division South title, he toured Canada with the FA, scoring six goals in seven games, including a hat-trick in a 9-0 win over Alberta.

In March 1951 Sheffield Wednesday stunned the football world by signing Jackie for a then British record fee of £34,500. This beat the previous record of £30,000 paid by Sunderland for Villa's Trevor Ford in 1950.

'I got drunk on cherry brandy trying to forget I was the costliest footballer in the country' recalled Jackie.

Unfortunately Jackie was unable to prevent the Owls from being relegated to Division Two, but his contribution of 23 goals in 1951-52 was a vital element in their Championship success. He spent four years at Hillsborough, netted 92 goals in 175 games and won six caps for England, scoring in that famous 6-3 defeat by Hungary at Wembley in 1953 and playing in the 7-1 defeat in Budapest the following year. He went on another FA tour, this time to Australia, and represented the Football League on four occasions, notching a hat-trick against the League of Ireland in 1954.

Aston Villa boss Eric Houghton signed Jackie for 20,000 in December 1955. After 18 months of exceptionally-fine play he gained an FA Cup-winners' medal in 1957 when Villa beat Manchester United 2-1 in the Final, Jackie getting the better of the midfield exchanges with United's Billy Whelan and Duncan Edwards.

After Villa had been demoted from the First Division in 1959, Jackie played only twice more for the first team before losing his place to Bobby Thomson.

At that point he was sold to Hull City for £5,000 (October 1959), where he remained until September 1961 when he was appointed senior player-coach of Zambia-based Lusaka City, a position he held until May 1964.

Thereafter he served as player-coach/manager of Zambia's national team, skippering the side twice. He also coached in the Northern Rhodesia and Belgian Congo and celebrated the latter country's independence before returning to England, where he worked as a car salesman for Bristol Street Motors in West Bridgford, Nottingham (1973 to 1987). Jackie now lives in retirement in the village of Wilford, Nottingham.

One interesting point is that Jackie was relegated from the top Division on four occasions: twice with Sheffield Wednesday (1951 and 1955) and once each with Aston Villa (1959) and Hull City (1960).

In a fine career, Jackie netted almost 250 goals in 550 matches, 228 coming in 510 League games alone and this despite suffering a baffling loss of form when least expected.

His son, Paul, became a top-flight golfer in Nottingham.

Gary Shaw

Date of birth: 21 January 1961, Castle Bromwich, Birmingham

Aston Villa record:
Appearances: League 158+7, FA Cup 11, League Cup 16+1, European 17, others 2
Goals: League 59, FA Cup 4, League Cup 6, European 9
Debut: League, 26 August 1978 v Bristol City (a) lost 1–0

Also played for: North Warwickshire Boys, Erdington & Saltley Boys, Coleshill Town Colts, Coleshill Town, Warwickshire & District Schools, Blackpool (loan), BK Copenhagen (Denmark), FC Klagenfurt (Austria), Sheffield Wednesday (loan), Walsall, Kilmarnock, Shrewsbury Town, Ernst Borel FC (Hong Kong), England (9 Youth and 7 Under-21 caps)

Over the years Aston Villa have had some great goalscoring partnerships, especially between the two World Wars, and the Peter Withe-Gary Shaw pairing during the 1980-81, 1981-82 and 1982-83 seasons was one of the best, certainly since World War Two.

Although they didn't play together in every single game, those three campaigns brought Shaw and Withe a total of 58 goals apiece – and they helped Villa win the Football League Championship, European Cup and European Cup-Winners' Cup.

Football mad from an early age, the blond-haired Shaw represented his school and starred in all the local school's representative games as well as playing for his county (Warwickshire) and having a few games for Coleshill Town before joining Aston Villa as an apprentice in July 1977, turning professional on his 18th birthday in January 1979 – having already tasted League action in his first local derby against West Bromwich Albion.

He netted his first hat-trick for the club in December 1979 in a 4-1 win over Bristol City at Ashton Gate – against the team where he made his senior debut 16 months earlier – and the following season he and his ally Withe started giving experienced and world-class defenders up and down the country a torrid time, as Villa clinched the League title for the first time in 71 years.

In 1980-81 Shaw received the PFA Young Footballer of the Year award, and when Villa lifted the coveted European Cup in Rotterdam 12 months later he was voted as the Player of the Tournament, having once again teased and tormented some quality defenders on the European circuit.

Honoured by England at Youth-team level, he also gained seven Under-21 caps – the first against the Republic of Ireland – between 1980 and 1983, and he came mighty close to winning a full international call-up in 1981 when he was twice named as a reserve.

Sharp, incisive, quick over the ground with a distinct knack of being in the right place at the right time (in sight of goal), Shaw scored some cracking goals during his professional career, which spanned 13 years before he was forced to retire in 1992 through injury at the age of 31 after having six knee operations.

He averaged a goal every two-and-a-half games for Villa and had his best season, in terms of marksmanship, in 1982-83 when he netted 24 times, including 17 in Division One, a hat-trick in a 4-2 European Cup home win over Dinamo Bucharest, when Villa went out in the quarter-finals to Juventus, and one against Barcelona, which helped set up a 3-1 aggregate victory in the Super Cup.

Forced to miss the whole of the 1984-85 season because of that niggling right knee of his, Shaw was never the same player again, and after a loan spell with Blackpool (February-March 1988) he left Villa Park to join BK Copenhagen at the end of that 1987-88 season. He later assisted clubs in Austria and Hong Kong, had brief spells with Sheffield Wednesday, Kilmarnock and Walsall (February-May 1990), before spending a season with his last club Shrewsbury Town. He ended his playing days with just over 100 goals under his belt in 302 club appearances – and one feels that he would have had a greater goal return if injuries hadn't affected his game as they did.

In recent years, Shaw, still looking young and reasonably fit, has worked as a match summariser for local radio stations, covering mainly Villa matches, home and away.

Nigel Sims

Date of birth: 9 August 1931, Coton-in-the-Elms, near Burton-on-Trent, Staffordshire

Aston Villa record:
Appearances: League 264, FA Cup 31, League Cup 14, FA Charity Shield 1
Debut: League, 19 March 1956 v Burnley (h), won 2-0

Also played for: Coton Swifts, Stapenhill FC, Wolverhampton Wanderers, Arsenal (guest), Peterborough United, Toronto City (Canada), Toronto Italia (Canada), England XI (1 app)

Initially, goalkeeper Nigel Sims was third choice at Molineux, behind England international Bert Williams and Dennis Parsons, but when the latter moved to Villa Park in September 1952, Sims became Williams's deputy.

Joining Wolves as a youngster and signing professional in the summer of 1948, he made his first League appearance against Sheffield United at Bramall Lane in April 1949 when Williams was sidelined with a back injury.

Signed up for National Service, Sims played in several representative games for the army and in April 1954 played for an England XI against Young England at Highbury, in the then annual challenge match ahead of the FA Cup Final. Later in his career he kept goal for the Football League against the League of Ireland at Elland Road, Leeds (October 1957).

After spending almost eight years at Molineux, during which time he managed only 39 competitive appearances, Sims followed in the footsteps of his former teammate Parsons and signed for Aston Villa in March 1956.

Manager Eric Houghton handed him his senior debut against Burnley almost immediately, Sims taking over the duties from Welsh international Keith Jones. He remained first choice in the side until 1962 and went on to serve the club for just over eight years.

Extremely agile for a big man – he stood 6ft 1in tall and weighed 14st – Sims had a massive pair of hands, was a fine shot-stopper, and he was certainly both brave and confident, always giving assurance to the defenders in front of him.

In a game against rivals West Bromwich Albion at The Hawthorns he went up to collect a high ball from a left-wing corner and in doing so took out two of his own defenders, full-back Doug Winton and centre-half Jimmy Dugdale, both of whom required lengthy treatment from the trainer.

Sims was quite outstanding during the 1956-57 season, which ended in triumph for both himself and Aston Villa when the FA Cup was won at Wembley, double-chasing Manchester United being defeated 2-1. That afternoon Sims pulled off some terrific saves, including one superb effort from Duncan Edwards, and was only beaten late on by a looping header from Tommy Taylor when United were throwing everyone forward in search of an equaliser.

Over a period of four and a half years, from his debut day in March 1956 until December 1960, Sims missed only nine games out of a possible 201 played by Villa in senior competitions, and in 1958 his efforts earned him the Villa Terrace Trophy award (chosen by the supporters). He helped Villa win the Second Division Championship in 1959-60, conceding a fraction over a goal a game, and the following year he was the recipient of a League Cup-winners' medal after Rotherham United had been eclipsed 3-2 over two legs in the first-ever Final of that tournament. Sims, in fact, played in the first game at Millmoor, which Villa lost 2-0, but missed the return fixture through injury, replaced by yet another former Wolves 'keeper, Geoff Sidebottom.

Continuing to perform with authority, Sims contributed greatly to Villa's cause during the early 1960s but eventually, after appearing in well over 300 first-class matches, he was replaced between the posts on a permanent basis by Sidebottom, and then, after Colin Withers had joined the club, he knew his time was up and switched his allegiance to Peterborough United in September 1964, signed on a free transfer. He later spent several years plying his trade with two Canadian clubs before returning to England in 1971 where he subsequently entered the insurance business, based in Wolverhampton, before retiring to Swansea, where he resides today.

A regular visitor to Villa Park during the 1980s and 90s, Sims is still regarded by many as one of Villa's finest post-war goalkeepers.

Tommy Smart

Date of birth: 20 September 1896, Blackheath, Worcestershire
Died: 10 June 1968, Dudley

Aston Villa record:
Appearances: League 405, FA Cup 47
Goals: League 8
Debut: League, 14 January 1920 v Everton (h) drew 2–2

Also played for: Blackheath Town, Halesowen Town, Brierley Hill Alliance, England (5 full caps)

Standing 6ft 2in tall and weighing 13st, the barrel-chested Tommy Smart – nicknamed 'Tic' – was a solid, uncompromising full-back, strong in all aspects of defensive play, fearsome in the tackle, a fine kicker of the ball, resilient in his approach and totally committed. One football correspondent wrote 'He was built like a buffalo and kicked like a mule.'

On the field of play Smart was always urging his teammates on, clapping his hands and giving them encouragement, and quite regularly supporters would hear him shout out his personal war cry of 'Thik Hai' (Hindustani language) when clearing his lines, having first heard this saying during his army service with the Staffordshire Regiment in India during World War One. He also served in Greece and Belgium and was a real character in the typical Black Country tradition, and the fans loved him.

After spending quite some time playing local non-League football with Blackheath Town and Halesowen, Smart, perhaps surprisingly, was signed by Aston Villa in January 1920 at the age of 25, and within three months he starred in an FA Cup Final, helping Villa beat Huddersfield Town 1-0 at Stamford Bridge. Four years later he played in his second Final, this time against Newcastle United in the first all-ticket game at Wembley, but on this occasion he had to settle for a runners'-up medal.

He certainly made rapid progress after taking over the right-back berth from the out of form Jack Thompson. He remained in the side as first choice for practically 12 years, injuries apart, and he proved to be one of the most consistent players in the side. Initially partnering Tommy Weston and then Ernest Blackburn, he was joined by Tommy Mort in 1922 and they quickly developed into one of the finest full-back pairings in the entire country, being affectionately known as 'Death and Glory.'

He scored eight goals, all penalties, for Villa, half of them in 1927-28. And four of his spot-kicks earned his team a point – the first from a 2-2 draw with Bolton in April 1926, his third in the local derby with Birmingham in March 1928 (1-1), his sixth at Bury in February 1929 (2-2) and his last at Manchester City in November 1933 (3-3).

In April 1921, after some outstanding displays for Villa, Smart was selected to play for England against Scotland at Hampden Park – the first of five full caps he gained for his country. He also represented the Football League versus the Scottish League in 1928 and played in three international trails (once for an England XI against Cradley Heath in 1929), and if it hadn't been for the likes of Tommy Clay (Tottenham, Hotspur), Warney Cresswell (Everton) and Eph Longworth (Liverpool), he would surely have won more senior caps than he did.

Smart, who would often turn up for a morning's training session wearing a grubby-looking flat cap, eventually handed over his right-back duties to Danny Blair in 1933, after making over 450 senior appearances for Villa – the second highest by a full-back in the club's history (behind Charlie Aitken). In fact, Smart currently lies in seventh place in the all-time list of appearance makers for Villa, and that is some achievement considering that during his playing days only two major competitions were in existence – the Football League and FA Cup.

Smart left Villa in May 1934 to join Brierley Hill, whom he served as player-coach. He then took a similar position with his former club Blackheath Town (August 1938) but quit football on the outbreak of World War Two. He was later employed at Marsh and Baxter, the famous sausage and pork pie manufacturers, for 17 years.

Smart was almost 72 when he died in 1968.

Leslie Smith

Date of birth: 23 March 1918, Ealing, London
Died: 20 May 1995, Lichfield, Staffordshire

Aston Villa record:
Appearances: League 191, FA Cup 16, Wartime 22
Goals: League 31, FA Cup 6, Wartime 3
Debut: FA Cup, 5 January 1946 v Coventry City (a) lost 2-1

Also played for: Horn & Petersham FC, Brentford (2 spells), Wimbledon, Hayes, (wartime guest for Chelsea, Leicester City, Manchester City, West Bromwich Albion), England (1 full, 10 Wartime and 3 Victory caps)

Outside-left Leslie Smith was only 17 years of age when he played for Wimbledon against Bishop Auckland in the 1935 FA Amateur Cup Final in front of almost 100,000 spectators at Wembley. He finished on the losing side that afternoon, but the experience of playing in such a high-profile match set him in good stead for a splendid career, especially with Aston Villa.

Born at the end of World War One, Smith played for Horn & Petersham FC in the Middlesex League before signing as a junior with Brentford in 1933, transferring to Wimbledon in August 1934. He moved to Hayes in July 1935, then returned to Griffin Park to sign as a full-time professional with the Bees in March 1936.

During the war he played as a guest for four big-name clubs, including Villa's near neighbours West Brom, and in October 1945 he was lured to Villa Park by manager Alex Massie, who paid £7,500 for his signature, money well spent, so it proved.

Smith went straight into the first team, accompanying Bob Iverson on the left wing in a Football League North encounter at Plymouth, setting up one of George Edwards's goals in a 3-0 win. He went on to play in 30 games that season, eight in the FA Cup when he scored four times in both legs against Coventry City in the third round and the two matches versus Millwall in round four, the second of which resulted in a 9-1 win.

A precocious talent, Smith (the fans called him 'Schmidtz') was certainly Villa's 'Will-o'-the-Wisp' winger, and he thrilled the crowds with his confidence, exquisite ball control, wing wizardry, dash and goalscoring technique that had earned him England recognition at senior level.

He appeared in 13 Wartime and Victory internationals and gained one senior cap for England in a 2-0 win over Romania in Bucharest in May 1939, when he was joined in attack by Villa's Frank Broome. He also represented the FA in Romania, Italy and Yugoslavia, and played for the Combined Services and the RAF during World War Two.

In his first season at Villa Park he collected a League North runners'-up medal, and after that he went from strength to strength, proving to be a constant thorn in opposing defences' sides. An ever present in 1946-47 and 1947-48, during which time he scored seven and nine goals respectively, he missed only four League games in 1948-49 but was sidelined with a niggling knee injury in 1949-50, allowing Billy Goffin to have a few outings on the left flank.

Sidelined again during the 1950-51 campaign, when he missed 20 League matches, Goffin once more acting as his deputy. Smith's last season at Villa Park saw him appear in only eight games. He was transferred back to Brentford in June 1952 and 14 months later returned to the Midlands to take over as player-manager of Kidderminster Harriers, a position he held until June 1954 when he was asked by his former international colleague Stan Cullis, then manager of Wolves, to do some scouting for the club. In later years Smith organised charity matches for the Aston Villa old stars team (1960-65) while also running a thriving electrical business in Aston.

In later life he retired to live in Lichfield, where he died at the age of 77, having attended his last game at Villa Park as the match sponsor's guest in 1993.

Gareth Southgate

Date of birth: 3 September 1970, Watford

Aston Villa record:
Appearances: League 192+1, FA Cup 20, League Cup 17, European 13, others 2
Goals: League 7, FA Cup 1, League Cup 1
Debut: Premiership, 19 August 1995 v Manchester United (h) won 3–1

Also played for: Crystal Palace, Middlesbrough, England (57 full caps)
Managed: Middlesbrough

Gareth Southgate began his career playing in central midfield as captain of Crystal Palace, leading the Eagles to the 1994 Division One title. After the south-London club's relegation from the Premiership, he moved to Aston Villa for £2.5 million in July 1995, having made over 150 appearances over four seasons for the London club.

At Villa Park he was immediately converted into a centre-back and formed part of a formidable defence, playing alongside Ugo Ehiogu and Paul McGrath initially, and later with the Turk Ozalan Alpay, occasionally Gareth Barry and Colin Calderwood.

In his first season he gained a League Cup-winners' medal when Villa qualified for Europe by defeating Leeds United 3-0 in the Final, and in 1997-98 he was outstanding as Villa reached the quarter-finals of the UEFA Cup, beaten over two legs by Atletico Madrid.

Southgate played in every Premiership game during the 1998-99 season, and he continued to star at the heart of the defence in 1999-2000 when Ehiogu was still his main partner. However, he handed in a transfer request just before Euro 2000, citing a desire to move to a more ambitious club. John Gregory, the then manager of Villa, attempted to keep his club captain, but after a year on the transfer list he let Southgate move (perhaps surprisingly) to Middlesbrough for £6.5 million (July 2001), becoming Steve McClaren's first signing for the club.

This move, no doubt, was due to the fact that two of his former colleagues, Ehiogu and midfielder George Boateng, were by now bedded in at the Riverside Stadium, and he immediately became a firm favourite with the fans, winning the club's Player of the Year award in his first season after a series of assured displays.

Handed the captaincy for 2002-03 when Paul Ince left, he became the first Middlesbrough captain to lift a major trophy when he helped them win the League Cup in February 2004, although his season ended soon after that triumph when he suffered knee ligament damage. There were strong rumours that Southgate might move to Manchester United following Rio Ferdinand's ban for missing a drug test in January 2004, but it turned out to be nothing more than paper talk, and he later committed his final playing years to Middlesbrough, eventually taking over as boss from McClaren at the Riverside in the summer of 2006 – although he didn't hold a UEFA Pro Licence (to become a Premiership manager). Southgate, who became the first player-manager in the Premiership for seven years, did well in his first season in charge at Boro.

Capped 57 times by England at senior level, Southgate won his 50th at Villa Park against Portugal in September 2002. He made his debut as a substitute against Portugal in 1996, was in Terry Venables's squad for Euro 1996 and played a towering role as England reached the semi-finals. However, Southgate's missed penalty against Germany in the semi-final sent the hosts crashing out. He later played in the 1998 World Cup and Euro 2000 tournaments but failed to get a game in the 2002 World Cup in Japan and South Korea.

During 2003-04 Southgate became an author, penning *Woody & Nord: A Football Friendship* with his very good friend Andy Woodman. The book describes an enduring friendship between them both, initially forged in the Crystal Palace youth team, and the publication won the Sporting Book of the Year award for 2004, presented by the National Sporting Club.

Besides his obvious footballing interests, Gareth is also a keen fan of the New York Mets.

Howard Spencer

Date of birth: 23 August 1875, Edgbaston, Birmingham
Died: 12 January 1940, Sutton Coldfield

Aston Villa record:
Appearances: League 259, FA Cup 35, Charity Shield 1
Goals: League 2
Debut: League, 13 October 1894 v West Bromwich Albion (h) won 3-1

Also played for: Albert Road School (Handsworth, Birmingham), Stamford FC (Birmingham), Birchfield All Saints, Birchfield Trinity, England (6 full caps)

Howard Spencer was one of Aston Villa's all-time greatest players. An incredibly-gifted defender, he was known as the 'Prince of full-backs' and 'Gentleman Howard' during his hugely-successful time at the club and was renowned for his sportsmanship.

He gained three League Championship-winning medals, in 1896, 1897 and 1900, and appeared in three FA Cup-winning teams, in 1895 versus West Bromwich Albion, 1897 against Everton and 1905 versus Newcastle United. He captained the side in the latter victory when he was accompanied at full-back by the evergreen Albert Evans. Indeed, this pairing was quite magnificent when Villa completed the coveted League and Cup double in 1896–97. Prior to that Jim Welford had played alongside him.

Howard was also capped six times at senior level by England, playing in his first international against Wales in March 1897 along with his Villa teammates Charlie Athersmith and Jack Reynolds, and his last against Scotland in April 1905 when two more Villa stars, Alec Leake and Joe Bache, also featured.

Many felt this was paltry reward for a player of his quality, although he did have several other great full-backs to contend with for a place in the national team, among them Billy Williams (West Bromwich Albion), his Villa colleague Jimmy Crabtree, Billy Oakley of the Corinthians, the great Bob Crompton of Blackburn Rovers, Harry Thickett of Sheffield United and cricketer-footballer Charles Fry of Southampton.

He did, however, represent the Football League on nine occasions between 1896 and 1906 and played in five international trials (1896–1903).

Signed by Villa as an amateur from Birchfield Trinity in April 1892, Howard turned professional two years later and became a regular in the side in 1894, remaining so (injuries, illness and international call-ups excluded) until 1906.

Spencer was a brilliant positional player, never giving his winger much space at all and always seeming to control the threat of top-class outside-lefts such as internationals Alf Milward of Everton and Fred Spiksley of Sheffield Wednesday.

He was scrupulously fair and was never known to commit a ruthless foul. He gave away only two penalties, one for handball, and his forté was his anticipation. He was also a strong kicker of the ball and when in possession, and not under too much pressure from an opponent, he always tried to find a colleague when clearing his lines rather than just thumping the ball aimlessly downfield and hoping it would land near a teammate. However, Howard did, at times, take the easy way out, playing safe by simply belting the ball high into the crowd so that his defence could get back into position.

He scored only two senior goals for Villa, both against Midlands rivals Wolves – the first in the 2–2 home League draw in April 1895 which helped salvage a point from a 2–2 draw, and his second which clinched a 2–1 victory at Molineux on Boxing Day 1896.

He did, though, come mighty close to scoring twice more – firstly against Burnley (away) in November 1895 when he bent the crossbar and then against Derby County at the Baseball Ground in September 1899, when his long-range effort crashed against an upright.

Howard continued to play for Villa until November 1907. He immediately became a shareholder of the club and in July 1909 was elected to the Board of Directors, remaining in office until May 1936.

In all, Howard's association with Aston Villa football club lasted 42 years.

Nigel Spink

Date of birth: 8 August 1958, Chelmsford, Essex

Aston Villa record:
Appearances: League 357+4, FA Cup 28, League Cup 45, Europe 25+1
Debut: League, 26 December 1979 v Nottingham Forest (a) lost 2-1

Also played for: West Ham United, Chelmsford City, West Bromwich Albion, Millwall, Forest Green Rovers, England (1 full and 2 B caps)
Managed: Forest Green Rovers (joint)

Goalkeeper Nigel Spink began his career as a schoolboy with West Ham United but soon moved to Chelmsford City in 1974 and then, five months after his 18th birthday in January 1977, he joined Aston Villa on a five-year professional contract for a fee of £40,000, although at the time he was told by manager Ron Saunders that he would be a reserve team player for perhaps two years or more!

Surprisingly, but realistically owing to the excellent form shown by first John Burridge and then Jimmy Rimmer, and occasionally Jake Findlay, it was almost five years before Nigel got his big break in the first team, and it arrived on the biggest stage of all – in the European Cup Final.

Barely 10 minutes into the 1982 Final against Bayern Munich in Rotterdam, Villa's first-choice goalkeeper at the time, Rimmer, was injured and Nigel, one of the named substitutes, was called off the bench to take his place – having made only one previous appearance in the first team against the reigning European Cup holders Nottingham Forest on Boxing Day 1979. Nigel performed superbly, keeping a clean sheet and helping Villa win the game 1-0, courtesy of a tap-in goal scored in the second-half by Peter Withe. The following season he helped Villa beat the crack Spanish side Barcelona over two legs to win the European Super Cup.

Nigel eventually gained a regular place in Villa's League side halfway through the 1982-83 season but then came under pressure from Mervyn Day before Nigel bounced back to reclaim the number-one position, which he held confidently and virtually unchallenged for seven years – until Les Sealey arrived during the 1991-92 season. He was in excellent form in 1987-88 when promotion was gained to the First Division (following demotion the previous season) and he was an ever present when Villa finished runners-up to Liverpool in the First Division in 1989-90, conceding a goal a game.

Thereafter he had the Australian Mark Bosnich to contend with and eventually – after accumulating just over 450 senior appearances, including the 1994 League Cup Final victory over Manchester United – Nigel moved to arch-rivals West Bromwich Albion on a free transfer in January 1996 (almost two decades after first joining Villa). He was, at that time, the oldest player ever to join the Baggies – aged 37 years, 176 days.

He spent 18 months at The Hawthorns and then had a two-and-a-half year spell with Millwall (from September 1997), playing his last League game against Wigan Athletic in January 2000 at the age of 41 years and 160 days. This was, in fact, Nigel's 540th game in all club competitions.

He retired from first-class football in the summer of 2000 and became a goalkeeping coach with Birmingham City, later holding a similar position with Swindon Town and then Northampton Town before assisting Conference side Forest Green Rovers in August 2001, taking over as joint team manager for season 2002-03 while also assisting various clubs in a coaching capacity.

Nigel, 6ft 2in tall and weighing almost 15st, was an apprentice plasterer before joining Villa. He could withstand the fiercest of challenges, handled the ball well (especially the high-floated crosses), was a fine shot-stopper, commanded his area with authority and, above all, was always confident in his own ability.

In June 1983 he was capped by England during a tour of Australia, coming on as a second-half substitute for Peter Shilton in a 1-1 draw in Melbourne. His Aston Villa colleague Gordon Cowans and ex-teammate John Gregory played in the same match.

Nigel is also a very useful cricketer, and he now lives in Sutton Coldfield.

Ronnie Starling

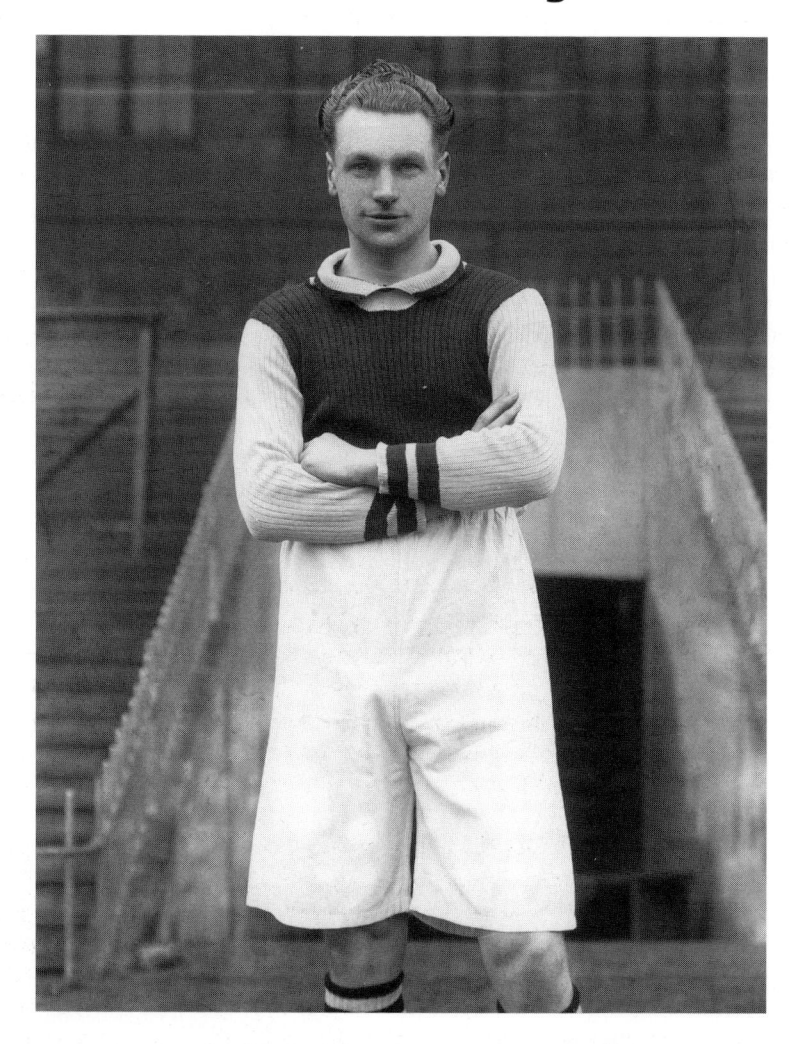

Date of birth: 11 October 1909, Pelaw-on-Tyne, near Gateshead
Died: 17 December 1991, Sheffield

Aston Villa record:
Appearances: League 88, FA Cup 11, Wartime 142
Goals: League 11, FA Cup 1, Wartime 4
Debut: League, 9 January 1937 v Burnley (h) drew 0-0

Also played for: Usworth Colliery, Washington Colliery, Hull City Newcastle United, Sheffield Wednesday, (wartime guest for Northampton Town, Hereford United, Nottingham Forest [also player-coach], Walsall), Sheffield Wednesday, Beighton FC, England (2 full caps)

Norton Jones, writing in the Aston Villa versus Wolverhampton Wanderers programme, printed on the 24 February 1976, described Ronnie Starling as being 'A star of skill, class and international ability....a gifted artist who rose from the humble launching pad of a local miners' team in the North East to reach the pinnacle of his profession.'

Nicknamed 'Flutterfoot', he once netted eight goals in a junior game while registered with Usworth Colliery and notched 45 in one season playing for Washington Colliery. After an unsuccessful trial at St James' Park, Newcastle, he signed as an amateur for Hull City in July 1925, turning professional two years later. He scored 16 goals in 53 appearances for the Tigers and followed up with eight in 53 outings for the club that had rejected him, Newcastle United (from May 1930), before giving Sheffield Wednesday tremendous service for almost five years, signed for a bargain fee of just £3,250 in May 1932.

A huge favourite with the supporters, he was Wednesday's skipper in their 1935 FA Cup Final victory over West Bromwich Albion, and he also helped the Owls win the FA Charity Shield at Arsenal's expense that same year.

A terrific footballing strategist whose tactics could turn the course of a game in a matter of minutes (even seconds), he possessed all the tricks of the trade and often produced them to the full out on the field of play.

At his peak Ronnie was rated better than the great Scottish international Alex James and one biography noted that he was a 'ball-playing genius'.

He left Hillsborough for Villa Park for a record fee of £7,500 in January 1937 and helped Villa win the Second Division Championship the following season. Then in April/May 1944 he starred as Villa won the Wartime League (North) Cup, beating a very strong Blackpool side 5-4 on aggregate over two legs. Ronnie, in fact, lined up at inside-left in the first game and at left-half in the second.

During his professional career Ronnie appeared in both wing-half positions, in the three centre-forward berths (preferring inside-left) and also had the off game as a left-winger. An ever present in 1937-38 (when Villa won the Second Division title), Ronnie was often headline news and reports state that he was outstanding in home victories over Luton Town (4-1), his former club Sheffield Wednesday (4-3, when he scored twice), Stockport County (7-1) and Swansea Town (4-0), and those away at Bradford Park Avenue (2-1) and Coventry City, when his goal proved decisive (1-0).

After successfully coming through an England trial (1932), Ronnie gained two full caps for his country, both against Scotland at Hampden Park – the first in April 1933 (lost 2-1 in front of 134,710 fans) and the second in April 1937 when a crowd of 149,547 saw the Scots win 3-1.

He also appeared for a selected International XI against a District XI in September 1940 and played in three FA Cup semi-finals with different clubs in the space of nine years: for Hull City versus Arsenal (1930), for Sheffield Wednesday versus Burnley (1935) and for Aston Villa versus Preston North End (1938). He was a winner just once, in 1935.

When he retired from first-class football in the summer of 1946, Ronnie had bagged 65 goals in 431 League and FA Cup games. He made over 200 more appearances during World War Two, including 142 for Villa. He actually went on playing at a lower level until he was 41 years of age, kicking his last ball in anger for Beighton in April 1952. He worked and lived in Sheffield for the rest of his life, running a newsagents shop near the Hillsborough ground for over 20 years, and was a regular at Wednesday's home matches.

It must be said that besides being a great footballer, Ronnie could preach a sermon as good as any vicar.

Steve Staunton

Date of birth: 19 January 1969, Drogheda

Aston Villa record:

Appearances:	League 270+11, FA Cup 23+1, League Cup 22+2, Europe 17+1, others 3
Goals:	League 16, FA Cup 1, League Cup 1, others 1
Debut:	League, 17 August 1991 v Sheffield Wednesday (a) won 3–2
Also played for:	Liverpool, Bradford City, Crystal Palace, Coventry City, Walsall, Republic of Ireland (2 Youth, 4 Under-21 and 102 full caps)
Managed:	Republic of Ireland

Steve Staunton was spotted by Liverpool playing for Dundalk, with whom he won an Irish League Championship medal.

Signed at the age of 17 by Kenny Dalglish for £20,000 in September 1986, he competed in the second XI and had a loan spell with Bradford City (late 1987) before making his first-team debut for the Reds in September 1988. Putting in an impressive performance, he stayed in the side for the remainder of the season, despite his relative inexperience compared with other senior players at Anfield.

Steve, in fact, helped comfort bereaved families after the Hillsborough disaster in April 1989 before producing an outstanding display when that fateful FA Cup semi-final was replayed a month later as Liverpool beat Nottingham Forest 3–1. He then did the business when rivals Everton were defeated 3–2 in the Final.

Steve also made his international debut for the Republic of Ireland in the same season, lining up against Spain in Seville, the first of a record 102 caps. And the following campaign he helped Liverpool win the Championship, having been bitterly disappointed to miss out on a winners' medal 12 months earlier when Arsenal won the 'last match' decider.

Steve, who was the youngest player in the Irish squad at the 1990 World Cup Finals, when Jack Charlton's men raised a few eyebrows with some impressive displays in Italy, spent one more season at Anfield before switching to Aston Villa in August 1991 on a free transfer.

He quickly settled in at Villa Park, scored the winning goal on his debut at Sheffield Wednesday and gained a League Cup-winners' medal in 1994, thus completing the domestic treble, and that summer he starred with his Irish teammates in another World Cup, this time in the US. Two years later he added a second League Cup-winners' prize to his tally, maintaining a high level of consistency in the process, as he took his senior appearance tally at club and international levels past the 350 mark.

Despite Ireland failing to qualify for Euro '96 and the 1998 World Cup Finals in France, Steve remained a regular in the national team, but with his contract set to expire at Villa Park he chose to move back to Anfield in July 1998.

His second spell with Liverpool lasted two years, and after a loan spell at Crystal Palace he returned to Villa Park in December 2000, while at the same time he took over the skipper's armband from Roy Keane at international level.

Steve announced his retirement from international football after the 2002 World Cup Finals, having been the only player to appear in all of the Republic of Ireland's 13 matches. He also became Villa's most capped player and took his overall tally of full caps to 102.

Never a prolific goalscorer from either defence or midfield, he nevertheless netted some spectacular long-range efforts with his trusty left foot, one memorable strike coming in the 3–0 defeat of Northern Ireland in March 1993 – direct from a corner.

Steve joined Coventry in August 2003 and two years later became player-assistant coach of Walsall. In January 2006 he was appointed manager of the Republic of Ireland, replacing Brian Kerr, having skippered the Saddlers to a 2–0 win over Blackpool on New Year's Eve 2005 – his 689th and final game as a professional.

On taking over his country, Steve appointed Villa's reserve-team coach Kevin McDonald as his senior coach and also asked Sir Bobby Robson to assist as a consultant.

He started well enough, seeing Ireland beat Sweden 3–0 in March 2006, but two defeats quickly followed, the second a 4–0 thrashing by Holland in August – Ireland's worst at home for 40 years.

Prior to the Dutch game, Steve was confronted by a man with a gun outside the team's hotel. The 31-year-old assailant was arrested at a nearby beach and released by police the following day. He apparently used an imitation Uzi machine gun and his motives remain unknown.

Ireland then suffered their worst defeat ever, whipped 5–2 by Cyprus in Nicosia in a European Championship qualifier. Steve witnessed the debacle from the stands, following his sending-off in a previous game versus Germany.

Clem Stephenson

Date of birth: 6 February 1890, New Delaval, County Durham
Died: 24 October 1961, Huddersfield

Aston Villa record:
Appearances: League 192, FA Cup 24
Goals: League 85, FA Cup 11
Debut: League, 25 March 1910 v Tottenham Hotspur (h) won 4–0

Also played for: Bedlington, New Delaval Villa, West Stanley, Blyth Spartans, Durham City, Stourbridge (loan), Leeds City (guest), South Shields & District, Huddersfield Town, England (1 full cap)
Managed: Huddersfield Town

Clem Stephenson captained Aston Villa, Huddersfield and England during a wonderfully-successful career. He twice won the FA Cup with Villa (1913 and 1920), then, as a Huddersfield player, gained three League Championship-winning medals in succession (1924, 1925 and 1926) and won a third Cup medal in 1922. He also collected two Cup runners'-up medals after defeats in 1930 and 1938.

Not the quickest of players, Clem joined Villa for £175 in March 1910 as an inside-forward, having previously occupied all five frontline positions with his previous clubs.

His career at Villa Park effectively covered 11 years, broken up by World War One and a spell with Stourbridge.

He appeared in 216 matches and scored 85 goals, his first on his debut in a 4-0 home win over Spurs a few days after signing.

Clem's career at Villa Park began just as goalscoring legend Harry Hampton's was nearing its end. He soon acquired a reputation for precise and skilful play; his passes were said to be 'as sweet as stolen kisses'.

His first piece of silverware came in 1913 when, playing alongside Hampton and Joe Bache, he helped Villa beat the League champions Sunderland 1-0 – this being the only occasion in English football history when the Final was contested between the top two clubs in the Football League.

Prior to the game Clem dreamed that Villa would win with a headed goal from Tommy Barber. That is precisely what happened – Barber steering home the decisive goal from Charlie Wallace's corner on 75 minutes in front of almost 122,000 fans at Crystal Palace.

In this same year Clem represented the Birmingham FA against London, and in 1914 he played in the Cup semi-final when Villa lost to Liverpool. After the war he gained his second Cup-winners' medal when his future club Huddersfield were defeated 1-0 thanks to another headed goal.

Clem remained at Villa Park until March 1921 when he was transferred to Leeds Road, manager Herbert Chapman paying £3,000 for his services. In fact, during the war, Clem had guested for Leeds City, who at the time were managed by Chapman.

As a result of making irregular payments to other guest players like Charlie Buchan of Sunderland, Franny Walden of Spurs and Billy Hampson of Newcastle, Chapman's career at Leeds came to an unhappy end and led to the dissolution of the club in 1919.

However, when Chapman took over the reins at Huddersfield (August 1920), one of his first tasks was to secure Clem. This caused controversy at the time, but within two seasons Clem became the first player in the 20th century to win three Cup-winners' medals when Huddersfield pipped Preston 1-0.

Clem scored 20 goals in 105 of the 126 League games during Huddersfield's three Championship-winning campaigns, and his manager was moved to say 'I want to thank you personally for your play, your wholehearted efforts both on and off the field. I have never had such confidence in any captain of a team I have been associated with.'

Chapman welded Clem's assets together astutely and soon fielded one of the most successful League sides of all time. It was stubborn, disciplined and highly mobile, with Clem – as he had been with Villa – at the heart of everything.

In March 1924 Clem gained his only England cap (it should have been more) against Wales at Blackburn. England lost 2-1, and he was replaced for the next game by his old teammate at Villa Park, Billy Walker.

Clem played his last game for Huddersfield against Bury in April 1929. Soon afterwards he took over from Jack Chaplin as manager at Leeds Road and went on to become Huddersfield's longest-serving boss, holding office for 13 years – from May 1929 until June 1942. In that time the Terriers claimed a record 10-1 win over Blackpool (1930), and a record crowd of 67,037 packed into Leeds Road to see an FA Cup-tie against Arsenal (1932).

After retiring from football, Clem became a caterer in Huddersfield and was 71 when he died in the Yorkshire town in 1961.

Clem's brothers George and Jimmy also played for Villa in the 1920s.

Alec Talbot

Date of birth: 13 July 1902, Cannock, Staffordshire
Died: 13 August 1975, Stourbridge

Aston Villa record:
Appearances: League 240, FA Cup 23
Goals: League 7
Debut: FA Cup, 2 February 1924 v Swansea Town (a) won 2-0

Also played for: West Hill School (Cannock), Cannock Colliery FC, Hednesford Prims, Hednesford Town, Bradford Park Avenue, Brierley Hill Alliance, Stourbridge (later player-manager)

Alec Talbot, a product of the coal-mining area of Staffordshire, learned his footballing skills by dribbling a ball in and out of sticks two feet apart on a patch of land in the upper part of Bradbury Lane in Hednesford.

This was typical of the application and attention to detail of a man with football in his blood.

His father, Jack, played wing-half for Hednesford Town in the 1890s and two of his uncles, inside-forward Alf and goalkeeper Arthur, also played at a junior level. Another relative, Ezekiah, was registered with Hednesford prior to 1914 and later played for Stafford Rangers, while Alec himself was the elder of four brothers, Ray, Horace and Les, who all played in the local district league. The youngest, Les, followed Alec into League football with first Blackburn Rovers, then Cardiff City and finally Walsall (1946), later coaching FC Haarlem in Holland.

Alec, the best of a very good and respected footballing family, served as a wing-half and centre-half with Hednesford Town from August 1921 before joining Aston Villa for £100 in April 1923, along with his best pal Teddy Bowen.

Alec made his first senior appearance in the claret-and-blue strip (in place of the injured George Blackburn) against Swansea Town in an FA Cup tie at the Vetch Field in February 1924, and did well in a 2-0 win.

That was the first of 238 senior games Alec played for the Villa, whom he served for 13 years, up to June 1936 when he was transferred to Bradford Park Avenue a month before his 34th birthday.

Long-striding, head held high, Alec was a supreme defender, a credit to the game both on and off the field. Teddy Bowen described him as being a player of 'poise, pluck and shrewdness with an artistic streak to go with free consistency.'

Unflurried, neat and sharp in style, Alec could also be a forceful player when the situation warranted, and he could ping out a pass with great precision up to 40 yards. He had confidence to spare but was never showy.

Surprisingly, for five years he was unable to hold down a regular place in the first team at Villa Park, making only 36 senior appearances in his first five years at the club. But after replacing Vic Milne at centre-half in November 1928, Alec remained a regular at the heart of the Villa defence until 1934 when Jimmy Allen was signed from Portsmouth.

Part of a wonderful middle line comprising Jimmy Gibson, himself and Joe Tate, and known affectionately as 'Wind, Sleet and Rain', Alec was an ever present in successive seasons of 1930-31 and 1931-32, and, in fact, had a run of 136 consecutive League appearances in the side from September 1929 to November 1933.

Unfortunately he failed to win a major prize with Villa, twice gaining League runners'-up medals in 1931 and 1933 and playing in two FA Cup semi-final defeats, by Portsmouth in 1929 and Manchester City in 1934. He appeared in an England international trial in 1931 but failed to get any further recognition, although he did represent the Football League against the Scottish League a year later.

After leaving Villa Park, Alec made only six appearances for Bradford Park Avenue before returning to the Midlands to sign for Brierley Hill Alliance, later assisting Stourbridge, firstly as a player and then as manager, before finally quitting football in 1947. He was then a vehicle inspector at the Austin car factory at Longbridge, Birmingham, where he worked until 1967.

Alec and Horace Talbot

Joe Tate

Date of birth: 4 August 1904, Old Hill, Worcestershire
Died: 18 May 1973, Cradley Heath, Worcestershire

Aston Villa record:
Appearances: League 180, FA Cup 13
Goals: League 2, FA Cup 2
Debut: League, 26 December 1927 v Derby County (a) lost 5-0

Also played for: Birch Coppice Primitives, Grainger's Lane Primitives, Round Oak Steelworks (Brierley Hill), Cradley Heath, Brierley Hill Alliance (player-manager), England (3 full caps)

Joe Tate, one-time inside-left, developed into an outstanding left-sided defender (an old-fashioned left-half) and a master tactician who always tried to play the ball on the ground rather than sending it high and not so handsome downfield in the hope it might find a teammate.

Described as being 'strong in attack and quick in recovery', he loved to participate in a triangular movement involving his inside-forward and winger (usually Billy Walker and Eric Houghton, at times his full-back Tommy Mort).

A member of Villa's famous middle line that also comprised Jimmy Gibson and Alex Talbot, he was quite outstanding for around five years (1928–33) and was an ever present in 1930-31, having missed just two League games the previous season.

The youngest of five brothers, Tate joined Villa for just £400 from Cradley Heath in April 1925. He was nurtured along in the reserves for nearly two and a half years, and he made his senior debut at centre-half in place of Dr Vic Milne in a 5-0 League walloping at Derby on Boxing Day 1927. He followed up by playing in two further defeats over the next four days before gaining a regular place in the first team in October 1928, following Frank Moss's departure to Cardiff City. Indeed, during that season he scored his first Villa goal – a real beauty in a resounding 6-1 home FA Cup win over Cardiff.

Tate's first League goal followed in October 1929 in a 3-0 home win over Leicester City and his second (and third strike overall) was scored in February 1931 against near-neighbours and FA Cup Finalists of that season, Birmingham, in a 4-0 win at St Andrew's. His last goal for the club proved to be the winner in a 2-1 home FA Cup victory over Bradford City in January 1933.

An England international trialist (playing for the Whites versus the Colours), Tate was regarded as one of the best players in his position in 1931 and, as a result, gained the first of his three full caps, lining up alongside the Sheffield Wednesday pivot Alf Strange and another debutant, Tommy Graham of Nottingham Forest, in a 5-2 defeat by France in Paris. He played in a 4-1 win over Belgium in Brussels 48 hours later and appeared in the goalless draw versus Wales at Wrexham in November 1932, when he made two goalline clearances.

Unfortunately, a series of niggling knee and ankle injuries, along with a tedious back strain, interrupted Tate's progress, and he played his last first-team game against Newcastle United in November 1933. Slipping gracefully into the second team, having been replaced at senior level by Bill Simpson and later by Tom Wood, he left Villa Park in May 1935 (after a decade of dedicated service) to become player-manager of Brierley Hill Alliance, retiring as a player two years later after breaking his right leg during a Birmingham League game against Moor Green.

In September 1937 Tate was appointed coach at Birmingham University, a position he held throughout the war before being replaced by ex-Villa colleague Norman Young.

Tate later ran a successful tobacconist shop in Brierley Hill, which he initially opened in 1936.

He was also a very fine club cricketer and played for Warwickshire Club and Ground, Stourbridge (in the Birmingham League), Oldswinford and Netherton, and once scored a century in 55 minutes as well as claiming four catches in one innings while fielding at slip. His best bowling return was 4-14 playing for Netherton.

Ian Taylor

Date of birth: 4 June 1968, Birmingham

Aston Villa record:
Appearances: League 202+31, FA Cup 14+3, League Cup 19+2, Others 18+1
Goals: League 28, FA Cup 2, League Cup 7, Others 5
Debut: League, 24 March 1990, substitute v Crystal Palace (a) lost 1–0
Also played for: Moor Green, Port Vale, Sheffield Wednesday, Derby County, Northampton Town.

For many years during his lengthy spell at Villa Park, the name of tall midfielder Ian Taylor was the first on Aston Villa's team sheet, certainly when John Gregory was manager between 1998 and 2001.

Blessed with a terrific engine, he was a workaholic, who covered acres of ground during a game and, more often than not, was battling away just as tenaciously at the end of his 90-minute stint as he was at the very start.

He began his career in local non-League football with Moor Green, whom he served for four years before transferring to Port Vale in July 1992, for an initial payment of £15,000. In addition, he earned further instalments based on appearances which eventually amounted to an extra £25,000.

He went on to play in 111 first-team games for the Valiants, scoring 38 goals. He was voted the club's Player of the Year in 1992–93, when he was also selected in the PFA Second Division team, in the season when Vale won the Autoglass Trophy (versus Stockport County) but lost in the Play-off Final (versus West Bromwich Albion), both at Wembley Stadium. He helped the Staffordshire club gain promotion the following season and was again included in the PFA team.

After two years at Vale Park, Ian moved to Sheffield Wednesday for a tribunal-fixed fee of £1 million, plus an extra £100,000 if he gained a full England cap and £25,000 for every 10 goals scored (up to a maximum of 50), in addition to 15 percent of the profit of any future sale. Unfortunately, he never settled down at Hillsborough, appearing in only 18 senior games (scoring two goals) before switching his allegiance to Villa Park, signed by manager Ron Atkinson for £1 million in December 1994. Striker Guy Whittingham joined the Owls as part of the deal.

Over the next eight and a half years, Ian became a huge favourite with the Villa Park fans, recouping the money spent on him many times over with some sparkling displays in midfield.

Ian scored on his Villa Park debut versus Chelsea and initially linked up in the centre of the park, with Andy Townsend and Ray Houghton and then again with Townsend and Dwight Yorke.

He had a decent first season, making 24 appearances. The following campaign he improved further, having 34 outings and scoring five goals, including one in the 3–0 League Cup Final victory over Leeds United.

Playing alongside Mark Draper and Townsend, Ian continued to impress, and early in 1997–98 he reached the milestone of 100 senior appearances for Villa, progressing to top the 200 mark in July 2000 versus Marila Pribam in the Intertoto Cup.

In October 2001 manager Gregory was replaced by Graham Taylor, who placed Ian on the bench, and began with Lee Hendrie, George Boateng and the Moroccan Hassan Kachloul in midfield. As time progressed, Taylor introduced Garth Barry on the left and the German Thomas Hitzlsperger into the action. At this juncture, Ian was finding it hard to hold down a regular place in the side.

Consequently, in July 2003, after scoring 42 goals in 290 competitive games for the club, Ian moved to pastures new, joining Derby County on a free transfer. He did well at Pride Park, claiming 15 goals in 88 appearances before moving to Northampton Town, again on a free transfer, in July 2005.

He continued to produce the goods for the Cobblers, and when he retired at the end of the 2006–07 season his record with the Sixfields club stood at eight goals in 74 games and his career statistics boasted 581 club appearances and 111 goals.

Ian, at one point during his time with Aston Villa, was voted the fourth best player in the Premiership, but, disappointingly, he never gained international recognition for his brilliant efforts.

Andy Townsend

Date of birth: 23 July 1963, Maidstone, Kent

Aston Villa record:
Appearances: League 133+1, FA Cup 12, League Cup 20, European 10
Goals: League 8, League Cup 2, European 1
Debut: League, 14 August 1993 v Queen's Park Rangers (h) won 4–1

Also played for: Welling United, Weymouth, Norwich City, Chelsea, Middlesbrough, West Bromwich Albion, Republic of Ireland (1 B and 70 full caps)

Midfielder Andy Townsend began his playing career in non-League football, serving with Welling United from August 1980 and Weymouth from March 1984, before becoming a full-time professional with Southampton, signing the appropriate forms at The Dell in January 1985 in a deal worth £35,000.

After more than 100 games for the Saints, he joined Norwich City for £300,000 in August 1988. He had 88 outings with the Canaries before switching to Chelsea for £1.2 million in July 1990. He played superbly well at Stamford Bridge, partnering Dennis Wise, hard man Vinnie Jones and Nigel Spackman in centre-field.

He signed for Aston Villa for £2.1 million in July 1993, having scored 19 goals in 142 appearances for the London club.

Andy spent four complete seasons at Villa Park before transferring north to Middlesbrough for £500,000 in August 1997. In the engine room on Teesside he played alongside Paul Merson, Robbie Mustoe and Craig Hignett, and he scored two crucial goals – in the 1–1 draws at Crewe and at home to Portsmouth – during his first season, which ended with promotion.

Andy then assisted West Bromwich Albion for a short time, starting in September 1999 as a player. On retiring in September 2000 at the age of 36, he was appointed reserve-team coach in place of Cyrille Regis. He held that position for six months before ex-Villa star Gary Shelton took over his duties.

Andy accumulated 682 appearances at club and international levels. His international career with the Republic of Ireland ran for nine years, from 1989 to 1998. He won one B and 70 full caps, scoring seven goals in the latter category. His first senior start was against France as a Norwich City player and his last versus Belgium when he was registered with Middlesbrough. He gained 28 caps with Villa.

Hard working with an eye for goal, most times Andy was seen battling away at the end of a game just as he was at the start, a terrific 90-minute competitor whose effective use of the ball made him one of the best in his field during the 1990s, especially when skippering his country in the 1994 World Cup Finals.

He also played in Aston Villa's League Cup-winning side that same year (against Manchester United) and added a second winners' medal to his collection in the same competition two years later (versus Leeds United). Then in 1998 he helped Middlesbrough clinch promotion to the Premiership.

During his time at Villa Park, Andy manned midfield with Gordon Cowans, fellow countryman Ray Houghton, Kevin Richardson and Garry Parker. Mark Draper and Ian Taylor then joined the ranks, and they were followed by Sasa Curcic and Lee Hendrie, with a handful of others slotting in from time to time.

Andy missed 10 Premiership games in each of his first two seasons. He was then absent from five in 1995–96 and four the following season before moving to the Riverside Stadium after three outings in 1997–98.

Patron of the George Coller Memorial Fund, Andy was initially against the development of the new Wembley Stadium, stressing that the national stadium should be built in the Midlands, where he lives.

Andy now works as a television pundit and is regularly seen on ITV covering live matches. He also hosts the channel's *Soccer Night* programme alongside Peter Beagrie, *Talk Sport's Weekend* breakfast programme along with Mike Parry, and occasionally co-hosts the same station's drive-time show when resident presenter Adrian Durham is not available.

Andy's father Don played as a full-back for Charlton Athletic and Crystal Palace.

Billy Walker

Date of birth: 29 October 1897, Wednesbury
Died: 28 November 1964, Sheffield

Aston Villa record:
Appearances: League 478, FA Cup 53, Wartime 5
Goals: League 214, FA Cup 30, Wartime 2
Debut: FA Cup, 10 January 1920 v Queen's Park Rangers (h) won 2–1
Also played for: Kings Hill School (Wednesbury), Walsall Boys, Fallings Heath, Hednesford Town, Darlaston, Wednesbury Old Park, Wednesbury Old Athletic, Birmingham (guest), England (18 full caps)
Managed: Sheffield Wednesday, Chelmsford City, Nottingham Forest

Billy Walker was born into a footballing family; his father George was a full-back with Wolves (1900–04) and two of his brothers were amateurs.

Billy was a prolific marksman as a schoolboy, netting 80 goals in the Walsall Boys' League in 1910–11 and over 100 more during the next three years, when he also had an unsuccessful trial with Aston Villa (1913).

After serving Wednesbury Old Athletic he was signed by Villa in March 1915, but World War One halted his progress. He had a few outings during the hostilities and played three games in the Midland Victory League prior to the recommencement of senior competitions in 1919–20.

Billy developed fast and scored twice on his major debut against Queen's Park Rangers in a first-round FA Cup tie in 1920, the first of 246 goals for the club (only Harry Hampton, with 247, scored more). He does, however, hold the record for most League and Cup goals for Villa (244).

Establishing himself in the first team during the second half of that initial post-war campaign, he helped Villa beat Huddersfield Town 1–0 in the FA Cup Final.

The following season, when he had Clem Stephenson alongside him, he top scored with 31 goals, bagging another 50 over the next two years.

He represented the Football League, going on to make six appearances at this level. He also played in the FA Cup Final versus Newcastle United in 1924, which Villa lost.

In 1926 Billy was appointed Villa's captain, a position he held for six years, during which time he also netted nine goals in 18 internationals for England, leading his country to a famous win over Austria in 1932. He played for England versus the Rest at Tottenham in 1929 and captained the Staffs Jubilee FA XI against the Football League in 1926.

Billy had tremendous ability, possessed a cracking shot, was a fine header of the ball, a superb tactician and, above all, was a champion marksman. He netted 11 hat-tricks, including four versus Arsenal in August 1920 and three penalties in the League game versus Bradford City in November 1921. He was also an exceptionally talented goalkeeper and deputised for both club and country on many occasions.

Retiring in November 1933, having made 536 appearances for Villa, he went into management with Sheffield Wednesday. He guided the Owls to FA Cup glory over West Bromwich Albion in 1935, but after that success things started to turn sour, and two seasons later Wednesday were relegated. They were languishing in 21st place in Division Two when he quit in November 1937.

An intelligent man, he loved his football and, absorbing information like a sponge, he spent hours talking to the coaches of the Austrian 'Wunderteam', eventually adopting their ideas.

Returning to the game as boss of Chelmsford City in January 1938, he remained in charge until February 1939 when he again resigned.

Soon afterwards he accepted the manager's job at Nottingham Forest, but within six months of arriving his long-term plans had to be put on indefinite hold due to World War Two.

In 1945 Billy began the task of rebuilding his Forest side. However, things were somewhat shaky to start, and they were relegated to the Third Division South in 1949.

He battled on, moulded the side and got them to play in the style he wanted. The rewards started to come. Forest won promotion in 1951 and six years later climbed into the First Division.

Forest won the FA Cup in 1959 when they beat Luton Town 2–1, but after that the team struggled, just avoiding relegation. Billy, now aged 63, was feeling the strain, and he immediately announced his retirement, joining the club's committee.

Brian Clough (with 18 years) is the only manager to get close to Billy's record for the longest-serving Forest manager (with 21 years), and in these modern times it is unlikely that another manager will get anywhere near it.

Billy's health slowly deteriorated and in 1963 he suffered a stroke, from which he never recovered.

Charlie Wallace

Date of birth: 20 January 1885, Southwick, Sunderland, Wearside
Died: 26 January 1970, Birmingham

Aston Villa record:
Appearances: League 314, FA Cup 35, FA Charity Shield 1
Goals: League 54, FA Cup 3
Debut: League, 2 September 1907 v Manchester United (h) lost 4–1

Also played for: Sunderland and District Schools, Southwick FC, Crystal Palace, Oldham Athletic, England (3 full caps)

During the 12-year period from 1909 to 1921, Aston Villa were a lively, exciting team, their forward-line being quite brilliant at times, full of attacking ideas and goals.

One of the star performers was outside-right Charlie Wallace – direct, speedy, clever and competitive. He helped the team win their sixth Football League title in 1910 and lift the FA Cup in 1913 (1–0 versus Sunderland, his home-town club, whom he supported as a lad) and 1920 (1–0 versus Huddersfield Town), although he did have the misfortune to become the first player to miss a penalty in a Final when he screwed his spot-kick wide in the victory over the Wearsiders at Crystal Palace in front of a record crowd for a game of football anywhere in the world – 121,919. But Wallace, obviously disturbed, quickly made amends by swinging over the corner, from which left-half Tommy Barber headed home the all-important winning goal with 15 minutes remaining.

Wallace also missed a penalty in the penultimate League game of the 1910–11 season at Blackburn. The game ended goalless and, disappointed not to win at Ewood Park, Villa knew they had to win their last game at Liverpool to retain the Championship crown. They lost 3–1 and the title went to Manchester United by a single point (52–51).

Wallace gained three full caps for England, starring in a 4–3 win over Wales in March 1913 when he had a hand in teammate Harry Hampton's goal. He then played in a 3–0 defeat in Ireland in February 1914 and performed superbly well in front of Villa colleague Andy Ducat in a thrilling 5–4 victory over Scotland at Hillsborough in April 1920, when he set up two goals. He also represented the Football League on five occasions and appeared in three international trials when he was competing for a place in the England team with Fanny Walden (Tottenham Hotspur), Jack Simpson (Blackburn Rovers) and Sam Chedgzoy (Everton).

As a youngster, Wallace played for Southwick FC as a centre-forward and winger. He became a professional with Crystal Palace in July 1905 and scored nine goals in 51 games for the London club before transferring to Villa Park in May 1907. He took over the right-wing berth from Charlie Millington and held it (injuries and illness permitting) until handing over his duties to Dicky York in March 1921.

Wallace notched 57 goals in 350 first-class appearances for the club. He was twice an ever present (in seasons 1909–10 and 1910–11) and had his best scoring campaign in 1911–12 when he found the net 17 times, finishing second in the charts behind centre-forward Harry Hampton.

On leaving Villa, he joined Oldham Athletic for a fee of £1,000 and spent two seasons at Boundary Park, hitting three goals in 50 games, before retiring in April 1923 to become a self-employed painter and decorator. He worked part-time in the boot room at Villa Park until the summer of 1960, and he also acted as a scout, ground steward and mentor to the youngsters, who played in the Junior Ordnance Corps team during the later 1930s, guiding them to the runners'-up spot in their respective League in 1939.

Remaining an avid supporter of the team, Wallace served Aston Villa football club in various capacities for more than 50 years. He attended his last match at Villa Park in 1965 and died five years later at the age of 85.

Mark Walters

Date of birth: 2 June 1964, Birmingham

Aston Villa record:
Appearances: League 168+13, FA Cup 11+1, League Cup 20+1, European 7+3
Goals: League 39, FA Cup 1, League Cup 6, European 2
Debut: League, 28 April 1982, substitute v Leeds United (h) lost 4–1

Also played for: Glasgow Rangers, Liverpool, Stoke City, Wolves, Southampton, Swindon Town, Bristol Rovers, Ilkeston Town, Dudley Town, Aston Villa Old Stars, England (1 full, 4 Youth and 9 Under-21 caps)

Mark Walters was an attacking winger who preferred to raid down the left flank. He made his name as a highly-rated youngster with Aston Villa, whom he joined as an apprentice in June 1980, turning professional in May 1982 – just as Villa won the coveted European Cup.

Blessed with good, close ball control and devastating pace, he could shoot using both feet but preferred his right, and he was able to deliver a perfect cross on the run as well as being an expert at dead-ball situations. He had one favourite trick whereby he used to drag his foot over the ball, feint one way before leaving his marker for dead as he shot off in the opposite direction.

After representing Aston and District Boys and Birmingham Schools, Mark went on to play for England at both Schoolboy and Youth-team levels before going on to gain one full, one B and nine Under-21 caps, his senior debut coming against New Zealand in 1991 when he was registered with Glasgow Rangers.

Establishing himself in Villa's League side at the age of 19, having already starred in the European Super Cup victory, he was excellent in 1983–84, scoring 11 goals in 48 appearances and playing in the losing League Cup semi-final against Everton.

The following term he netted 10 times in 39 outings and added 13 goals to his tally in 53 games in 1985–86, when, once again, Villa lost a League Cup semi-final – this time to Oxford United.

This latter campaign was, in fact, Mark's best with Villa. He was on the fringe of the England team after some superb wing displays in a struggling team that just managed to squeeze clear of relegation by registering three wins in their last five matches.

After scoring 48 goals in 225 games for Villa, Mark joined Glasgow Rangers for £600,000 in December 1987 and thus became the first significant black player in Scottish football since Andy Watson of Queen's Park in the 19th century.

Mark became a huge hit with the Rangers supporters and is the only honorary member of the Rangers Supporters Trust.

Subjected to racist abuse from Celtic fans on his debut at Parkhead, the display of overt hostility towards him was described at the time as the worst in relation to racism ever seen on a British ground.

Gerry Britton, a Celtic apprentice, recalled 'I was appalled at the hideous racist goading of winger Mark Walters during his Old Firm debut. I was even more sickened on the morning after the match when I was told to help clear the Parkhead trackside of the dozens of bananas that had been thrown onto the field by so-called Celtic supporters, intent on upsetting the on-field focus of the Ibrox wing wizard.'

Mark quickly put that incident behind him and went on to score 52 goals in 143 games for Rangers, gaining three Premier League and two Scottish League Cup-winners' medals before following his manager Graeme Souness to Liverpool in a £1.25 million deal in August 1991. The move was somewhat ironic as Mark shared his middle name (Everton) with Liverpool's fierce city rivals.

It was hoped that Mark would emulate his fellow winger John Barnes at Anfield, but equalling a player of Barnes's ilk was to prove too tough a burden for the winger and the task was made doubly difficult by the emergence of Steve McManaman.

Mark did, however, gain an FA Cup-winners' medal (as a non-playing substitute) in 1992 and a League Cup-winners' medal three years later.

He certainly found it hard going on Merseyside, and after loan spells with Stoke and Wolves he moved to Southampton in January 1996, having netted 19 goals in 125 games (42 as a substitute) for the Reds.

After assisting Swindon, Bristol Rovers, Ilkeston and Dudley, Mark retired in 2004 with almost 170 goals to his credit in over 750 appearances.

He still plays in Masters Football competitions for Rangers as well as coaching the youngsters in Aston Villa's Academy.

* Aston Villa became the first club to score 6,000 League goals when Mark Walters netted against Bournemouth in October 1987.

Tom 'Pongo' Waring

Date of birth: 12 October 1906, Birkenhead
Died: 20 December 1980, Liverpool

Aston Villa record:
Appearances: League 216, FA Cup 10
Goals: League 159, FA Cup 8
Debut: League, 25 February 1928 v Sunderland (a) won 3-2 (scored)

Also played for: Tranmere Colts, Tranmere Celtic, Tranmere Rovers (two spells), Barnsley, Wolverhampton Wanderers, Accrington Stanley, Bath City, (wartime guest for New Brighton, Wrexham, Everton, Crewe Alexandra), South Liverpool, Ellesmere Port, Grayson's FC, Birkenhead Dockers, Harrowby FC, England (5 full caps)

Tom 'Pongo' Waring is one of Aston Villa's all-time greats, having scored 167 goals in 226 League and Cup games, including an amazing record haul of 50 in 1930–31 with 49 coming in the First Division, which still remains Villa's club record.

'Pongo', as he became affectionately known throughout the world of football (a nickname he got from a 1920s cartoon character), started out with his local junior club Tranmere Colts, and after assisting Tranmere Athletic he then did well with the bigger boys of Tranmere Rovers, for whom he netted 23 goals in just 24 games before Aston Villa forked out £4,700 for his signature in February 1928 – certainly money well spent.

A 6ft tall long-striding centre-forward, Tom developed into a wonderfully-consistent goalscorer, supremely confident in his own ability. He was certainly a colourful character and a huge favourite with the supporters, and the stories about him, apocryphal or otherwise, are numerous.

A crowd of 23,440 turned out to watch him make his debut for Villa in a reserve-team game against Birmingham when he scored a hat-trick in a 6–3 win, soon after he had netted a double hat-trick for Tranmere in an 11–0 win over Durham in a Third Division North match.

A former chocolate-bar seller at Tranmere's Prenton Park ground, he actually took over from the great Dixie Dean as leader of the Rovers attack, and within two years he was playing in front of 50,000 fans in top-flight League action.

He spent 10 years at Villa Park and his terrific goal tally included nine hat-tricks (nine in the First Division). Also known as the 'Gay Cavalier', 'Pongo' played in five full internationals for England (1931 and 1932) and scored on his debut against France in Paris (lost 5–2), then whipped in two goals in a 6–2 win over Ireland and added a fourth goal to his tally in a 3–0 victory over Scotland at Wembley.

Around this time every kid who supported Villa wanted to be 'Pongo' Waring, and at one point it was said that he was more popular than the King and even the Prime Minster.

Unfortunately he never won a prize with Villa, and the nearest he came was to gain First Division runners'-up medals in 1930–31 and 1932–33 when Arsenal were declared champions on both occasions.

One sad note in his Villa career came at White Hart Lane in January 1934 when he was sent off for the first and only time in his career – and as he walked from the pitch, head bowed, he received a bigger cheer than the whole of the team would have if they had won the FA Cup.

He had little success after leaving Villa Park, and played in just 18 games (seven goals scored) for Barnsley and found the net three times in 10 outings in his brief spell with Wolves, before returning to Tranmere. Here he seemed to have regained a little of his goalscoring touch, striking 42 goals in 74 games and helping Rovers win the Third Division North title in 1937–38.

Accrington Stanley signed him in November 1938, and he responded with 10 goals in 22 League games for a very poor Reds side. Although he had some obvious disciplinary problems at Peel Park, Accrington still wanted to keep him, but he would have none of it, his relationship with the club's directors being irreparably poor.

He opted to sign for non-League Bath City in August 1939, thus depriving Stanley of a fee. He played in 80 of New Brighton's World War Two fixtures between 1939 and 1942, scoring 52 goals, but the Rakers then closed down for the duration of the hostilities. After the war he went into non-League football, eventually retiring in 1950. He later worked in the Merseyside dockland and was 84 when he died.

Fred Wheldon

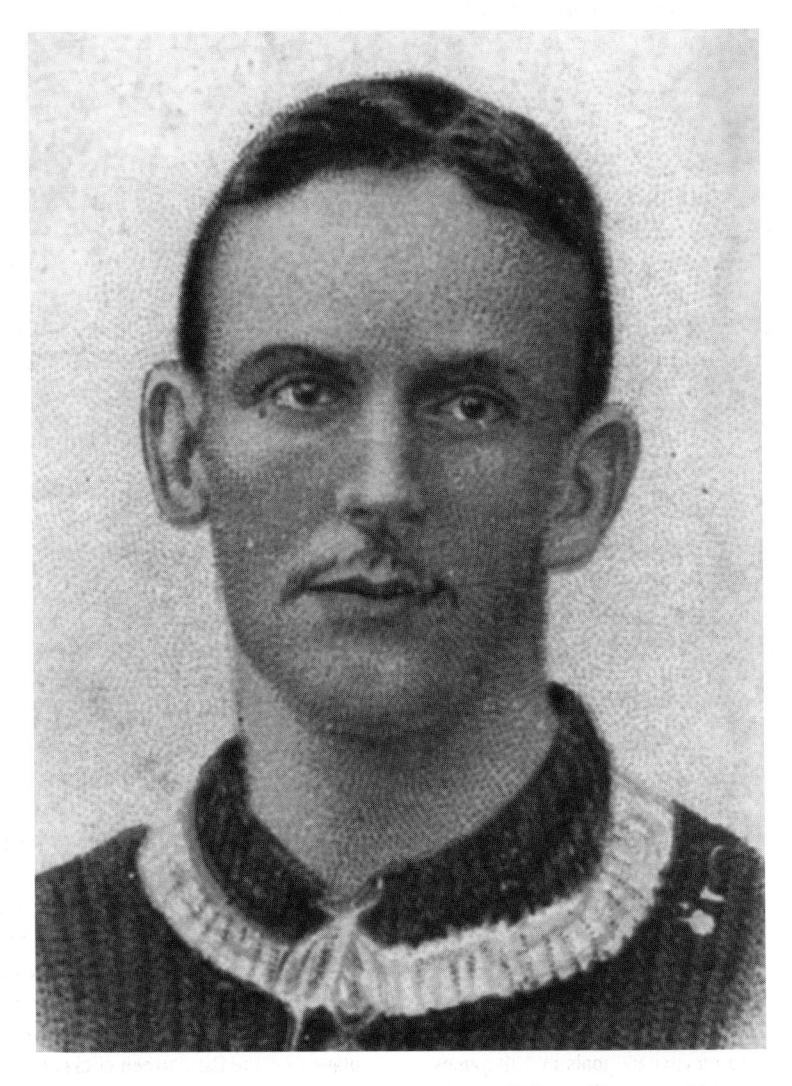

Date of birth: 1 November 1869, Langley Green, Oldbury, Worcestershire
Died: 13 January 1924, St George's, Worcester

Aston Villa record:
Appearances: League 124, FA Cup 14, others 2
Goals: League 68, FA Cup 6
Villa debut: League, 2 September 1896 v Stoke (h) won 2-1

Also played for: Rood End White Star, Langley Green Victoria, Birmingham, West Bromwich Albion (2 spells, first on trial), Queen's Park Rangers, Portsmouth, Worcester City, England (4 full and 2 XI caps)

The youngest of 10 children, Fred 'Diamond' Wheldon was a brilliant footballer, an exceptional talent and a tremendous goalscorer whose career spanned 16 years. In fact, he was the first player to appear in a League game for three major Midlands clubs – Blues (then known as Small Heath), Aston Villa and West Bromwich Albion.

Regularly seen in a pair of golfing stockings instead of the traditional footballing type, he had a month's trial with the then FA Cup holders West Bromwich Albion in 1888 but was turned away. Two years later, in mid-February 1890, he signed as a semi-professional for Birmingham, for whom he scored twice on his debut in a 6-2 home win over Darwen in a Football Alliance fixture.

In May 1890 Fred became a full-time professional and was an ever present that campaign, scoring 14 goals, including his first hat-trick at senior level in his first FA Cup tie – an 8-0 qualifying-round win over Hednesford.

He helped Blues gain a place in the Football League and actually played in their first-ever game in Division Two, scoring twice in a 5-1 victory over Burslem Port Vale in 1892. He weighed in with 26 goals that season, helping Blues clinch the title, but the team missed out on promotion after losing to Newton Heath (Manchester United) in two Test Matches (today's equivalent of the Play-offs).

Superb again in 1893-94 with 24 goals, his efforts this time were rewarded as Blues again won the Second Division title, and with it promotion, after beating Darwen in the vital Test Match, Fred scoring one of the goals.

He had the pleasure of scoring Blues' first-ever penalty in a 2-2 draw with Aston Villa in October 1894 and went on to register 82 goals in 129 games for the club before moving to Villa Park in June 1896 for a fee of £350.

Now plying his trade on a much bigger stage, he maintained his form and scored 74 goals in 140 games over the next four seasons, helping Villa win three League titles (in 1897, 1898 and 1900) and the FA Cup (also in 1897), when, of course, the double was achieved.

Fred was an ever present that season, top scoring with 22 goals, including one in the 3-2 Cup Final win over Everton and a hat-trick in a 5-1 League victory at Blackburn.

He was outstanding on the field, delivering perfect passes to his colleagues, creating chances galore and scoring some wonderful goals. He inspired players around him and was forever battling away, never giving up a lost cause.

Fred won four full caps for England – the first in 1897 versus Ireland and the next three in 1898 against Ireland, Wales and Scotland. He twice starred for an England XI and appeared in two matches for the Football League against the Irish League and Scottish League – having earlier lined up against the Irish and the Scots in 1893-94 as a Blues player.

In August 1900, at the age of 30, Fred moved four miles down the road to neighbours West Bromwich Albion for £100. He appeared in the first League game at The Hawthorns, against Derby County, but struggled in a poor team, the Baggies being relegated for the first time.

In December 1901 Fred signed for Southern League side Queen's Park Rangers and later spent two seasons with Portsmouth (August 1902 to July 1904) before ending his career in May 1906 after two years with Worcester City.

Besides his footballing exploits, Fred was also a splendid cricketer who, between 1899 and 1906, scored 4,938 runs for Worcestershire at an average of 22.50 per innings. He struck three centuries and claimed 95 catches, some as a wicketkeeper. He also played for the Carmarthen cricket club.

He remained in Worcester for the rest of his life, working as a publican prior to his death in January 1924 at the age of 54.

Fred's brother, Sam, played for Albion while his son, Norris, assisted Liverpool.

Gary Williams

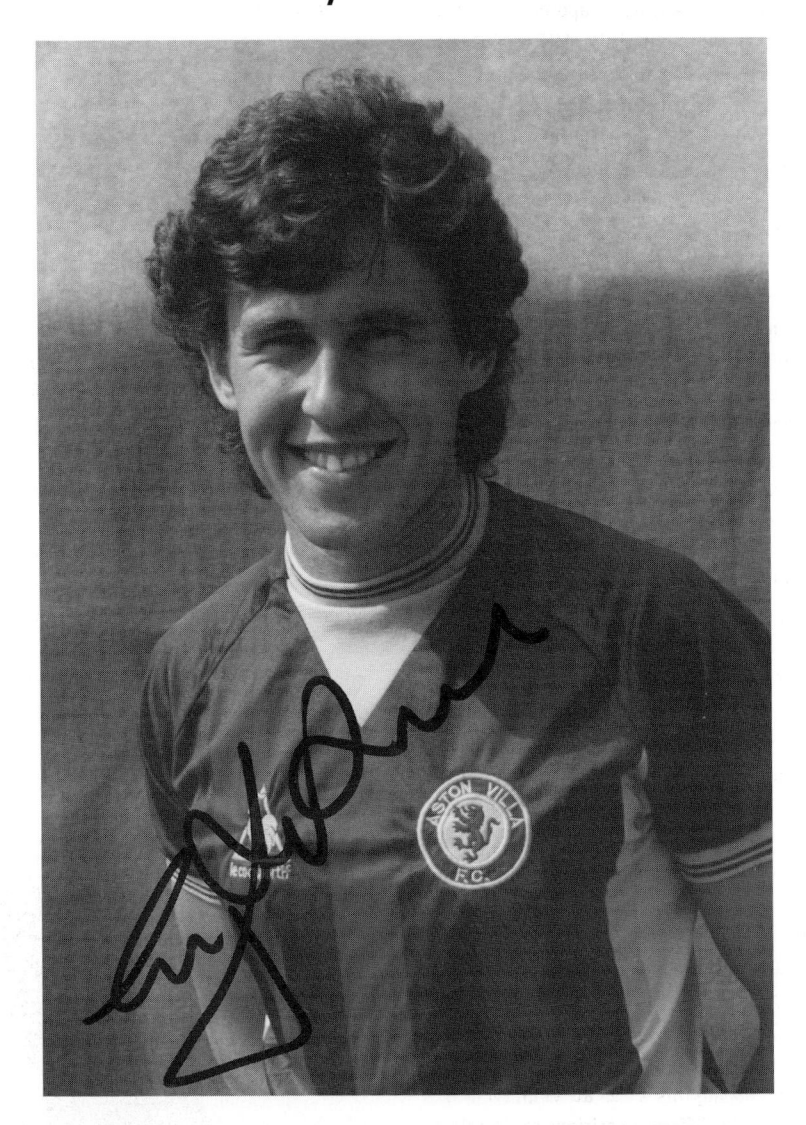

Date of birth: 17 June 1960, Wolverhampton

Aston Villa record:
Appearances: League 235+5, FA Cup 14, League Cup 29, European 17, others 2
Goals: League Cup 2
Debut: League, 16 September 1978, substitute v Everton (h) drew 1–1

Also played for: Wolverhampton and South Staffordshire Boys, Walsall (loan), Leeds United, Watford, Bradford City

After representing Wolverhampton and Staffordshire Boys, Gary Williams spent 11 pretty good years with Aston Villa. He signed initially as an apprentice under manager Ron Saunders in July 1976, turned professional in June 1978 (shortly after helping the youngsters win the FA Youth Cup), and remained at the club until July 1987 when he became Billy Bremner's first signing for Leeds United, having earlier had a successful two-month loan spell with Walsall in March and April 1980, during which time he helped the Saddlers gain promotion from the Fourth Division.

Always performing with consummate ease and authority, Williams was a sure kicker of the ball, had excellent positional sense, was quick over the ground, a strong header of the ball and a dedicated club man. He gained a League Division One Championship medal in 1981 (making 22 appearances, mostly alongside Kenny Swain), collected a European Cup-winners' medal the following season (when the West German champions Bayern Munich were defeated 1-0 in the Final in Rotterdam), won a European Super Cup-winners' prize in 1982-83 when Villa eclipsed the Spanish giants Barcelona 3-1 over two legs and played in the World Club Championship encounter against the South American side Penarol in Tokyo, a game Villa lost 2-0.

During this period (the early 1980s) he was linked with a possible move to Arsenal, Glasgow Rangers, Brian Clough's Nottingham Forest and even Manchester United, as he was playing so well at that time.

A key figure in Villa's senior side for some seven years, from 1980 until his departure in 1987, Williams could play, and play well, in several positions, but he preferred either the right or left-back spot, although he was equally at home on the left-hand side of midfield. In fact, during his time at Villa Park he actually occupied eight different positions for the first team and made in excess of 300 senior appearances, scoring just two goals. These both came in the same League Cup game in October 1985 when Villa thrashed luckless Exeter City 8-1 in the return leg of a second-round tie at Villa Park.

Williams was on the brink of representing England at Under-21 level in the early 1980s. He was selected for the game against the Republic of Ireland but had to withdraw at the 11th hour due to a tedious leg injury and, disappointingly for him, he never got another chance, although he was named as stand-by reserve on two occasions.

Villa remained a very efficient First Division side for several years, and the slide from their lofty heights was slow to start, but by 1987 they had slipped agonisingly into the Second Division for the first time since 1975, at which point Williams was released and almost immediately snapped up by Leeds for just £235,000.

He immediately gained a regular place at Elland Road, but under new manager Howard Wilkinson, who took over from Bremner in 1988, his chances became more and more restricted, and, as a result, he was released on a free transfer in January 1990 and signed for Watford, having made 45 senior appearances for the Yorkshire club.

He added 47 appearances to his tally with the Hornets before ending his career with Bradford City, whom he served from December 1991 to May 1994 and played in 96 competitive matches.

Williams retired after making over 500 club appearances during his 18 years in the game.

His son, who is hoping to follow in his father's footsteps, has just turned professional for a Finnish First Division club.

Peter Withe

Date of birth: 30 August 1951, Liverpool

Aston Villa record:
Appearances: League 232, FA Cup 9, League Cup 19, Europe 22, Charity Shield 1
Goals: League 90, FA Cup 2, League Cup 5, Europe 9, Charity Shield 2
Debut: League, 16 August 1980 v Leeds United (a) won 2-1

Also played for: All Hallow's School (Speke), Smith Coggins FC (2 spells), Skelmersdale United, Southport, Preston North End, Barrow (trial), Port Elizabeth, Arcadia Shepherds, Wolverhampton Wanderers, Portland Timbers, Newcastle United, Nottingham Forest, Sheffield United, Birmingham City (2 spells), Huddersfield Town (player-coach), Evesham United, England (11 full caps)
Managed: Thailand and Indonesia national teams, Wimbledon

At various levels, much-travelled striker Peter Withe served with 16 different clubs between 1966 and 1989, scoring 232 goals in 640 games in all competitions.

After two spells with Smith Coggins and Skelmersdale United, he joined Southport, turning professional in August 1971. Brief sojourns with Preston North End and Barrow preceded a move to South Africa, where he played for Port Elizabeth and Arcadia Shepherds, returning to England to sign for Wolverhampton Wanderers in October 1973.

He spent the summer of 1975 playing for Portland Timbers in the North American Soccer League (NASL), scoring 17 goals and adding seven assists in 22 games as the Timbers won their respective Division.

The Timbers also played two home Play-off games, each in front of more than 30,000 fans – attendances unheard of in American soccer circles at the time. They advanced to Soccer Bowl '75 (the League Championship) but lost to Tampa Bay Rowdies 2-0.

Birmingham City boss Willie Bell paid £50,000 to bring Peter back 'home' in August 1975. He spent 13 months at St Andrew's before switching to Nottingham Forest for £42,500. He won a League Championship medal under Brian Clough before leaving The City Ground on the verge of their European Cup glory to join then Second Division side Newcastle United, recruited by manager Bill McGarry (his old gaffer at Molineux) for £200,000 in August 1978.

Ron Saunders then persuaded Peter to join Villa on the eve of the 1980-81 season, paying £500,000 for his services – the club's record incoming transfer at the time.

Peter proved to be a real snip of a signing, considering the service he gave the club over the next five years.

Tall, strong in the air and positive on the ground, he scored 20 goals in his first season with Villa Park, helping the team win the League Championship for the first time since 1910. He then netted the only goal of the 1982 European Cup Final defeat of German champions Bayern Munich in Rotterdam, having bagged both goals when Villa held Tottenham Hotspur to a 2-2 draw in the FA Charity Shield game at Wembley a few months after they had won the League crown. Peter also played his part in Villa's Super Cup win over CF Barcelona.

Taking over from David Geddis as leader of the attack, he linked up superbly well with Gary Shaw and, cashing in on the precise crosses from the left by winger Tony Morley and defence-splitting passes delivered by Gordon Cowans, Des Bremner and skipper Dennis Mortimer, Peter was regarded as one of the best strikers in English football at the time.

Capped by England 11 times at senior level and scoring once, he was the first English-born player from Aston Villa to feature in the World Cup Finals, going to Spain in 1982.

He remained with Villa until July 1985 when he left to join Sheffield United on a free transfer. There followed a loan spell with his former club, Blues, before he switched north to become player-coach of Huddersfield Town (July 1988). He returned to Villa as assistant-manager/coach under Josef Venglos (January-October 1991) and then had a brief spell as coach of the English Premiership club Wimbledon, being promoted to manager following the resignation of Ray Harford.

However, Peter's time with the Dons was not a successful one. His team won only one of 13 League games, and after 105 days at the helm he was replaced by the youth-team coach Joe Kinnear.

After assisting Evesham United, working as a Football in the Community officer at Port Vale and a Community Liaison Officer in the West Midlands and also for Birmingham City (1993), Peter was Villa's Youth Development Officer before propelling the Thailand national team towards some success, later doing likewise as head coach (manager) of Indonesia, remaining in the Far East for over seven years. He is now living in Australia.

His brother Chris Withe played for Bradford City and his son Jason was on the books of West Bromwich Albion.

Dicky York

Date of birth: 25 April 1899, Villa Cross, Handsworth, Birmingham
Died: 9 December 1969, Handsworth, Birmingham

Aston Villa record:
Appearances: League 356, FA Cup 34
Goals: League 79, FA Cup 7
Debut: League, 30 August 1919 v Sunderland (a) lost 2-1

Also played for: Friends Hall FC (Hockley, Birmingham), GEC Works (Birmingham), Birmingham Boys, Handsworth Royal, Birchfield Rangers, (wartime guest for Chelsea and Boscombe Town), Port Vale, Brierley Hill Alliance, England (2 full caps)

Dicky York was born directly opposite where Aston Villa football club was founded on Heathfield Road, Villa Cross, Handsworth.

He played locally for several years – and once scored six goals in a game for Birchfield Rangers – before being engaged by Villa, initially as an amateur in March 1915 and then as a full-time professional two months later. However, due to the wartime hostilities in Europe, when he served in the Royal Flying Corps, receiving a commission, he played very little football over the next four years, having only a handful of games here and there, and he even missed out when Villa took part in the Midland Victory League so that clubs could get their players prepared, fit and ready for the resumption of domestic League and Cup football in August 1919.

A strong, hard-running, fast-raiding and orthodox right-winger with a powerful shot, York could also play as a right-half and centre-forward. He made 17 senior appearances in the first full season after the war, scoring one goal in a crushing 5-1 defeat at Blackburn in April, but sadly he failed to make Villa's Cup Final team, Charlie Wallace retaining his place.

The following term York had only 11 outings on the right flank, but in 1921-22 he firmly established himself in the forward line, taking over from Wallace and missing only one game as Villa edged up to fifth in the First Division table, their highest placing since 1914.

With Billy Kirton now starring as his inside-partner, York was again in fine form in 1923-24 as Villa reached their second FA Cup Final in four years, but this time they slipped up, losing 2-0 to Newcastle United in the first all-ticket game staged at the old Wembley Stadium.

York scored seven goals in 1924-25 before registering his best-ever return as a Villa player, weighing in with 25 in 1925-26. His haul included a smart hat-trick in a 3-3 League draw at Bury and braces in a 3-1 win at Bolton Wanderers, in a 2-2 draw at Tottenham, in a 3-2 victory at Burnley, in another 2-2 draw with Leicester City at home and a 3-1 triumph over Everton, also at Villa Park.

A player who simply loved to cut inside his full-back and have a crack at goal whenever he could, he was precise and sure when taking a corner or a free-kick and was also very effective when centring on the run, often whipping the ball across the face of the goal head high. He once scored direct from a flag-kick and twice found the net with crosses that became shots.

An ever present in 1926-27 and 1928-29, York remained first choice on Villa's right wing until shortly after the start of the 1930-31 season when he was replaced by Jack Mandley as Villa began to fire on all cylinders in what was to be a goal-happy campaign.

York, who gained schoolboy honours for his country versus Wales and Scotland in 1913, played twice for England in senior internationals, lining up against Scotland in April 1922 and April 1926 – each game ending in a 1-0 defeat. He also appeared in one junior international (1919) and played twice for the Football League versus Irish League and Scottish League, in 1925 and 1926 respectively.

On leaving Villa Park in June 1931, York signed for Port Vale, switching to Brierley Hill Alliance in August 1932 and retiring as a full-time player two years later, although he did return to action with Villa's third team in 1948-49 when serving as a part-time coach.

From 1942 onwards York was employed as a technical advisor (buildings) on the Birmingham war damage Committee; he later managed a Coventry-based plumbing, building and decorating company and was also a director of the Brecon tennis club in Handsworth, where I met him for the first time in 1964.

Dwight Yorke

Date of birth: 3 November 1971, Cannan, Tobago

Aston Villa record:
Appearances: League 195+36, FA Cup 22+2, League Cup 20+2, European 9, Other 1
Goals: League 73, FA Cup 14, League Cup 8, European 2, Other 1
Debut: League, 24 March 1990, substitute v Crystal Palace (a) lost 1–0

Also played for: Signal FC (Tobago), Manchester United, Blackburn Rovers, Sydney FC (Australia), Sunderland, Trinidad and Tobago (58 full caps)

By far the most famous footballer ever to have come out of the Caribbean nation of Trinidad and Tobago, Dwight Yorke has not only won the UEFA Champions League (with Manchester United), but he was the only player at the 2006 World Cup Finals to have a major stadium already named after him in his native homeland.

Discovered by former England manager Graham Taylor on Aston Villa's tour of the Caribbean in 1989, the Birmingham club subsequently shelled out £120,000 to bring the speedy, skilful striker to Britain in December that same year. And what a bargain buy he turned out to be. He spent nine years at Villa Park and averaged a goal every three games.

Despite occasional injury worries and bouts of inconsistency – which all players suffer – Dwight netted 98 times in 287 senior appearances and tasted victory in the 1996 League Cup Final when he scored in a 3-0 win over Leeds United at Wembley.

Dwight made only two substitute appearances in his first season with Villa; he played in 21 games the following season and 40 in 1991–92 when he also top scored with 17 goals, including his first-ever senior hat-trick in a 4-3 FA Cup win at Derby County.

The Premiership came into force in 1992–93 and Dwight was again in good form, scoring six goals in League action as Villa finished a creditable second to champions Manchester United.

Unfortunately he missed quite a chunk of the 1993–94 campaign, starting only two matches while coming off the subs' bench 12 times. But in 1994–95, when he was used mainly as an attacking midfielder, he struck top form again and appeared in 43 competitive matches, netting eight goals including an excellent winner at Coventry, a beauty in a 3-0 home win over Chelsea and two in a fine victory over Liverpool at Villa Park when the Holte End terraces were used for the very last time.

Then we come to 1995–96, which proved to be Dwight's best-ever season with Villa. He again topped the scoring charts with 25 goals (13 more than Savo Milosevic), and, of course, he bagged a goal in the League Cup Final.

At this time, Dwight's silky touches and strike rate at Villa Park sparked an interest from Manchester United's boss Alex Ferguson, who enticed him to Old Trafford for £12.6 million in August 1998. In his first three seasons with United, he formed a wonderful strike-partnership with Andy Cole and played a crucial role as United won three consecutive League titles – not to mention the 1999 Champions League and FA Cup as part of a historic treble.

In all, Dwight hit 47 goals in 96 League appearances for United before switching to Blackburn Rovers for £2 million in July 2002.

The goals seemed to dry up for Dwight at Ewood Park, and after a spell with Villa's arch-rivals Birmingham City (from August 2004) he took his toothy smile to Australia where he joined Sydney FC, whom he captained to the inaugural A-League Grand Final in March 2006.

Revered in his beloved Trinidad and Tobago, Dwight, blessed with great determination and spirit, was inspirational as he led the 'Soca Warriors' in their first-ever World Cup Finals in Germany in 2006 – an honour that made him akin to a demigod in the Caribbean.

Described as a 'special player' by Trinidad and Tobago coach Leo Beenhakker, Dwight's roaming role just behind the front line allowed his experience and tactical knowledge to shine through. And despite his veteran status, he retained a touch of class, which was clearly visible when he returned to English football with Sunderland at the start of the 2006-07 season, helping them win the Championship and their place back in the Premiership.